Stock Market Capitalism: Wel

'Professor Dore has written a thoughtful and provocative book on how global capitalism may evolve. Whether or not you agree with him—and many economists and CEOs will not—if you are interested in the future of the world economy, you should read this book.'

Jeffrey E. Garten
Dean, Yale School of Management

Stock Market Capitalism: Welfare Capitalism

Japan and Germany versus the Anglo-Saxons

RONALD DORE

OXFORD

UNIVERSITY PRESS

OXFORD
UNIVERSITY PRESS

Great Clarendon Street, Oxford OX2 6DP
Oxford University Press is a department of the University of Oxford.
It furthers the University's objective of excellence in research, scholarship,
and education by publishing worldwide in

Oxford New York

Athens Auckland Bangkok Bogotá Buenos Aires Calcutta
Cape Town Chennai Dar es Salaam Delhi Florence Hong Kong Istanbul
Karachi Kuala Lumpur Madrid Melbourne Mexico City Mumbai
Nairobi Paris São Paulo Singapore Taipei Tokyo Toronto Warsaw

and associated companies in Berlin Ibadan

Oxford is a registered trade mark of Oxford University Press
in the UK and in certain other countries

Published in the United States
by Oxford University Press Inc., New York

British Library Cataloguing in Publication Data

Data available

Library of Congress Cataloging-in-Publication Data

Dore, Ronald Philip.
Stock market capitalism : welfare capitalism : Japan and Germany versus the
Anglo-Saxons / Ronald Dore.
     p.   cm.
Includes bibliographical references and index.
1. Management—Japan. 2. Management—Germany. 3. Management—United States.
4. Management—Great Britain. 5. Capitalism—Japan. 6. Capitalism—Germany.
7. Capitalism—United States. 8. Capitalism—Great Britain. I. Title
HD70.J3 D67 2000   330.12'2—dc21   00-025534

ISBN 0–19–924062–0 (Hbk.)
ISBN 0–19–924061–2 (Pbk.)

10 9 8 7 6 5 4 3 2 1

Typeset by BookMan Services
Printed in Great Britain
on acid-free paper by
Biddles Ltd
Guildford and King's Lynn

To Peter Parker

who may not share all the sentiments, much less
endorse the judgements of this book, but whose
warm support was invaluable at many points on
the road to its completion

Preface

... up to the present moment, mostly you were for the economy or for protecting the environment, you were for business or you were for labor, you were for promoting work or for promoting family life.... We come and say, well, we're for fiscal responsibility and social justice, we're for individual and group identity and the national community.

William Clinton, speech at the Florence Third Way Conference,
21 November 1999

Britain must leave behind the sterile century-long conflict between enterprise and fairness—between the left which promoted the good society at the expense of the good economy, and the right which promoted the good economy at the expense of the good society.

Gordon Brown, pre-Budget speech, *Financial Times*, 10 November 1999

What sort of government wants to slash capital gains tax for entrepreneurs while limiting access to incapacity benefit? Britain's Labour government. ... In the past, the Chancellor seemed to view wealth creation as an abstract process which could occur without individuals getting rich.... Wait a few years and we may even hear Mr Brown talking about the trickle-down effect.

The Lex column, *Financial Times*, 10 November 1999

THERE you have it: the fluffy circle-squaring politicians and their plain-speaking interpreter who knows where he and his fellow wealth-creators are coming from. I suppose that if I were asked to explain in one sentence what I mean by the 'versus' in my subtitle, the answer would go like this. People in Germany and Japan, both those whom Gordon Brown and Bill Clinton would count on the political left and those they would put on the right, do not have quite the same views about money and motives as they or the Lex columnist have. They tend to believe that, although money is a splendid thing to have, and few people would not put themselves out to get some, if you want to know why people work hard, work conscientiously, work creatively, work entrepreneurially, money is only a small part of the answer; you need also to look at social structures, the perceived fairness of organizational arrangements, friendships, collegiality, obligations arising from personal relations, as well as the intrinsic satisfactions of the work itself.

And I hope this book will also draw attention to the fact that where people *do* believe that, their beliefs are more likely to be reflected in—and confirmed by—the way other members of their society actually behave. Conversely, a society in which people are always told that the only thing that counts is the bottom line is likely to become a society of bottom-liners. This is not a book about 'human nature' as embodied in that rational maximizing automaton who lurks in the pages of every neoclassical economics textbook. It is about living people whose families and schools and tobacco advertisements and sitcoms and politicians' speeches and work friendships have made them into individuals who, in spite of their infinite variety, can—most of them at least—be discerned to belong to the genus Americana, the genus Japonica, the genus Anglicana or Germanica.

Apart from the beliefs about money and motivation which I have singled out here, there is a long list of other concomitant differences between these societies which the following pages will enlarge on. But for the most part the book is not just about those differences themselves, but also about the very large number of people in both Japan and Germany who now believe, or profess to believe, that their countries have been *getting it all wrong*. What we need, these reformers argue, are all the things which over the last twenty years have made America and Britain the successful societies they are today—deregulation in the name of consumer sovereignty and of the moral as well as the efficiency virtues of competition, a change in corporate governance to make managers concentrate single-mindedly on creating shareholder value, a roll-back of the state and especially of the welfare systems which encourage dependency and idleness, tax adjustments to let the wealth-creators keep more of the wealth they create in their own pockets.

The debate has been more prominent, more strident, in Japan than in Germany, largely because Japanese society and economy were so much further from these 'Anglo-Saxon' ideals. But, during 1998 and early 1999, when this book was being written, the dominance of such reformist opinions in the media and in the pronouncements of business leaders and politicians was unmistakable.

The extent to which actual economic *behaviour* changed was far less dramatic. The *Financial Times* and *Wall Street Journal* correspondents were able, it is true, to find evidence for enthusiastic, celebratory, and often patronizing, reports that the Japanese were finally abandoning their quaint, irrational, cronyist habits. Firms were refusing to give profit-sacrificing help to banks just because they belonged to the same enterprise group, they were abandoning loyal suppliers in favour of cheaper ones, declaring lifetime employment to be at an end, proclaiming their conversion to doctrines of shareholder value. Much the same tale was told about Germany. And the Japanese media, more than the German, reflected the same general assumptions: few swallows here as yet, but the full Anglo-Saxon summer of which they were the harbingers was well on its way and bound to come.

Recently, in Japan especially, a badly bruised national self-esteem seems to be recovering. On 1 March 1999 a business magazine, *Nikkei Bijinesu*, splashed across its cover: 'The Japan which has not woken up to the power of the Net'. By 11 October it was proclaiming 'Second wave of the e-revolution: Japan and America towards a great reversal of roles' and describing how the number of Internet-connected mobile phones in Japan had gone from zero in January to a million and a half by August, while they were still hardly heard of anywhere else. And as confidence returns, the advocates of reform may be losing ground. Defenders of the system seem less daunted by the prospect of challenging what they have been told are 'global standards' (and what is indeed a globally dominant ideology), and they have begun speaking up more boldly. Toyota's chairman told an international business forum (at which Jack Welch from GE was the star turn) that his firm was not going to abandon lifetime employment however much Standard and Poor's lowered its credit rating (*Nikkei*, 8 October 1999). In Germany, too, the Vodaphone/Mannesmann battle (not exactly a clash between 'financial logic and the dictates of German nationalism' as the Lex column crassly put it) is sharpening issues as never before. Even such famous spokesmen for shareholder value as Schrempp of Daimler-Benz and Ackermann of Deutsche Bank, acting as shareholder representatives on the Mannesmann Board, seem unwilling to view the Vodaphone offer solely in terms of whether shareholders would ultimately benefit. (Their other considerations have less to do with 'German nationalism' and more to do with notions of corporations as organic entities and objects of loyalty; though if it turns out—ultimate irony and ultimate comeuppance for Mr Esser, the Mannesmann Chief Executive—that Mannesmann goes under because it has let 60 per cent of its shares get into foreign hands, the nationalist tap will obviously be turned on with a vengeance.)

Who knows whether, before this book reaches the bookstores in five months' time, the whole perspective on the issues it deals with will have been changed. After all, even the persuasive magic of Greenspan surely cannot much longer persuade fund managers that price–earnings ratios, outstanding margin loans, consumer debt, and the balance of trade deficit can all go on rising and rising—and carrying their dollar asset values into the stratosphere—for ever. And among the many and not necessarily pleasant effects of a jolting 'correction' on Wall Street would certainly be a deflation of the claims of the Japanese and German proponents of stock market capitalism. The reader of this book may know a lot more than the writer; the hazards of writing a book about the contemporary world to academic publishing timetables are obvious.

This one started, in 1991, as something quite different, a book to be written with a German colleague on how the capitalist economies of Japan and Germany differed, and differed in similar ways, from those of Britain and America, and how the countries of Eastern Europe might do well to question whether a flourishing stock market really was the key to rebuilding their economies on free market lines. We had no sooner started than we were scooped by Michel Albert, who made the central point about different types of capitalism in a much more entertaining, if less meticulously documented, way than we would have done. (Those were the days when I was less confident about people taking me on trust without meticulous documentation than I am now.) Then, the next year, Alan Blinder delivered what we had intended to be the 'message for emerging economies' forcefully and elegantly in an address to the International Economic Association in Moscow. It soon became obvious that nobody in Eastern Europe was in the least inclined to listen to Alan Blinder, much less to us—as the failed efforts of a Russian and a Hungarian friend to get a short article of mine translated for local journals demonstrated. But still, for the first half of the 1990s, although the zest had gone out of the intended book project, its intention of delineating a stable 'alternative form of capitalism' remained. That the final upshot should be a book whose central theme is whether or not there will *continue to be* an alternative form of capitalism is something which, even five years ago, I would never have imagined.

My debts are multiple: to the Centre for Economic Performance, its director Richard Layard, and its administrators Nigel Rogers and Marion O'Brien for giving me a home over those years; to the Leverhulme Trust, which long ago gave me a grant to start the work, and to Rex Richards and Barry Supple for being so understanding about a gestation period seemingly stretching to infinity; to those who taught me most of what I know about Germany: Wolfgang Streeck, my original intended collaborator and constant mentor over the years, Isabela Mares, whose guidance through my one and only 'field trip' to Germany was so eye-opening, Ansgar Richter for many enlightening conversations, and above all to Gregory Jackson, without whose control over statistical details and close reading of the typescript I would have been lost. I also benefited greatly from the chance to join the Japan/Germany project meetings organized by Kozo Yamamura and Wolfgang Streeck. My chief debt in Japan is to Inagami Takeshi, who provided a steady stream of faxes and e-mails to keep me abreast of what was going on, tipped me off about the web pages I should look at, and ran the Global Standards Study Group of senior academics, businessman, and officials which we formed during my stay in Japan in the spring of 1998. For that visit—three months in the stimulating environment of the Graduate Institute for Policy Research (GRIPS)—I have the kindness of the late and sadly missed Professor Sato Seisaburo to thank. Another steady source of mailed information and (wry) comment was Suzuki Fujikazu of the Rengo research institute, while Kamimura Yasuhiro and Fujimoto Makoto provided the occasional mail-order research assistance. Among the many lunch companions whose ideas I have shamelessly borrowed, several stand out—Asanuma Ken, Larry Duke, Kosai Yutaka, Namiwaki Yoshiyasu, Ogata Shijuro, Ono Kenichi, Takai Kunitake, Tanaka Masami, and Yoshitomi Masaru.

For helpful and sometimes crucial comments on various chapters at various stages, thanks go to more people than I shall, doubtless, succeed in remembering: Masahiko Aoki, Chris Beauman, Suzanne Berger, Andrea Boltho, Colin Crouch, Andrew Gordon, Gregory Jackson, Henry Laurence, Bill Lazonick, Mary O'Sullivan, T. J. Pempel, Henry Rosovsky, Mari Sako, Ulrike Schaede, Wolfgang Streeck, Ezra

Vogel, Robert Wade, Hugh Whittaker, and Oxford's anonymous copyeditor. I am particularly grateful to Andrew Gordon for organizing a seminar at Harvard to mull over a nearly final draft.

I also thank the editors of the *Journal of Japanese Studies* for their kind permission to use material first published in their journal.

All errors and quirky opinions are mine, of course.

RD, 24 November 1999

Contents

Chapter 1

Introduction

THERE are two ways of reading this book. One is as a study of recent developments in Japan—to be read with a touch of ironic *Schadenfreude*, perhaps. Is this the same Dore, the reader might ask, who was explaining,[1] a decade ago, as the doctrine of labour market 'flexibility' was on the way to becoming the orthodoxy which British Prime Minister Tony Blair would subsequently preach to the rest of Europe, that Japan's rigidities could also have flexibility of a different kind? The Japanese were indeed—so went the argument—much less free not only to change jobs and hire and fire, but also to invest and disinvest, to switch from one supplier to another, to buy a company on Monday and sell it on Thursday. But, at the same time, the security and predictability they gained from accepting the constraints of these long-term commitments—'jobs for life' and all—meant that they had far more flexible cooperation, fewer changes thwarted by clashes of vested interests, and hence, in the long run, greater efficiency, faster innovation and, to boot, a more cohesive and egalitarian society.

And is this the same Dore who showed his incurable nostalgia for all those discredited 1970s things like incomes policies, industrial democracy, and corporatism by telling us that we should take Japan seriously[2] as a source of hints as to how we, in spite of our very different values and cultural preferences, might arrive at a less conflictual, less authoritarian, and more egalitarian way of managing our affairs?

So what, some readers might ask, has he got to say now that the 'Japan as model' bubble has been pricked and nobody wants to listen to sanctimonious nonsense about taking Japan seriously any more? Clearly he can't let go. While in Japan clear-minded reformers, under the sound and disinterested guidance of the US Treasury and the Tokyo army of American and British financial analysts, are bravely shedding their trammelling rigidities and joining the real world of tough competition in globally flexible markets, here, now, is a new

Jeremiah Dore. In the guise of an objective account of the changes in economic structure—and in ideas about economic structure—over the last decade, he offers, in effect, a lament. Here he is, mourning, in the company of his septuagenarian Japanese friends, the passing of 'their' Japan, trying desperately to believe that the country will once again become a byword for quality and innovation, and that when it does so it will still be something like the opaque, cartelized, crony-ridden, hugger-mugger Japan they once knew.

Doubtless I caricaturize potential caricaturists, but it is certainly true that the story I present here of Japan's recent troubles and soul-searching is considerably different from, for example, the American triumphalist thrust of Richard Katz's recent—and in the United States much acclaimed—*Japan: The System that Soured: The Rise and Fall of the Japanese Economic Miracle*.[3] Different, in the first instance, in focus. Most discussions—including discussions among Japanese—are about the meaning of recent changes, both evolutionary and engineered, for Japan's competitive strength in the neomercantilist competition among nations. That is the question I address in the last chapter of the book, but it will be evident that my main concern is with the impact of change on the quality of life, the quality of social relations, and the distribution of income and life chances. That difference in focus leads to differences in evaluation and in interpretation—in assertions and speculations as to what causes what. I hope nevertheless that my de-scription of recent changes in economic practice and thought will also be of use to readers with a different focus of interest. And I also hope that I have by now had enough training in leaning over backwards to make it a reasonably fair description, so that even if I do make my prejudices clear by indulgence in the odd ironic aside, readers with different prejudices can find the information they need for counter-argument.

But, more importantly, the polemical thrust of this book is not simply about Japan.

Financialization

It is also—and this is the second and more important way of reading this book—about modern capitalism, about a pattern of gradual change common to all the industrial societies. What is happening in Japan is a rerun of trends which have long since been apparent, and in the last two decades have been greatly accelerated, in the United States and Britain. Call it postindustrialism, call it neoliberalism, call it the consequence of affluent individualism and globalization, call it, if you are a Fukuyama fan, a part of the Great Disruption. It has many strands, but the label which perhaps best captures the dominant common element is—though I shall be as sparing as possible with ugly neologisms—'marketization plus financialization'.

Perhaps 'financialization' alone would do, but it is a process rather different from the financialization of capitalism that Hilferding talked about in his 1910 book *Das Finanzkapital*. It is anything but 'organized' capitalism, offering much less of a role for individual powerful financiers, and much more for market forces and a vast financial services industry. Some of the major strands of the transformation are set out in Figure 1. The enormous cheapening of communication and transport and the possibilities of globalization inherent in the vast leaps in technology of recent decades (bottom left-hand corner) have made financial services (and the large part of the information services industry devoted to finance) potentially the greatest of all export industries. They have replaced traditional branches of manufacturing as a major focus of international competitiveness (today you could buy the whole American steel industry with 5 per cent of the shares of America Online). But in my causal map, that *facilitating factor* is only one of four *root causes*, the other three (the three at the top) being—however much they themselves are deeply rooted in social and technical change—more directly the result of political will. They are the salient features of the neoliberal radicalism of Reagan and Thatcher: first, the decision largely to withdraw the state from the business of supporting the old; secondly, the preoccupation with 'competitiveness', i.e. staking the nation's pride and well-being on its position in the international-growth league tables; and, thirdly, adoption as a matter of universal principle of the Smithian notion that profit-seekers, competing with each other, will always be led by the invisible hand (supplemented by a raft of telecoms regulators, Financial Services Agencies, electricity regulators, etc.) to add more to the sum of human happiness than salaried public servants.

The trends which result and whose working out in Japan—and

Figure 1. Neoliberalism and the rising dominance of the finance industry

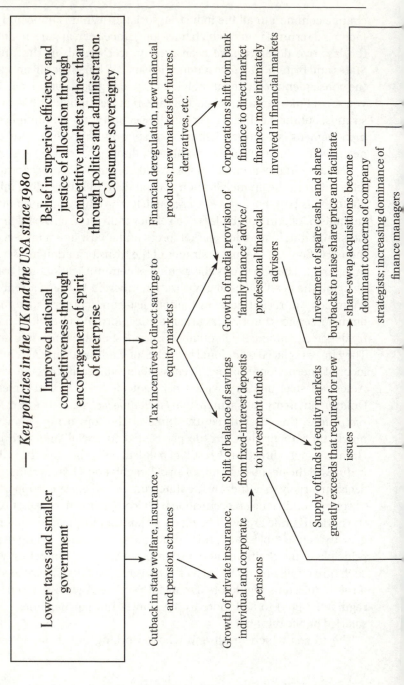

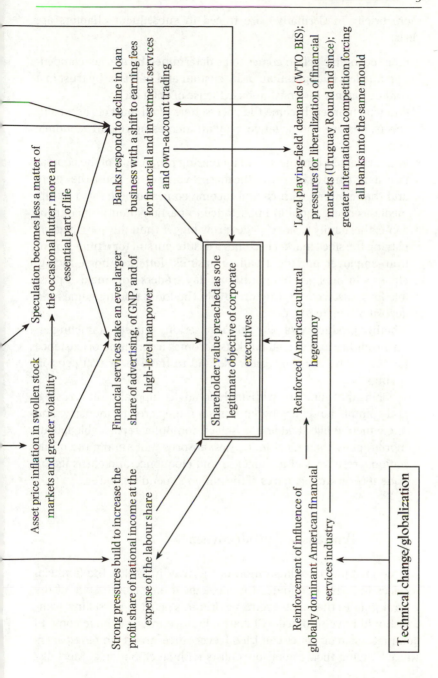

Speculation becomes less a matter of the occasional flutter, more an essential part of life

Banks respond to decline in loan business with a shift to earning fees for financial and investment services and own-account trading

Asset price inflation in swollen stock markets and greater volatility

Financial services take an ever larger share of advertising, of GNP, and of high-level manpower

'Level playing-field' demands (WTO, BIS); pressures for liberalization of financial markets (Uruguay Round and since); greater international competition forcing all banks into the same mould

Shareholder value preached as sole legitimate objective of corporate executives

Reinforced American cultural hegemony

Strong pressures build to increase the profit share of national income at the expense of the labour share

Reinforcement of influence of globally dominant American financial services industry

Technical change/globalization

more briefly in Germany—are traced in subsequent chapters are clear:

- more economic action comes to be determined by market competition and less by regulation, or by custom and habit, or by trust in a trading partner's friendship-based sense of obligation;
- financial markets become the pace-setters of all markets as wealth effects, positive and negative, play an increasing role in economic cycles;
- financial assets become, for an increasing proportion of the population, as much of a concern as the market value of the house they own;
- and that concern with capital income comes to be treated by the media as being equal in importance to participation in labour income; the 'family finance' pages grow bigger than the 'jobs' pages;
- playing the stock market becomes a leisure pursuit (or a time-stolen-from-employer pursuit) rivalling casinos, lotteries, horse-racing, etc. as a form of gambling: Internet day-traders now make it possible for housewives in Dayton to join the forex trading game for a deposit of a mere $10,000:
- whether productive of play fun or of serious anxiety, gambling on uncertainties in financial markets becomes a condition of existence for those who expect to grow old and to have to live off pension savings;
- servicing that gambling with analysis, advice, appraisal, advertising, and commission-charging becomes a major growth industry, and one which, while shedding unskilled computer-replaceable labour more rapidly than most industries, absorbs more and more of the nation's resources of intelligence and eloquence and earns its exponents ever-larger shares of the nation's spending power.

Pensions and productivism

Let me give just one illustration of the way in which the financial services industry dominates the ideological airspace in spite of the warning notes that such events as Britain's pension misselling scandal should have sounded. (Of course finance interests have come to dominate, said an American friend, ever since American newspapers started paying their senior journalists with stock options.) Most discussions of pensions start off, as if stating an unassailable fact, from the notion that it is impossible to continue the traditional pay-as-you-go system of paying this year's pension largely out of this year's contributions, with only a small invested float if any at all. Pay-as-you-go is dead. Today, the argument typically runs, we have three-and-a-half people working for every pensioner. In 30 years' time it will be only two-and-a-half. It is unreasonable to expect those two-and-a-half to bear the tax and social security contributions to pay a whole person's pension. So people must be self-reliant and save for their old age themselves. What few people bother to ask is where the returns on those savings are going to come from. The savers have a choice. Either they send their savings to China or Brazil and build up claims to the production of future generations of Chinese and Brazilians—which could be quite risky given the volatility of exchange rates. And, as a *Financial Times* leader-writer suggested, 'the successful Asians' . . . readiness to pay for pensions in the West rests on a rosy Western perception of mutual interest that could yet be confounded by realpolitik'. Anyway the savings might be needed for economic growth at home. But if they do keep them at home, it is still the work of the same two-and-a-half producers that they will be depending on for their rentier income as pensioners. Will their collective market power to extract rent and interest and profits from those two-and-a-half workers be so much greater than their collective political power to persuade the two-and-a-half to pay the necessary sums in taxes or social security contributions? Market and state are simply two alternative mechanisms by which those of working age support those who can no longer work. And for a 25-year-old for whom the crunch will come in 40 years, no greater certainty attaches to the one than to the other.

And it is not only a matter of certainty. Deciding what is the best balance between these two alternative methods is indeed a fearsomely complex matter, far beyond the simplicities of 'self-reliance' and 'not being a burden on the young'. It involves considering, for example, the way that the respective capital and wage shares of GNP are determined by market forces and the way that institutional arrangements can shape and bend those market forces; the effects of different institutional arrangements on work ethics and work motivation, as well as on the incentive to save; the effects on income distribution; the relative strength of property rights arguments and community cohesion arguments as a means of legitimating redistribution, and the relative faith that citizens have in promises embodied in the property system and the political system. But who cares about following through on such arguments when in Britain there is £60 million pounds a year to be made simply out of the advertising for Individual Savings Accounts, an amount which is doubtless peanuts compared with what is spent in the United States advertising the equivalent 401(k) plans?

Japan is one country where the pensions issue is a crucial one, likely to have considerable consequences for how far Japan goes down the financialization road. It is starting on that road 'further back', as it were, than Britain or the United States. On the one hand, its pattern of long-term commitments militates against arm's-length markets. On the other, what one might call its 'productivism' militates against financialization. One of Japan's Confucian legacies is a well-established 'productivism' vocabulary. Everybody understands the distinction between 'the culture of making things' and 'the culture of making money' (with 'things' and 'money' being conventionally put in the Japanese equivalent of quotes when the words are written). And those who use the distinction generally imply that the former—a culture geared to serving one's fellow-citizens by providing goods and services —is more worthy than, ethically superior to, a culture geared to 'mere' self-enrichment unlinked to any concern with the service or disservice one might be doing to one's fellow-citizens in the process. Which is not to say that there are no Japanese with the instincts and behaviour patterns of the Maxwells and the Rowlands, the Trumps and the Boeskys. Only that they just do not become celebrities and few people take them as role models.

I realize that in endorsing these productivist sentiments I risk putting myself in the company of Queen Victoria, who wrote, apropos of a peerage for Lord Rothschild, that 'she cannot think that one who owes his great wealth to contracts with Foreign Governments for Loans, or to successful speculations on the Stock Exchange can fairly claim a British Peerage . . . this seems to her not the less a species of gambling, because it is on a gigantic scale—& far removed from that legitimate trading which she *delights* to *honour*'.[4] (Since so many of her aristocratic favourites were equally the beneficiaries of speculation, it may be doubted whether she would have taken the same line had Rothschild not been a Jew.) The other doubtful association of productivism, particularly in the Confucian tradition, is with the agrarian fundamentalism whose Japanese exponents assassinated prime ministers and contributed to the collapse of civilian government in the 1930s—and which took a very similar form in Europe in the *Blut und Boden* element in Nazism.

Thus, that there are dangers in stiff-necked moralism about speculation, I recognize. Nevertheless, by my values there is an important distinction to be drawn between, say, running a betting shop—a service giving the punters a bit of fun—and what the Japanese call the 'money game' of hedge traders who make their money as often as not by destroying the hedges that prudent traders build, rather than tending and mending them.

Shareholder value

Speculation is a part of the story told in Figure 1, and pensions are an even more important part, but these are not the central focus of this book. That central focus is the centre also of the chart—the point of convergence of all the arrows: 'Shareholder value preached as sole legitimate objective of corporate executives'. And it is striking how rapidly, in the countries which are ahead in the financialization process, that objective is being achieved. A Goldman Sachs study of manufacturing value-added in the United States, Germany, and Europe in general, recently concluded that

> The share of gross value added going to wages and salaries has declined on trend in the US since the early 1980s. In fact, for the US, this appears to be an extension of a trend that has been in place since the early 1970s. . . . We believe that the pressures of competition for the returns on capital available in the emerging economies have forced US industry to produce higher returns on equity capital and that their response to this has been to reserve an increasingly large share of output for the owners of capital.[5]

One may cast doubt on the explanation (the subsequent collapse of the emerging markets seems not to have diminished the drive to increase capital's returns at the expense of labour), while accepting the paper's meticulous documentation of the fact.

And today, multiple voices are urging Japanese managers to go in the same direction. The transformation on the agenda may be variously described—from employee sovereignty to shareholder sovereignty; from the employee-favouring firm to the shareholder-favouring firm; from pseudo-capitalism to genuine capitalism. They all mean the same thing: the transformation of firms run primarily for the benefit of their employees into firms run primarily, even exclusively, for the benefit of their shareholders. And for the whole economy—and this is what the stock market capitalism/welfare capitalism contrast of my title is intended to convey—it means an economy centred on the stock market as the measure of corporate success and on the stock market index as a measure of national well-being, as opposed to an economy which has other, better, more pluralistic criteria of human welfare for measuring progress towards the good society.

Once upon a time the business schools of America and Britain debated the relative merits of the property or shareholder-value-as-maximand view of the firm (the one which has become the dominant Anglo-Saxon doctrine) and what was called in contrast the 'stake-holder' view. Unfortunately, in Britain, soon after a speech by Tony Blair in Singapore some five years ago when he seemed to be talking about just that, the term 'stakeholder' was appropriated for various foggy features of the new Third Way, such as a new system of pensions and profit-sharing in industry—both of which involve marginal rearrangements of property rights, but no qualification whatever of the assumed supremacy of property rights over other rights.

It is in this sense that the Japanese and German systems are distinctly different from the Anglo-Saxon system. The rights of owners in Japan and Germany are seen to be very properly circumscribed by the rights of other stakeholders—employees, customers, suppliers and subcontractors, creditors, local communities, etc. There is a difference between the two societies. In Japan, hitherto, there has been little doubt that employees come a clear first. To be sure, Japanese firms are indeed more prone than those in Anglo-Saxon economies to treat their suppliers as having a stake in trading relationships of long standing which should be respected. When they talk of giving good service to their customers, it is indeed the case that the ratio of earnest honesty to cynical manipulation is quite high. But the stakeholder which is of overwhelming importance to a Japanese manager is the community of *sha-in*, the 'members of the enterprise community': the firm's regular employees who, like himself, joined the firm, mostly at a very early age, in the expectation of making a career in it. In fact, the concern for suppliers and customers also springs in large part from that concern for the enterprise community. Decent treatment of customers and suppliers affects the reputation of the firm in the society at large; hence it affects the 'standing' which the manager himself has when he goes to seminars and meetings of his business federation, as somebody who is identified with, and identifies himself with, his firm.

In Germany, though the sense of the firm as a public institution with major responsibilities towards society as a whole is relatively stronger compared with Japan, it is still the employees who have hitherto been considered as the most important stakeholders, rather than the owners of shares.

In the 1960s, the golden age of managerial capitalism, Britain and America had a lot of businessmen with some sort of 'stakeholder' notion of their responsibilities at the top of some of the major enterprises and banks. True, the lifetime-employment pattern which dominated in the civil service and the police and armed forces was extended in private industry only to the managerial ranks of some of the larger firms like Unilever, BP, Kodak, IBM, and the major banks. The Anglo-Saxon societies always were more mobile than Japan has in recent decades (only in recent decades) become. Top managers may have been a good deal more flamboyant and domineering than top civil servants, but, like civil servants, they got their income predominantly from their salaries, and, like top civil servants, they owed their job partly to 'character', their ability to handle people and impress their fellows in the bureaucratic organization in which they spent their lives, but in large part, also, to the thoroughness with which they knew the business of the firm they ran—its products, its technology and the way it could be developed, its markets, its sources of supply, its employees.

That similarity, or cultural affinity, between the bureaucratic corporate manager and the civil servant was, indeed, one of the elements which inspired such 1960s predictions of a benign evolution towards a social democratic form of capitalism as those of Galbraith[6] or Shonfield.[7] These were the managers Burnham had in mind when, 20 years earlier, he wrote of *The Managerial Revolution*[8] as something that was transforming our notions of capitalism. Marx wrote about Capital and how it treated Labour in an England in which the family firm predominated. The paradigm capitalist was the owner-manager. Now, he was replaced by the technically competent salaried manager and organization-builder, notionally responsible to a fragmented mass of stockholders, but in effect, as Berle and Means pointed out,[9] with a wide range of discretionary autonomy, and (Robin Marris[10]) with a tendency to be more concerned about organization growth than about maximizing profits.

The capitalist-manager's counter-revolution

What we have been witnessing in recent decades, especially the last two, is the capitalist-managerial counter-revolution. The fat cats of British boardrooms are favourite topics for the financial press as well as for the tabloids. But it is not so much the size of their packages as the way they are calculated that is the nub of the counter-revolution. Increasingly the big rewards come, not from salaries, but sometimes from performance bonuses, linked to some measure of profits, and much more commonly from stock options. The fact that the value of the option depends on the share price is seen as incentive enough effectively to align the interests of managers with those of the owners to whom they are—exclusively, in modern doctrine—responsible. In the 200 largest American companies 'shares and share options still "live" in incentive schemes at the end of 1998 amounted to 13.2% of corporate equity', and American companies as a whole spent $220bn in that year buying back shares so that their employees could exercise their options.[11] Since in most cases the granting of options appears nowhere in the company's accounts as a cost, some people are beginning to wonder whether the cost to shareholders of aligning managers' interests with their own is more than it is worth—a point to which we will return in the last chapter when considering system efficiency.

This transformation in managers' financial incentives and in their perceptions of their responsibilities is the effect of many factors, some of which are hinted at in my chart. One is the concentration of ownership in insurance companies, pension funds, and mutuals, the direct influence of their representatives on Boards, and above all their decisive influence in takeovers. To that should be added the increasing incidence of takeovers as the investment banks' ability to mobilize large sums of money to facilitate them grows. Another factor is that prompting some firm to make a bid for another and earning vast commissions from managing their takeover battle strategy has become a major part of investment bank business. (In Europe, celebrates the *New York Herald Tribune*, 'a generation of young, talented and ambitious

Europeans [who were] educated and trained in the United States, [and] have embraced the concept of shareholder value and American financial techniques' are now dominant in the European offices of the 'two hottest firms in corporate finance', Goldman Sachs and Morgan Stanley. 'They are using their local knowledge and contacts to sell European companies on the merits of takeovers, leveraged buyouts, innovative debt and equity offerings and other restructuring tactics.'[12]) The increase in takeovers, and the increasing equation of 'corporate strategy' and 'corporate restructuring' with the buying and selling of companies and bits of companies, has led to the replacement of engineering by financial expertise at the top of corporations, which has provided feedback reinforcement for the trend which caused it. All of these evolutionary changes have had the effect of reversing the Berle and Means trend towards fragmented, powerless ownership. Shareholders have in reality become more powerful, and at the same time some spectacular boardroom scandals (the RJR Nabisco story, for example) have reinforced the popularity and legitimacy of shareholder activism.

Thence the urge towards greater shareholder power. The means have been provided by true-believer economists, working within what is known as principal–agent game theory to devise ever more ingenious uses of stock option and other remuneration devices, reinforced by the business school professors/managerial consultants who dominate the business press, vying with their MVAs and EVAs, their EBITDAs and their FCFs to produce *the* ultimate accounting measure of the extent to which a managerial team actually enhances shareholder value.

These exemplars of Davos Man, members of the new capitalist-manager class, are, to be sure, not quite the same as the robber-barons of old. Wherever they sit in the system they are constrained by the rules they have worked out for fair play among themselves—stock exchange disclosure rules, takeover bid rules, the Financial Services Authority in and out of which they rotate. And they are constrained by their investors. Their investors, however, are, effectively, other capitalist-managers—the managers of pension funds, merchant banks, insurance companies, and investment funds. They in their turn are paid by the same criteria, and at similarly generous levels to the people they supposedly control. They have the same constellation of interests and are fully cognizant of the community of interests which bind them to support of the system and of the financialization process which is consolidating it.

Come off it. Relax!

Some take a relaxed view of the financialization process and see it as possibly good for democracy. The so-called employee-favouring firms of Japan and Germany, this argument goes, may take care of their workers, not only paying them premium wages and fringe benefits above what would be their market-clearing price, but keeping them redundantly on the books at the expense of potential profits. This both lowers the efficiency of the whole system and also makes their employees a pampered labour aristocracy, at the expense of those who work in the less protected sectors of the economy. Much better to give efficient managers free rein to maximize the returns on the scarce capital they employ, to hire as much labour as they need at the price the market dictates, and to give as much of their revenue to shareholders as possible. That way the total cake is bigger. And if a bigger share thereby goes to the shareholder, well, aren't we all shareholders now? As shareholders via our pension funds we have—potentially at least—power in the system. We can make our fund trustees invest ethically; make them steer clear of firms making landmines or genetically modified foods. It's all—potentially—a wonderful process of 'empowerment'.

Like most arguments employing the word 'empowerment', the emotion is not in doubt, but the logic is faulty. First, it's just not going to happen. If ever there was a principal–agent problem never likely to be resolved it is that between the ordinary joe prospective pensioner and the hot-shot pension fund manager trying desperately to beat the index. And in any case the ordinary joe does want returns, not ethics nor—as several American efforts to use union influence on pension funds for other than revenue-maximizing purposes have shown—advancement of working-class solidarity. Secondly—my principal objection—for every person empowered and enriched, several are depowered and made, relatively if not absolutely, poorer. Those who work in employee-favouring firms may be a labour aristocracy, and a system of pensions (like the German one) which is based on final salaries may mirror existing inequalities, but paying for social security by pay-as-you-earn contributions to a central fund out of labour income *can* include a redistributive pooling of risks more egalitarian than a system which redistributes capital income through pensions and endowment policies. Private insurance and private pensions do more than reflect the inequality of the incomes out of which the contributions and premiums are paid; they greatly amplify them.

There is a third comment to be made on the 'relax!' argument. 'Give managers a free hand to manage the scarce capital they employ,' it says. This, a major premise of the argument, reveals one of the founding assumptions of modern capitalism—that it is indeed capital that is the scarce resource; that 'labour' will normally be in fairly abundant supply. It is amazing that anyone can seriously sustain this view in a world awash with so much liquidity that its movement from one country to another keeps exchange rates in perpetual motion. Or that it can be sustained in a world of skill shortages, in which the steadily increasing complexity of the technology we use, and the consequent steady increase in the learning time required to master it, and in the premium placed on scarce learning ability (i.e. brains), makes the human capital that can walk out of any manager's door at will a far more crucial factor of production.

The dominance of the free trade ideology at this millennium-end is nearly absolute, and Yergin and Stanislaw have traced in a fascinating and convincing manner how it has become so.[13] The rampant protectionist behaviour of governments is always excused as temporary weakness of the flesh compromising the spirit's willingness to do right. If only nobody sins, the free-traders urge, any sacrifice we make, any social disruption and painful loss to minority private interests in the short term, will eventually be rewarded with much greater prosperity for all; by definition we all have comparative advantage in something and even the rioters in Seattle streets will eventually find out what it is.

I have explained elsewhere my own view of where compromises ought to be drawn—and drawn explicitly and with confidence, not half-heartedly and apologetically—between free trade principles and conflicting values.[14] The debates about banking and corporate governance which I describe later in this book suggest another illustration of the position which I would want to advocate. It goes as follows. International institutions which seek to achieve genuine 'international public goods', such as confidence in the international banking system, are indeed highly desirable. But those institutions can be, and are in case of the BIS as in that of the WTO, shaped not merely by such public goods considerations—in the case of banking, for example, the prudential regulations—but also by the stronger players' appeal to 'level playing-field' arguments for rules which minimize all restraints on international competition to the clear and disproportionate advantage of their own national firms.

The banking crisis in Japan offered an illustration. The authority carried by the Basle committee rules enforcing criteria for the capital adequacy of internationally trading banks is nowhere greater than in Japan, a country whose determination to be internationally a 'good neighbour' cannot be in doubt. Short-term economic policy in the spring of 1998 and 1999 was constrained—there is dispute about how much—by the government's desire to ensure that the Japanese stock market achieved a price level that would allow Japan's internationally operating banks to value the shares they owned at a price which allowed them to reach their 8 per cent capital reserve requirement. Now, the *prudential raison d'être* of those rules was already fulfilled, one would have thought quite adequately, by the limited-term (until April 2001) guarantee the Japanese government had given for all deposits in Japanese banks, overseas as well as at home. Nevertheless the possibility of flouting, or asking for a temporary suspension of, the Basle committee rules was never canvassed. The prospect of retaliatory reactions on *level playing-field* rather than *prudential* grounds was doubtless too daunting for anyone to float the idea.

At the risk of belabouring the point, let us imagine what arguments a Japanese government might have deployed. They are not dissimilar to the arguments which the French or the Canadians deployed in refusing to accept free trade in films and television.

Financial services are indeed an internationalized industry, and since it is one built on confidence, and since with such a density of interbank dealings lack of confidence can be highly contagious, there is a need for prudential rules. We accept a duty of good-neighbourliness and will ensure that all our internationally dealing banks reach an acceptable standard of prudence, though we insist that the rules should be drawn such that alternative means of maintaining confidence—capital requirements or government guarantees—should be explicitly recognized in those rules.

As for competitiveness, we recognize no similar good neighbour obligation to achieve what is called a 'level playing-field' because it cannot in practice be attained. A genuine levelling would require other countries to receive compensating advantages to balance America's superior assets, such as its vast natural resources, the sheer size of its internal market, its great migration inflow (all those clever Chinese now, all those Jews given refuge from Europe in the 1930s and 1940s), and—another of its important assets—a trading ethic which allows banks to drop unprofitable customers overnight, even after 50 years of collaborative trading. What you seem to mean by 'level playing-field' is that we should conform to you. But how can we, and why should we? On the one hand, getting the natural resources or the immigrants is impossible. On the other, adopting a trading ethic of single-minded concentration on profits means accepting your view that our concern with collective goods is discredited socialism, and our concern with maintaining patterns of mutually considerate social relations is despicable 'cronyism'. We are not prepared to accept that. We value our way of life. If you assert that our collectivism and our willingness to guarantee our banks' depositors give us a competitive advantage, you may well be right. It might, in some measure, compensate for all your resource/size/in-migration advantages. But whether it does or whether it does not, that is not an argument that will persuade us to change our way of life. The playing-field analogy is a false one. We are not a team which has decided to enter for a sporting cup. We are a society which is happy to trade with whoever finds it rewarding to trade with us.

'An outmoded nostalgia for the nation-state', the gung-ho global-izers will say, and, as this book will document, the globalizers have already won over enough of the Tokyo and the Frankfurt banking communities to make the effective deployment of such arguments—for the moment, at least—unlikely.

The Goldilocks economy as the model for Japan

All very well in theory, the sceptical reader might say, but it works. Look at the American miracle. Sustained returns on equity of 20 per cent (a Japanese firm considers itself to be doing well if it returns 8 per cent) have driven the American stock market boom. The wealth effects of that, plus various other lucky conjunctures such as low oil prices, have helped to sustain buoyant consumer expenditure and maintain the exchange value of the dollar, thus attracting to its safe haven ever more of the world's liquidity to compensate for the growing balance of payments deficit and accumulating consumer debt. It has even produced the trickle-down effect of low unemployment and a slight rise in bottom-of-the-heap wages.

And if that is what works in America, then that is what we must do in Japan. Never mind if the up-sizing of profits is usually accompanied by the downsizing of employment and wages. Economic dynamism takes care of that in no time. Among the many arguments which, as the following chapters record, are used by those promoting a re-run of the capitalist-managerial counter-revolution in Japan, that is currently one of the most powerful. Whether the United States will still be providing the same glittering model of success when these words are read remains to be seen.

... and Germany

There is another society where there is a widespread belief that (to reverse Mrs Thatcher's classic expression of individualism) there *is* such a thing as society. Germans, too, tend to see the firm as something of a community of the people working in it, if also as a public institution with public responsibilities. Their firms, too, have traditionally been on the employee-favouring, rather than shareholder-favouring side of the divide. Germans, too, balance a concern to prevent abuse of monopolies with a belief that there *is* such a thing as excessive competition and that the state can usefully intervene to regulate and to promote cooperation. Germany, too, shares Japan's 'productivist' leanings and retains a strong manufacturing sector. It is also, like Japan, a relatively egalitarian society, with a generous welfare state playing an important role in maintaining compressed income differentials.

And Germany, too, is subject to all the pressures—and all the seductive temptations—which are promoting the 'Anglo-Saxonizing' processes of marketization and financialization in Japan. If anything, the debate over how far those pressures and temptations should be yielded to is more overt and more openly contested in Germany. But at any rate, a comparison between recent trends in the two countries with their similar concerns but rather different institutional backgrounds can illuminate the debate, and clarify the interconnections of institutions, for both countries. And that might, in turn, prove of some interest to those in other countries subject to similar pressures and faced with similar choices.

So, after Part I, which characterizes 'the Japanese model' in its heyday, and the more detailed survey of recent developments in Japan in Part II, Part III consists of a briefer account of developments in Germany with the comparisons with Japan explicitly drawn. All leading up to a final section which is a mixture of forecast, prophecy (in the Old Testament sense), and hope.

— PART I

The Original Japanese Model

Chapter 2

A Society of Long-Term Commitments

W HAT is fashionably called the 'Japanese model' is often a bit like Voltaire's China—a subjective amalgam, supposedly features of some admired distant society, but in fact of all those things those who use the phrase want to urge on their own fellow-citizens. ('Flat organizational hierarchies' is just one of the many characteristics falsely but once quite frequently attributed to Japan.) A better alternative title for this chapter would be 'The Japanese Economic System'. That, at any rate, is what it is about: an attempt to summarize what seem to me to have been the most important differentiating characteristics of that system around 1990, when the Japanese were relatively happy about the way things were, and before the more recent changes which the following chapters will describe. Also to say in what sense one can see it as truly a 'system' with its own internal coherence.

The firm

The best place to start is with the key economic institution, the joint-stock corporation. Of the many differences between a British or American corporation and a Japanese corporation, I single out two to begin with.

First, top management. Whether they are appointed from the external market—as a great many of them are—or from inside the firm, the appointment of a British or American CEO is usually preceded by salary negotiations between the prospective appointee and the Board's compensation committee: so much for salary, so much in stock options, so much in performance bonus calculated thus and thus, so much in retirement provision, so much in compensation if dismissed before the end of the contract term, etc. The most spectacular packages can be deemed perfectly acceptable since they are presumed to reflect an estimate on the part of the committee of how much the peculiar talents of the appointee will contribute to shareholder value.

In Japan, there is no *domestic* external market for executive talent. The head-hunting firms do nearly all their business poaching Japanese executives for foreign firms or from one foreign firm to another. When a Japanese CEO is appointed—unless the firm is in dire trouble, with almost 100 per cent probability from inside—there is no more negotiation than there used to be in pre-Thatcher days when a British civil servant was appointed a permanent secretary. As throughout his career, he would be paid by scales devised by the firm's personnel office (representing the consensual view within the firm of a fair structure). As a new graduate and member of the union, he would have been on the bottom rungs of the scale negotiated with the enterprise union. In his early to mid-thirties, he would have been appointed to a post of line responsibility which precluded union membership. Thereafter his salary would have risen in small annual increments (based in part on merit assessments as well as seniority) to double or triple its level in his early thirties by the time he was appointed to the Board as an 'ordinary' director at what would count as the 'early', high-flyer age of 50–51. (Your average director, not counted likely to make it to the very top level, might be appointed at as late an age as 56–57.) From there, there are usually four steps, at each of which it is up or out: if you are not promoted you retire. The first step, to 'managing director', gives (in the average large firm) a 30 per cent jump in salary. The second, to 'executive managing director', gives an extra 10 per cent jump. From there to 'vice-president' is a 20 per cent jump, and finally, there is another 10 per cent jump to 'president'. At that point he would be getting, on average, 11.3 times the starting salary of a new management-track graduate. (All the above figures are from a recent survey of over 700 firms.[1]) He would, of course, have that salary supplemented by a substantial entertainment allowance and a company car and driver—which he would keep for the rest of his career (unlike that of most of the company employees, his genuinely 'lifetime' career). After his (usually four-year) stint as president, he would choose his successor and move on to become chairman, and then after making way for the new chairman four years later, become an 'advisor' for the rest of his life. (Though in 1999 Toyota innovated by creating an 'honorary chairmanship' between the chairmanship and mere advisor status for Toyoda Shoichiro, in recognition of his achieving the singular honour of becoming president of the major business federation, Keidanren.) Part of the 1999 banking-crisis economies at Tokyo-Mitsubishi Bank involved cutting back on the perks of some of the eight surviving advisors who had once presided over one or the other of the two merged banks.

The second difference I single out is in an area where the last ten years may have seen rather more change. Wage negotiations between the enterprise union of a Japanese company and its managers, and those between the managers of a major British firm and one of its union negotiating committees, bear a superficial resemblance, although there may be some difference in the arguments used. In Japan they are more likely to turn, on the one hand on the firm's investment plans, and on the other on the particular stage of family lifecycles at which employees were feeling the pinch. But the major difference is the following. A British manager who succeeded in talking a union demand for 5 per cent down to 3 per cent would be entitled to feel that this left more leeway for managerial salary rises and that his negotiating skills might well earn him an enhanced bonus. A Japanese manager knows, instead (again like a senior British civil servant negotiating with the civil service union), that, although he may have clocked up merit which will count in his favour for promotion and even be marginally reflected in his summer bonus, his own basic salary will, as a result of his negotiating skill, go up by only 3 per cent instead of 5 per cent. Managerial salary scales, as just described apropos CEOs' salaries, are extensions of those negotiated for junior managers by the union.

These two differences are symptomatic of a general difference between Japanese and Anglo-Saxon firms. The latter are 'properly' capitalist. The managers are there to do their best for the owners, and the owners want them to buy as much high-quality labour as they need, at as cheap a price as possible, just as they want them to get the best deal on their electricity and raw materials. It is naturally assumed to be in accordance with the owners' wishes that those skilfully negotiating managers who save them a lot of money should be rewarded and thus given an incentive to do the same next time. In Japanese firms, by contrast, nobody gives a great deal of thought to owners. Firms are not seen as anybody's 'property'. They are organizations—

bureaucracies much like public bureaucracies—that people join for careers, become members of. They are more like communities. And, as in most other communities, some people are more important than others, though rarely is the hierarchical ranking more explicit than in a Japanese bureaucratic firm community. The president, the vice-presidents, and the (large) Board are treated as, and see themselves as, the elders of the enterprise community. Their primary concern is the reputation of the community and the welfare of its members—not only of their juniors who might fill their shoes one day, but also of the people who are on career tracks which are likely to end as only (white-collar) section chief or (blue-collar) supervisory foreman. And not only of the people currently employed in the firm, but also, to some extent, of their 'descendants', those who will join the firm later and carry its reputation refulgently into the future—provided they, the current elders, themselves do their duty.

One can call this the Community View of the firm as opposed to the Property View; the Entity View as opposed to the Profit Instrument View; the Corporate Membership View as opposed to the Matrix of Contracts View; the Shareholder Firm versus the Stakeholder Firm. Instead the dichotomy which will be used throughout this book is a simpler one, which has the advantage of suggesting more-or-lessness rather than a sharp dichotomy: the employee-favouring firm versus the shareholder-favouring firm. Here, in tabular form, are some of the other differences between the typical Anglo-Saxon firm (left side) and its Japanese counterpart (right side) which follow from that overall characterization.

Mergers and acquisitions

Common, including hostile takeovers. Possibilities of acquiring and being acquired (together with the question of how to present company results in a way least damaging to share price) a major agenda item of Boards, a major preoccupation of top managers, and a key item of news in the financial press.

Low concern with M&A by Boards, CEOs, press. Agreed mergers not uncommon, but more likely to be inhibited by explicit concerns as to whether the 'cultures' of the merged entities will meld. Hostile takeovers exceedingly rare; frequent attempts to corner shares but nearly always with 'greenmail'[2] rather than restructuring intentions.

Personal objectives of managers

Above all, delivering profits to the shareholders, thereby enhancing their own claims to financial rewards within the firm and their reputation in the labour market, which determines their access to alternative sources of reward. Secondarily, fulfilment of promises they have personally given to suppliers or employees. Possibly also, in long-established firms, preserving the identity and reputation of the firm.

Working for the long-term prosperity of 'the firm' (i.e. all its employees, present and future), thereby enhancing their own reputation within the firm, and hence their chances of being one of the division directors appointed to the Board, then the one of their generation appointed as president, and finally the kind of president who goes on to be a respected, not disregarded, chairman and public figure, member of many Good and Great committees.

Indices used to measure managerial performance

Primarily share price as a combined index of earnings and growth prospects. Managers turn to the share prices in their newspapers much as academics do to citation indexes—as much to see how they and their friends/rivals/enemies are doing as to see how much money their shares are making.

Market share, sales margins, value-added per employee, growth in all these, plus total sales growth, and ability to avoid any deliberate reduction of employee numbers. Of these, market share, being the most direct measure of the firm's competitiveness in the product market on which its success crucially depends, is the most important.

Disciplinary constraints on managers: accountability

For CEOs and Board-level managers, a performance which loses the confidence of shareholders, reflected in a fall in the firm's share price, can lead to dismissal, either at the shareholders' AGM or by a successful takeover bidder. For lower-level

Managers are accountable to, and need to maintain their reputation among, (a) a group of personally known individuals representing their banks and other committed shareholders, (b) their peers and juniors within the firm, on their managers, dismissal if they lose the confidence of their superiors.

reputation with whom their further promotion and post-retirement livelihood depends.

Social perception of the firm

Popularly, as the place where, for the moment, one earns one's living, where one might or might not also have an active and enjoyable social life and the satisfaction of interesting work; as a legal entity to which one owes obligations which are time-bound by the period of notice specified in the employment contract.

Popularly, as a community of people, which is slowly renewed in composition as the old retire and new school-leavers are recruited, but which has an identity and, indeed, an 'interest' which transcends, and is not simply an aggregation of, that of individual employees. Company presidents can talk, and not expect a cynical reaction when they talk, of 'the future of our great firm', in much the same way as a king or president can talk of 'the future of our great nation'.

Academically, 'theorizing' that popular concept, as a web of contracts, the nature of which is constrained only by law and convention; all such contracts, even those which have legal entities as contractors (the firm, a trade union), being ultimately dissolvable into the contracts of individuals.

The only distinctive *academic* theorizing growing out of these popular concepts known to me is that of Aoki, in whose 'cooperative game theory' firm managers are the arbiters of the interests of shareholders and employees.[3]

Behaviour in a recession

Strenuous efforts to maintain profitability, in order to maintain dividend and share price levels, primarily through attempts to cut costs to match the fall in sales. This frequently involves redundancy dismissals, restrained in their 'ruthlessness' only by legal controls,

Energies directed more towards redoubled efforts to increase sales, the prime objective being to maintain employment and money rewards to employees (though the latter may well be sacrificed for the former, especially through reduced bonuses), even if this means a marked decline fear of reputational effects dictated by whatever are the locally current concepts of 'job rights', and fear of skill shortages in an upturn, known pejoratively as 'labour hoarding'.

in profitability and, eventually, a reduction in dividend levels.

Responses to secular decline of industry sectors

Rapidly liquidate loss-making divisions, usually thereby making their workers redundant. Downsizing possibly offset by acquisitions of firms in growth industries; shift to higher-value-added ends of traditional market.

Gradual withdrawal from the declining business, compensating by internal diversification—seeking new markets and products in growth industries chosen to capitalize on existing technological skills or market expertise. Transfer of the maximum possible number of employees to new activities—often undertaken in the expectation of a long gestation period and chosen at hurdle rates of return on investment well below market interest rates, even on the most optimistic estimate of eventual returns.

Wages and salaries

The distinction between the wage and the salary, as a dividing line between the 'trusted and responsible' and the 'hourly rated worker', is still the norm, in spite of much 'harmonization'. For both categories of employee, the principles of 'the rate for the job' (the market version) and 'equal pay for equal work' (the justice version of the same principle) have overwhelming acceptance.

No wage/salary distinction in form of pay, but only between those who record and are paid for overtime and those of higher rank who do not. Relatively predictable pay-rise trajectories, levelling off after age 40. These trajectories only loosely correlate with job functions (see below) and are at different levels and have different degrees of steepness for different 'grades' of worker—grade usually being determined by educational level (high-school-leavers, arts graduates, science graduates, etc.).

Nature of the employment contract

Except for new graduates recruited in the 'milk round', when employers visit universities—and even for many of these—the contract is a 'job contract', specifying a certain salary/wage for a defined job function. Promotion takes place through an internal labour market—bids, frequently competitive bids, for vacant posts, the assumption of a new post involving the fixing of a new wage (re-contracting).

Career contracts; recruitment of most 'normal' new employees at the beginning of their work careers. There is no internal labour market; promotion is not through *market* processes of competition. POCADS—the Personnel Office Career Deployment System—works, as in almost any country's army or police or civil service, to 'post' employees to a succession of (*a*) ranks and (*b*) functional positions and (*c*) salary grades. That posting is heavily constrained by seniority as well as the merit of demonstrated performance. The three dimensions of rank, job, and pay only roughly correlate: one might be given promotion in one dimension with no movement in the others.

Reward dispersion

Large

Small

Role of workers' unions

To maximize a worker interest seen as essentially antithetical to that of the shareholders, to make sure that their members get the full market rate for the job and to provide them with assistance as much when they are in the market looking for a job as when they are in employment.

Uniting the lower-ranking members of the firm (including future managers under about 35) to protect individual rights against arbitrary managers and to speak up for the claims of wages (as against investment or payments to shareholders) when decisions are made about the disposition of the firm's revenues.

Effort-inducing incentives

Mostly individual, in cash form, and short term—i.e. the reward is not too long delayed after the effort output. Range from 1 week in the case of manual piecework to 3–4 years for stock option cash-ins. Group bonuses can reward cooperativeness—helping others—as well as individual work performance, but still in the form of individual, cash payments.

Individual rewards are more long term—building up the reputation which (enhanced by the halo effect) may get one a crucial appointment in 20 years' time, for instance. Rewards are less exclusively in cash form; fast-track promotion up (a) the job-function/power track and (b) the rank track can be correlated only loosely with promotion up the pay track and can carry their own intrinsic non-monetary rewards.

Altruistic collective incentives (of the football fan type, springing from 'involvement'—i.e. the pleasure of seeing a firm with which one emotionally identifies doing well) may work marginally for senior long-service employees. Managers hesitate to try to evoke such sentiments for fear of the ribald cynicism which might greet such departures from the principle of the employment contract as hard-nosed arm's-length bargain.

Altruistic collective incentives are probably quite important as a determinant of effort for a high proportion of, particularly older, employees. No hesitation about seeking to evoke such sentiments.[4]

Nature of authority relations

Because the relation between manager and worker is based on explicitly adversarial contract, the organizational hierarchy is perceived more as a hierarchy of ability/licence to command obedience and cooperation than as a hierarchy of

The sense of shared membership in the community (plus the near guarantee of *some* promotion for all) modifies the adversarial nature of hierarchical relations and allows more importance to be given to technical competence when technical competence. Among technical competencies, the overwhelming importance attached to dealing with financial markets tends to devalue all other forms besides the financial. (Accountants get on Boards more easily than engineers.)

allocating authority, rather than to the possession of a steely authoritative eye. This, plus the lesser importance of financial markets, makes for Boards of manufacturing companies more dominated by experts in production or product markets. (More engineers than accountants.)

Pension funds

Pension savings are seen as the property of the eventual recipients, and the trustees of those funds have a fiduciary duty to promote their interests alone, not that of the firm which sponsors the scheme. It is held to be generally undesirable to have both present earnings and future pensions dependent on the fortunes of a single company—too many eggs in one basket.

Funds for the payment of retirement bonuses and pensions are frequently held within the firm, and are available to the firm as investment capital.

The facilitating environment

What makes these differences all the more striking is the fact that the legal environment—the company law's designation of the share-holders' general meeting as the supreme organ appointing the direc-tors, its definition of the shareholders' property rights, and so on—is not so very different in Japan from what it is in Britain or the United States. Lifetime employment has support in case law: employees' claims to unfair dismissal can only be countered by demonstrating that the firm did all it could—explored all reasonable market opportunities for diversification, for example—to find alternative employment for re-dundant workers. Not only back wages, but claims to be compensated for loss of job rights get high priority in bankruptcy proceedings. But by and large the status of the firm as shareholders' property is firmly enshrined in Japanese law.

How the conventions of actual practice came to deviate so widely from the legal model is a long story, but a brief outline follows. Before the war, Japanese firms were more like Anglo-Saxon firms. The stock market played a much bigger role in their financing; many of their directors were outsiders with only a financial interest who made sure that dividends and directors' bonuses took a goodly share of profits. Management–union relations varied between the antagonistic/co-ercive and the cooptative/manipulative. What primarily changed all this was the war. The stock exchange was shut down. Dividends were controlled. The munitions ministry bureaucracy took control of Board appointments and made into the general practice what was beginning to become the dominant pattern only in the constituent firms of the big *zaibatsu* concerns, namely the appointment of senior lifetime employees, qualified by their expertise not by their financial interest. After the war the practice stuck: it did, after all, find many justifying themes in traditional Japanese cultural values (Confucian values, if you like, since it was mostly in the aphorisms and proverbs of Confucian writings that they were expressed).

The second factor of enormous importance in shaping the modern corporation—extending the 'managerial-community firm' model, nurtured in the *zaibatsu*, into the 'employee-community firm' model—was the postwar labour movement and its militancy. To cut short a long and complex story, the first postwar years saw a communist-led, militant, transenterprise labour movement aimed at a transformative shift from capitalism to socialism. Its impetus was blunted by the combined efforts of managers and the Occupation army, and it was 'domesticated' by granting blue-collar workers essentially the same status—the same pattern of monthly wages paid by similar criteria, the same guarantees against dismissal, the same guarantees of sick pay and retirement allowances proportionate to salary, membership in the same enterprise union—as white-collar and managerial employees. In other words, shopfloor workers were given the same reason that managers had to identify themselves as members of the enterprise community.

So, an important part of the environment which keeps Japanese firms the way they are is the fact that nearly all other firms are in the same mould. Custom and practice are society-wide custom and practice.

The other crucial part of the story is financial. In two spurts—one after the war, when the shares of the big *zaibatsu* firms were impounded and dispersed, and the second in the 1960s, when the prospect of capital liberalization raised fears of wholesale takeovers by powerful American firms—a pattern of cross-shareholdings was developed which gives most large firms 'stable shareholders' who can provide a safe guarantee against the possibility of a hostile takeover. Typically, Japanese firms have up to 60 or 70 per cent of their shares in the hands either of the banks with whom they do their loan business, or of the insurance companies with whom they do their insurance business, or of other industrial and commercial companies with whom they do a lot of their trading. And with these latter, as with their banks, a good deal of their shareholding is on a reciprocal basis: Hitachi owns several million Nissan shares and vice versa. The crucial point about these 'stable shareholdings' is that the shareholders are more interested in the *other* business they do with the issuing firm than they are in the profits to be made from the shareholding itself. The holding is an expression of a multistranded relationship, rather than a property right to be exploited to the full. And where, as between Hitachi and Nissan, say, the holding is reciprocal, neither has an interest in pressing for higher than conventional dividends: if either did, the answer would be 'you too'.

Add to this the pattern of relational banking. Japanese firms rely a great deal on debt finance. Until the 1980s their debt–equity ratios were higher than elsewhere. Most big firms deal with a number of banks, but one of them is usually recognized as the 'main bank', which keeps track of a firm's performance, plans, and needs, and gives a lead to the other banks in providing investment funds. It is also the bank which has to pick up the pieces when a firm gets into trouble and needs a restructuring rescue from the brink of bankruptcy. This rescue is frequently a highly loss-making activity which is undertaken less for profit than from obligation—obligation not so much to the firm itself as to the banking community, to all the fellow-bank creditors, who are equally concerned to minimize losses.

It is easy to see what an enormous difference this makes in determining the shareholder-favouring or employee-favouring character of firms. The power of shareholders over Anglo-Saxon firms is mediated by the share price and the takeover mechanism. Disappoint your shareholders so that some of the more disillusioned sell and your share price goes down; you become a cheaper and easier prey for a takeover predator. So not disappointing your shareholders becomes a major preoccupation. (Many Boards spend as much time discussing how to present their results as the results themselves.) Japanese firms can disappoint the active buyers and sellers of the 'floating' portion of their share issue—because they go through a bad patch owing to a sudden price shift, say, or make long-term investments which hit short-term profits—and see their share price fall with considerable equanimity. If they give the impression of knowing what they are doing, their bankers are not going to charge them more for credit, and they are in insignificant danger of a consequent takeover.

The other way that shareholders impact on management—through the annual shareholders' meeting—has a special significance in Japan. Speculation, share-dealing, and thuggery (primarily menacing blackmail) have traditionally been closely associated. The practice grew up before the war of hiring one lot of thugs to suppress other thugs, not to mention consumer groups, environmental groups, and naïve concerned individuals who might make trouble at AGMs. The so-called *sokaiya* (AGM wallahs) made a reasonably stable living out of the practice. Strenuous efforts were made—part of the clean-up process described in following chapters—to make the payment of re-tainers to such people illegal, but the persistence of such practices in a number of major firms was, as we shall see, one factor in the corporate governance debates in the 1990s. A more modern way of neutralizing them has been found: the great majority of firms hold their half-hour AGM at the same time on the same day in June.

Relational trading

If the structure of the corporation and the assumptions of its man-agers are the prime way in which the Japanese economic system is differentiated from others, the second most significant way is the pat-tern of inter-firm trading. Along with relational banking and relational employment goes relational trading.

Anglo-Saxon common sense suggests that efficiency depends on keeping a sharp eye on market trends. No supplier should be immune from constant market-testing. You should always be comparing the deal you are getting from a particular supplier with what you could get elsewhere. Switch without compunction if you find a better combination of quality and price, without much damaging your chance of switching back again if advantage dictates—because suppliers understand and accept that that is the name of the game. 'Market-testing' is the guarantee of fairness, not just of efficiency. The Japanese, by contrast, operate with a greater sense of the advantages, particularly in areas of rapid technical change, of the cooperativeness and willingness to oblige, to give and take in a loose exchange of favours, which a long-term relationship with a supplier can bring. Along with that goes a greater sense of obligation, greater recognition of how difficult you make life for your supplier if you suddenly refuse expected orders. (To be sure, this is a statement about central tendencies. The degree to which such a recognition affects decisions varies from firm to firm, and varies also for any one firm, depending on how prosperous or pressured its situation is.)

Trading relations, that is to say, are seen as generating mutual obligations—as long as the supplier is fulfilling its side of the bargain. If it is 'genuinely and sincerely doing its best' to maintain quality and delivery times, to sink capital into the relationship in order to speed up the development of new products, and to cooperate in cost-cutting when the market turns down, it has a right not to be simply abandoned because, perhaps for circumstances beyond its control, another supplier offers a better deal.

To be sure, it may suffer a percentage cut in orders; large manufacturers usually double-source or triple-source. If there are three producers of soda ash and five glass-makers, the pattern of sales, *ceteris paribus*, is likely to vary little from year to year: glazier A buys 55 per cent from producer X, 20 per cent from Y, and 25 per cent from Z. Glazier B gets 75 per cent from Z, etc. Shifts in those percentage volumes may be a response to price changes beyond the control of the supplier, but in normal times they are 'punishments' or 'rewards' for performance, where performance depends on showing evidence of maximum *effort* to give good service, not just in discounts, but in such things as delivery promptness, quality, and readiness to accept short-notice orders. Percentage reductions, then; but unless the failure in effort and goodwill is grievous, rarely summary abandonment. A list of the 60-odd members of Toyota's first-line suppliers' club in 1990 had only two or three names not present in 1970, and only two or three of the names that figured in the earlier list had disappeared.

Especially in the case of the more traditional firms like Toyota, there is an explicit hierarchical ordering of suppliers, who are ranked on the basis of performance. There are ceremonial awards of certificates when a firm goes up a rank. The higher the ranking awarded, the greater the security of orders in the case of crisis, the greater the propensity of the customer to propose joint development projects, and the greater the likelihood of getting the higher-value-added jobs.

This greater stability of hierarchical supplier relations is reinforced by the lifetime-employment character of the corporation discussed earlier. Lifetime employers carefully recruit the personnel they offer careers to. Top firms get top people from the top schools and universities. They offer them not only the social cachet of membership in a firm that is a household name, but also premium wages. So most workers in smaller supplier firms on lower wages would indeed have preferred to work in a top firm if only they could have managed to be accepted for a job. The fact that this is universally known to be so is one factor which socially legitimates those lower wage levels. And the lower wage cost is one reason why outsourcing is so prevalent, one reason why more Japanese production is the result of cooperation between firms—more production through hierarchically organized markets than in pure hierarchies or through pure markets, to put it in transaction-cost analysis terms. One indicator of that is the ratio of the sale of intermediate goods to the sale of retail consumer goods of 4:1—about double the ratio in Britain.

Markets for intermediates, consequently, *are* contested and contestable, but within severe limits. The terms of competition involve not just price and quality, which a supplier can control, but the purchaser's subjective assessment of *willing effort* to improve price and quality. The stickiness of trade relationships makes entry barriers high even for Japanese who know the verbal and body language which affects purchasers' subjective assessments; *a fortiori* for foreigners who do not. This, along with the volatility of exchange rates and a bit of, not so much xenophobia as the discomfort of dealing through a foreign language, explains most of the complaints about the 'closed' nature of the Japanese domestic market, which is a preoccupation of such a high proportion of the American literature on Japan—*the* reason, according to Katz's *Japan: The System that Soured*, why Japan is now paying dearly for its sins against free trade rationality.

Inter-competitor relations:
cooperation, collusion, competition

A once popular characterization of Japan—'Japan Incorporated'—
went like this. Japan is (Edith Cresson used the phrase) an ant-hill.
The interests of private individuals are subordinated to a coordinated
national drive to capture world markets. Japanese firms are, consequently, intensely competitive abroad when they vie with foreign
firms, but collude at home to reap the excess profits which finance
their external activities.

A more reasonable view is the following. The Japanese are—a
feature of 'national character', 'modal behavioural disposition', or
whatever one likes to call it—more disposed than Americans and
most Europeans (though the Germans may be counted an exception)
to cooperative rather than to competitive, adversarial patterns of relations. All societies draw the line somewhere between cooperation and
competition (even in the most contested markets, participants cooperate in maintaining the law of contract, the validity of weights and
measures, etc.). The Japanese just tend to seek to draw that line closer
to the cooperation end of the spectrum. At the same time, the Japanese are also smart; they tend, consequently, to be good at discerning
possibilities of cooperation which can be of general benefit, and at
devising organizational forms which can reap those benefits in ways
which all participants can consider fair. Among other things this
means that they are good at forming viable cartels (see below).

As for the explanation of such 'national character traits', who
knows? Is it because of centuries of experience of collectively irrigated
rice agriculture, or because of the teachings of Confucian ethics, or
because of the nature of the population gene pool, or whatever? It is
undoubtedly linked to a general tendency to avoid face-to-face con-
frontations. 'A great relief to be back in Japan,' said a manager who
had spent some years running his firm's subsidiary in Italy. 'Less stress.
You don't get up every day with the possibility that some meeting is
going to turn into a nasty confrontational argument.' The whole discussion of modal behavioural dispositions as a factor in the functioning of economic systems tends to be avoided among economists who
wish to believe that what they teach their students are theorems
about THE economy, determined by the universal utility function of
MAN; so, too, is it avoided among those politically correct social

scientists who stick rigorously to 'structuralist' arguments for fear of the demon racism which they see as lurking in the thicket of any argument which gives causal importance to notions of 'culture'.

To return to competition, there is one matter to be cleared up at the outset. The word *keiretsu* is often heard in foreign complaints about Japanese anti-competitive behaviour. It is used in two senses in Japan. Sometimes it refers to the network of subsidiaries spawned by a major firm and bound to it by some capital relationship, together with, usually, its major long-standing suppliers, who are bound in the sort of long-term trading relationships just described. In this sense one hears talk of the Hitachi or the Toyota *keiretsu*. Sometimes (what started as ignorant foreigners' misuse of the word but has since become conventional even among Japanese) it refers, by contrast, to non-hierarchical groupings of major firms which share a common origin in one of the prewar *zaibatsu* concerns (Mitsui, Mitsubishi, Sumitomo) or share a common main bank (the Daiichi Kangin group or the Fuji group), and which may give a preference to fellow-group members as trading or joint-venture partners. What the term *keiretsu* does not refer to is our subject here, the pattern of relationships between competitors.

But what about cartels—the universal tendency of businessmen, according to Adam Smith, to end up forming a conspiracy against the public even when they get together primarily for their own merriment and diversion? I said that the Japanese have a leaning towards co-operation rather than competition and are clever at finding organizational arrangements for fairly sharing the gains of cooperation. Does this mean that there is more cartelization in Japan than elsewhere, and more damage, therefore, to the public interest?

My answers would be: yes, marginally more cartelization; and no, probably not more secret conspiracies against the public, because many cartel arrangements are regulated by guardians of the public interest—the Ministry of International Trade and Industry (MITI) and the other ministries which have regulatory or 'administrative guidance' powers. In Europe, of course, these were the salient characteristics of medieval guilds—even if their serving of the 'public interest' often meant no more than sharing their monopoly profits with the king or local baron. Japan had guilds of exactly that type only 150 years ago, with elaborate regulations limiting the forms of competition (banning the stealing of fellow-members' customers or craftsmen, outlawing stealing a march by secretly working on saints' days, insisting on collective quality seals and inspection, etc.). These guilds have their direct heirs today in the producers' cooperatives in those industries, such as textiles and ceramics, which are composed mainly of small family businesses. A weaver in some of the weaving districts might still have to answer to the cooperative's disciplinary committee if his looms are heard chattering on Sundays or after 11 pm.

In the large-scale corporate sector, the same role is played by industry associations, which are, in most industries, rather more active than their counterparts elsewhere in gathering statistics, in diffusing technological and market information, in promoting joint research projects, and so on. In the case of industries subject to voluntary export restraint agreements, of course, foreign protectionists often *force* them to be more active. In 1999 (though supposedly for the last year) some body still had to decide the allocation among producers of, say, the 11 per cent of the British car market allocated to Japan.

There are two factors which work against cartelization:

1. Concentration ratios are not high, as a result of (*a*) the absence of hostile takeovers because of the pattern of shareholding; (*b*) the care with which MITI used foreign exchange controls to manage technology imports in the postwar period in order to maintain domestic competition; (*c*) the tendency of the second type of *keiretsu* mentioned above—the non-hierarchical ones such as Mitsui, Mitsubishi, Daiichi Kangin, etc., which have loose coordinating mechanisms such as regular lunches of their CEOs—to want 'their' group to be *wansetto* ('one set', i.e. to be represented by a major player in every important industry) and their willingness to nurture such a player; and (*d*) the use of government-sponsored recession cartels to nurse the weaker players through recessions.

2. Lifelong employment, the nature of the firm as a committed community, does have the consequence of breeding inter-firm rivalry. An electrical engineer is a Hitachi man first and an engineer second. If he wants a change he might, say, switch to a major textile firm. But it would be quite unusual if he were to go to work for another *electrical* firm, or, indeed, if a rival firm among the big five were to contemplate employing 'deserters'.

As a generalization, illustrating what I called the capacity to discern where to draw the line between competition and cooperation, one could say this. Competition tends to be fierce (*a*) in consumer industries producing for anonymous markets, rather than in small-numbers intermediate markets, and (*b*) where demand is expanding rather than stagnant. Thus cartelization—the avoidance of price wars—sets in rapidly in the cement industry when demand is stagnant and there is oversupply: competition is restricted to quality, packaging, promptness of delivery, etc., and there may well be concerted efforts to prevent cheaper imports by blacklisting customers who resort to them.

One thing which both illustrates and reinforces the high degree to which Japanese managers and engineers perceive their firm as belonging to 'the XY industry', with the belonging having a semi-community character, is the quantity and variety of the trade press, often in the form of a daily or thrice-weekly newspaper. Moreover, in the industry association, as in most Japanese communities, the hierarchical structure is often explicit: the presidency of the association may, by formal agreement, be taken in turn by the chairmen of, say, the four 'leading firms' of the industry. The pecking order of those leading firms may also be seen as part of the order of nature when their market shares have been more or less stable for some time. In the 1980s the open declaration of the determination of the number two motor-bike manufacturer to supplant the number one led to unusually bitter competition, generally frowned on as offending against the norms of decent behaviour. Likewise, it is part of these norms that, while one tries hard to take market share from one's competitors, there is no cause for rejoicing if they are driven to bankruptcy.

The role of government

The notion of 'norms of competition' is highly relevant to the fourth major characteristic of the Japanese system: the role of the bureaucracy. 'Excessive competition' may be a term incapable of precise definition, but Japanese bureaucrats believed that they knew it when they saw it. Thus, for example, early in the postwar period they modified the severity of the anti-trust law which the occupying American forces had insisted on, by amendments which permitted cartels where they might serve the public interest by restraining excessive competition. One such type were the investment cartels for industries with lumpish investments, like steel and chemicals and artificial fibres, where simultaneous rival investments might lead to a wasteful excess of capacity. Another was the recession cartel: production cutbacks by every firm in an industry for a fixed period until inventories were cleared and the price recovered. Apart from the greater egalitarianism of a 'share-the-pain' solution, this was deemed better than a recession price war which might destroy a lot of potentially useful capacity and leave the industry short of capacity and liable to excessively high prices and profits after the recovery.

Vast quantities of polemical writing have been devoted to the question of whether industrial policy was, or was not, beneficial for Japan's growth. The market's 'true believers' have tried to show that bureaucratic interference did nothing to help, and may have hindered, a pattern of growth which owed everything to entrepreneurial excellence and open competition. On the other hand, for Americans (which was what most of the true believers were) it was hard in the 1980s to swallow the argument that Japan's steady encroachments on world markets owed nothing to 'unfair competition' in the form of state aid and interference.

The effect on growth rates and growth patterns—and on 'competitiveness'—can be endlessly disputed, but Johnson's characterization of Japan's post-Meiji state as a 'developmental state', as opposed to America's 'regulatory state', captures a real distinction.[5] Selective subsidies and credit at favourable rates—sometimes for targeted 'strategic' industries, sometimes for generic expenditures such as energy conservation devices or specific forms of training—have been among the devices used. Another device has been the research club: cooperative, state-organized but only marginally state-financed, research programmes at 'pre-commercial' level—i.e. at a level of speculative risk that a single firm would be unlikely to fund alone. These clubs have been particularly important since 1970, when the lifting of foreign exchange controls ended the powers that had been used to put conditions on the import of foreign technology—partly to strengthen firms' bargaining power, partly to make sure that all available rival technologies were imported and distributed among competitors.

But 'developmental' versus 'regulatory' captures only part of the difference between the roles of the administrator in Japan and in societies such as those of Britain and North America where 'nightwatchman state' prescriptions have long been a staple of political philosophers. Many Japanese interventions—for example, much of the extensive administrative machinery built to provide modernization grants, under many guises, for small and medium firms—had distributive (and political) as well as developmental intentions. Thus, clearly, did the recession cartels already mentioned. Likewise the 'declining industry' cartels, which allowed for orderly, staged cuts in capacity distributed among firms and provided subsidies for diversification and retraining—'positive adjustment programmes', the OECD called them. The first run-down was in the coal industry after cheap oil imports became available; steel, textiles, plywood, and a host of other industries affected by cheap imports from third world countries followed in the 1970s and 1980s.

For some state initiatives the term 'the umpire state' might be most appropriate—bargained trade-offs which allow the industry some extra profit from cartelization, in return for behaviour which is deemed to be in the national interest (or sometimes in the interests of the officials who administer the rules, or of the politicians who have to consent to the rules the officials initiate). The condoning of bid-rigging for public works contracts (*dangō*), for example, which became the object of fierce public denunciation in the 1990s, had the merit of preventing a lot of costly unsuccessful bid preparation, of helping to maintain the quality of work done, and of shifting some of the cost of specification planning from the public body to the private firm. All this was deemed to be in the public interest and to justify *to some extent* the additional cost to the public budget. However, everyone knew that *another part* of the balance sheet was the channelling of sizeable chunks of construction company profits into the private funds with which politicians bought votes, and the enhancement of those firms' willingness to make officials nice job offers when they came to retirement age.

Another example. The refining industry had a serious overcapacity problem. It was allowed to maintain a high price for gasoline through an informal ban on imports. In return it agreed to a price structure for heavy oil and kerosene other than the one which market forces might have produced, but one which was deemed to be desirable for (*a*) its industrial investment incentive effects and (*b*) its income distribution effects (kerosene, used for home heating, is also, of course, a vote-sensitive commodity).

The refining example is a good illustration of another particular feature of the role of the state in the Japanese economy. Along with relational contracting, relational banking, and relational employment, went relational regulation—the widespread use of 'administrative guidance' as well as statutory coercion. The strength of the industry associations was a precondition for this to happen, and it was at its most pronounced in industries such as refining and banking where there were few major players. Arrangements could be reached—and implemented—on an informal basis between the officials of an industry association and those of the relevant government department (MITI for most of manufacturing, the Ministry of Posts and Telegraphs for information technology, the Ministry of Transport, the Ministry of Construction, etc.). The refinery deal held up as a mere 'administrative guidance' arrangement for several years, until a maverick operator tried to take advantage of the absence of any legal ban to import cheap gasoline. This forced its transformation into legislation in the mid-1980s, as a limited-period law whose expiry led in 1999 to fierce gasoline price wars. (This clearly market-distorting piece of state intervention never got onto the agenda of the endlessly acrimonious United States–Japan trade talks. The American majors all have, or share an interest in, Japanese refineries and were major beneficiaries.)

So what is all this except the pork-barrel politics particularly familiar in Anglo-Saxon societies—the anti-competitive, growth-dampening favouring of firms which happen to be in the constituency of powerful politicians, and of interest groups which provide the votes for them? The answer is, a not unimportant bit more. Part of the equation was a political system in which bureaucrats ruled and politicians reigned. The bureaucracy had a century-old tradition of being *la crème de la crème*, a prime example of the way in which (think of France, also) elite arrogance can combine naturally with a sense of public duty. Until the 1960s that tradition included regular passage of the most able among them from bureaucrat to statesman with only a brief intervening decade or so as politician—and that, often, as a politician of such high prestige that he could leave most of the dirty work of politics to underlings. Politics started dirty with the first Constitution, in the 1890s, and has largely stayed that way, though the gradual widening of the franchise in the first half of the twentieth century, the formal adoption of representative, parliament-based democracy at mid-century, the slow 'legal-rational' fight against corruption, and the transition from face-to-face personal influence to media influence as a mechanism of vote-getting have all gradually wrought their changes—with consequences for the authority of bureaucrats, and for their insulation from sectional-interest-driven politics, which, as the next chapter will show, still have to be worked out.

A system?

Among social scientists a favourite way of characterizing much of what has been described above is to say that economic transactions in Japan are, as compared with other societies, much more commonly 'embedded' in face-to-face social relations. But note that this is not at all the Polanyi type of social embeddedness, the disentangling of which he sees as the precondition for the emergence of modern market capitalism.[6] Polanyi was talking about what sociologists call 'ascribed social relations'—those one is more or less born into, between uncle and nephew in an extended family or neighbours in the same village, for example. The social relations in which Japanese economic transactions are embedded are, by contrast, *achieved*—membership in the firm, for instance, through selection tests designed to make sure that each set of new employees starts off on its appropriate career track as a relatively ability-homogeneous group. As a subcontractor, one has to work one's way through Categories C and B before one gets to be a Category A supplier of Toyota. The greater tendency of Japanese associations to develop community-like characteristics is part of this more general tendency for economic transactions to be 'embedded' in this kind of (achieved) social relationship.

But to be more systematic about it, it seems useful to distinguish between two different mechanisms which create the system-ness of Japan's economic system—institutional interlock and motivational congruence.

Institutional interlock

The most obvious way in which the institutions of any country's capitalist system may be described as a system is through the jigsaw-puzzle-like 'fitting' of one institutional practice with another. Take, for example, the three salient features of the Japanese system:

1. lifelong rather than highly mobile employment relationships;

2. long-term, obligated, customer-market rather than mobile, auction-market supplier relations;

3. patient, long-term-committed rather than short-term-returns-sensitive equity capital, and the consequent absence of takeovers.

Some of the obvious interconnecting 'fits', already hinted at above, are:

1. Supplier relations can more easily rest in part on verbal under-standings and trust, because the assembler's purchasing manager, who identifies with the firm of which he is a lifelong member, can commit not just himself but the firm. Although he is likely to move on to something else at his next posting, his successor will see himself as bound by promises his predecessor gave, and he himself will still be around in the firm to give his version of what those promises might have been. Lifetime employees have a strong and shared interest in the firm's reputation.

2. Wage differentials between the high-prestige, high-market-power leading firms in an industry and lesser supplier firms—the 'premium wage' paid in top firms—are made legitimate by the selection pro-cesses that go along with lifetime employment. Because first jobs are start-of-career jobs, you aim for the best firms. Top firms can therefore select the best workers, and they invest a great deal in recruitment selection (surveys show recruiting budgets to be bigger than training budgets) because they are recruiting for very long tenures.

3. The length of tenures and the nature of the internal promotion system motivate individuals to train themselves: the top firms recruit the best learners and so maintain their top status and market power vis-à-vis subcontractors.

4. People who have committed their working lives to a particular firm are more prone to take a long-term view, to have a low time-discount. The firm's future is their future—an important precondition for the long-termism which informs both the supplier relations and stable shareholding.

5. Managers who have to watch their share prices in volatile stock markets to avoid takeovers cannot afford to keep underemployed workers on their books through recessions. Cross-shareholdings, committed capital, and the absence of takeovers are, therefore, pre-conditions for lifetime employment.

6. Maintaining cross-shareholdings may involve sacrificing gains available from investing in something with higher returns in order to retain the long-term business relationship with the issuing firm. That long-term interest is more likely to be appreciated by lifetime managers. Lifetime employment was thus a precondition for the initial creation of the cross-shareholdings and of the conventions which surround them.

There is, also, of course, institutional interlock between economic and not primarily economic institutions—between the structure of the family and employment institutions, for example. The distinctness of male and female roles in the marriage relationship, and in society generally, determines the acceptability of the sharp difference between the terms and conditions under which young unmarried and older married women are usually hired; and the 'male as breadwinner' assumption affects the acceptability of the lifetime distribution of male wages. It may well be, also, that the first-generation industrial workers from farm families were attracted into initially low-wage career employment patterns because their families (which gave an assured future to their eldest sons, who inherited the farm) accepted the need to 'set younger sons up for life'.

Motivational congruence

But there is another mechanism which can make for coherence in social systems. It could be called, on the analogy of 'cognitive dissonance', 'motivational sonance'—the *consistency* of the motivating maximands which lie behind behaviour over a wide range of social/economic situations. Is there in all these institutional practices a similarity in the values which seem to be maximized, in the moral constraints that seem to be obeyed, which would make it plausible to say: Well, it's just that people brought up in Japanese families and schools *are largely predisposed* to behave in this way, and to take happily to this kind of institutional practice, whereas people brought up in British or American schools and families are predisposed to behave differently and to fit into different kinds of institution? (Japanese or Britons and Americans, *on average*, that is to say. There is no need to postulate that no one brought up in America could fit happily into a Japanese-type firm, or that no Japanese could fit into the individualistic short-term life of a British company. The normal-curve distribution of behavioural predispositions spreads around the median in both societies. It is just that the median is at a different point on the various scales/dimensions involved.)[7]

The following three seem to me the chief of those dimensions.

1. Anglo-Saxons behave in ways designed to keep their options open—to keep their freedom to change jobs and loyalties, to shift investments, as soon as ever the prospect of advantage offers. Japanese are much more willing to foreclose their options by making long-term commitments from which, they accept, they can only with great difficulty disengage themselves.

2. In making their choices, Anglo-Saxons give greater weight to their own immediate welfare or that of their family or personal friends. Japanese are much more likely, by virtue of their long-term commitments, to have diffuse obligations to promote the welfare of others— the other members of the firm they have joined, their partners in long-term trading relationships, etc. Put starkly, this is a difference in the selfishness/altruism dimension.

3. The third difference, which is rather more often made into an explicit cultural norm than the other two, is in the 'productivist' dimension already elaborated in Chapter 1.

Part II of this book is devoted to the multiple factors which might make (or manifestly are making) these dispositions change and the consequent changes in the institutions which mould those dispositions—that is, to the forces changing the 'system'. The factors range from unwilled social evolutionary changes in class structure, or in the distribution of material and social capital, to changing interest-group objectives based on changing perceptions of self-interest, ideological influences, technological change, and globalization. They cover the whole gamut of modes of coercion, modes of persuasion, and modes of production (to adopt Runciman's useful basic classification[8]).

— PART II

Change and Controversy in Japan

Chapter 3

Sources of Change

C HAPTER 2 listed four dominant features of Japanese capitalism, four dimensions on which it differed by some degrees from the Anglo-Saxon model: first, firms which on the 'stakeholder', employee-favouring/shareholder-favouring dimension lean heavily towards employees; secondly, relational trading (as opposed to impersonal spot-market trading); thirdly, a greater tilt towards cooperation in the cooperation/competition balance among competitors; and, finally, a strong role for government as producer of public goods and umpire arbitrating clashes of private interests in matters where Anglo-Saxon countries would leave the market to sort things out.

In all four respects Japan is under pressure to change—or at least the Japanese see themselves as under pressure to change—towards the Anglo-Saxon pole of these dimensions. Let us start with the sources of these pressures for change—changes in the economy, the recession and the renewed authority of the American model, and long-term shifts in values and behavioural dispositions.

Changed economic parameters

The reasons for believing that the 'high-growth era'—the era of even 3–4 per cent annual growth rates—has gone for ever are not trivial.

1. High growth rates were sustained until 1990 by four factors, of diminishing or now zero force, which are unlikely to be reinforced or reproduced: (*a*) growth in the labour force; (*b*) a rapidly expanding share of world markets, fuelled initially by Japan's reaching world standards of technological capacity at a time when its standard of living was low and its labour cost advantage consequently great; (*c*) the momentum generated by that initial high growth: high savings

rates from rising incomes, high 'habitual' rates of investment, a high level of 'animal spirits' built on expectations of continued growth (continued capture of world markets as well as growth in domestic demand); (*d*) consequently young average capital vintages, permitting rapid incorporation of new technology, which helped to sustain productivity growth.

2. A steady rise in asset prices was generated, partly by population growth (especially in the case of land), partly by the rising productivity of industrial assets, and partly by the fact that they were increasing in volume more slowly than the accumulated savings competing to own them. The 'wealth creation' of this asset price rise both created extra resources for investment and meant that a large part of the value added by Japanese corporations could be absorbed by labour, giving (by the standards of other countries) small shares to capital, since the shareholder-owners were rewarded by the steady increase in the price of shares and other assets. This meant that pension funds and life insurance companies could obtain viable returns within the Japanese economy itself by adding the profits of asset-trading to their modest returns in dividends.

Absent population and labour force growth, absent the momentum effect deriving from the period of labour cost advantage, absent, hence, the benign effects of slow-but-steady asset inflation and the supplementation of the rewards to capital which it provided, it is not surprising that the process of adjustment should lead people to question whether the Japanese firm can continue to favour employees at the expense of shareholders in the distribution of current value-added. Indeed, of the four dimensions of the Japanese 'model' as listed above, the structure of the firm and its employee-favouring character is clearly the key one, and it is the one on which this discussion will concentrate.

Renewed force of the American model

Complacency and self-sufficient pride are not, on the whole, common Japanese sins. Complacent self-congratulation has been a widespread popular sentiment perhaps only twice in recent Japanese history— once between the fall of Singapore and the battle of Midway in 1942 and then in the late 1980s, at the time of the bubble boom, when the world seemed to be at Japan's feet, Japanese banks provided half the short-term lending for California, Mitsubishi owned the Rockefeller Center, and American scholars were writing articles on a possible future Pax Japonica. By the late 1990s the Japanese had reverted to their normal state; as the *Analects* instruct, 'three times a day critically contemplate your conduct'.

And nowadays there seems to be a lot to be critical about. Nothing could be more effective in reinforcing a sense that things must change than the economic stagnation of the 1990s. To begin with, it was simply the after-effects of the bubble—or at least of the decision to handle the adjustment process, not by the surgical means of mass bankruptcies, but by tightening belts, treading water, pushing slowly on against what Alan Greenspan called in one of his happier phrases 'the headwinds of balance sheet restructuring', until such time as the bad debts could be liquidated out of profits. The profits were a long time coming, in spite of the Bank of Japan's manipulating interest rates in the banks' favour; but with the 3.6 per cent growth rate of 1996 it looked as if the recipe was working. At that point the rise, to over 80 per cent of GDP, of the national debt accumulated as a result of the Keynesian budget-deficit years brought on what in retrospect was a fatal attack of traditional fiscal prudence which stopped the fragile recovery in its tracks. The Ministry of Finance is said to have expected that its 'for the sake of our grandchildren' measures in the spring of 1997—the sales tax increase, the end of a temporary income tax cut, and increases in health charges and social security contributions— would slow the economy down for six months or so. It had not reckoned on the collapse of the Thai economy, followed by all the other Asian dominoes, just as those six months were up.

The increase in saving, and the fall in consumer spending which followed, choked off the recovery of the banks and securities houses; and the collapse of the Hokkaido Takushoku Bank and of Yamaichi Securities added to the alarm. For inducing anxiety in consumers there is nothing like big bankruptcies and the sight of the president of a major securities company weeping on television. (Significantly, the tears came after an otherwise impassive performance, when he was asked what would happen to Yamaichi's 7,500 employees.)

Apart from procrastination—the difficulty all politicians have in admitting 'we misjudged it'—for a complex legal reason (namely, that the Public Finance Restructuring Law of the autumn of 1997 had firmly entrenched the balanced-budget principle) the government was unable to revert to reflationary measures until after the passage of the regular budget in April 1998. By this time, despite the size of the package—the equivalent of $113bn of extra spending, equal to 2 per cent of GDP—its effect was blunted by the rubbishing it got from the foreign financial community. The same thing happened to the autumn package, which raised the prospective level of deficit to an astonishing 9 per cent of GNP. As this is written, in the autumn of 1999, the signs of recovery remain uncertain.

Meanwhile, of course, the United States, where all the hand-wringing had been in the 1980s, and where the President's Council on Competitiveness had issued reports full of references to Japan as a model of what ought to be done, had entered its 'new economic growth era', which only intensified the demand for fundamental change. It was small comfort for the Japanese that a substantial flow of Japanese savings, channelled through the life insurance companies and the Trust Fund Bureau, was an essential element in making it possible for the United States to enjoy its fabulous prosperity with a negative savings rate and a ballooning trade deficit.

If 'beware complacency; there is always room for self-improvement' has been a constant theme in Japanese history, not only the intensity of the quest for improvement, but also its reference standard—the identification of the model—has constantly changed. The Confucian scholars of the eighteenth and early nineteenth centuries, writing their admonitory manifestos to their feudal lords, lamented the extent to which society and government had fallen below the standards of China in the age of the Sages, and sometimes even of contemporary China. After 1870, with the anti-complacency drive for self-improvement intensely reinforced by nationalism, it was no longer China but 'the West', predominantly the European countries, which were there to be emulated and caught up with. After 1945 it was predominantly the United States, and still is.

For a while, the nationalist drive to emulate and overtake was tot-ally discredited by the utter failure of its military form. But the 1950s resumption of growth and the prospects of catch-up reawakened and reinforced it in an economic form. The collective determination to be modern, competitive, and at the top of as many league tables as poss-ible should not be underestimated as a factor in Japan's astonishing

growth: it was not all market forces and individual self-interest maximization. The admiration for the American model has been fraught
with ambiguity, however. It has been matched by an equally nationalist sentiment of deep resentment, first, of the objective situation
of dependency on the United States, both military and diplomatic
(dependency on American support in WTO, G8, UNO, etc.), and,
secondly, of the way in which Americans flaunt their dominance in
self-righteous arrogance in trade talks, and in hectoring advice on
economic policy.

Nevertheless, it is the American model which the Japanese have
most clearly in their sights. It may be that the most common clichés of
the 'we must change' literature are 'in this new age of intensified
global competition' and—in arguments about change in anything
from pensions and corporate governance to patterns of childcare—'in
the advanced countries of America and Europe (*Obei-senshinkoku*), reform has already advanced to the point at which . . .'. But it is 60 years
since that phrase might have been elaborated with a European—usually German—example. Today, in matters economic, the dominance
of the United States increases steadily as its global cultural hegemony
is reflected back, not only from the homeland itself, but from the
academies of Western, Central, and Eastern Europe, not to mention
Latin America and the rest of Asia. And it increases, too, as the
proportion of young US-trained Ph.D.s staffing Japanese economics
departments and teaching from American textbooks (or their local
derivatives) steadily grows, along with the number of American-MBA
Japanese businessmen. When Moody's downgrades a Japanese bank,
it has not just practical effects but also *moral* authority, at least among
all except a small minority circle of cool Japanese who see it as one
more example of America Inc. getting its own back for the days when
the uppity Japanese were sweeping all before them. For most, whatever the defects of American society and whatever the excesses of
American boardroom salaries, in all things to do with competitiveness,
America is the model. The exemplars of self-reliant entrepreneurship
are to be found in Silicon Valley; of bold and effective risk-taking in
American venture capitalists; of effective and honest corporate governance in American corporations; of 'transparency' in financial
transactions in the American stock exchange; of consumer protection
in American courts. Once, Japanese businessmen used to be sent to
get their MBAs at American business schools for 'know thine enemy'

purposes, and they used to come back to their firms as loyal participants in a consciously different Japanese system. Nowadays more of
them either go under their own steam or desert their sponsoring firm,
to come back as 'consultants' teaching how to maximize shareholder
value. (Ten people in Hays Consultants' Japan office are said to rack
up a billion yen a year in fees advising companies on the fashionable
'annual salary system' for managerial salaries.)

And there are always some 'native-speaker' Americans around to
tell the Japanese where it is at. Hardly a day goes by without some
business lunch being addressed by one. For example, R. Taggart
Murphy, author of a mid-1980s *Foreign Affairs* article pointing out that
a Pax Japonica was not likely because the Japanese did not have the
moral backbone that hegemons need to have, told the assembled
businessmen at an executive lunch in April 1998 that

> only when we see less well-performing Japanese companies taken over by
> real owners can we expect to see a thorough purging of excess capacity.
> Only when the Tokyo Stock Market becomes a genuine stock market, with
> shares that represent real ownership of corporate assets changing hands,
> can we find out what Japanese companies are actually worth. And only
> when owners capture the residual returns of business can we expect them
> to shoulder the full risks of bankruptcy.[1]

There is no indication that he was listened to with anything but the
greatest respect, or that anyone suggested that employees who lose a
'lifetime' job might actually be taking more risks than a shareholder
who buys a few thousand pounds' worth of shares.

There is also, of course, direct pressure from American official
sources as well as luncheon speeches. A March 1999 paper for a
Council on Foreign Relations study group speaks of the tendency of
Japanese firms to 'chase growth in revenue, market share, and stable
employment' as the source of 'many of the practices which irk US
competitors and stoke trade disputes, including predatory pricing, production capacity "binges", vertical restrictions that foreclose imports,
horizontal collusion to exclude imports, and resistance to acquisitions,
especially by foreigners'. All those negotiations at the time of the
Structural Impediments Initiative brought nothing but empty promises. But now it is different: 'pressure now from the United States can
encourage the growing internal constituency for reform in Japan; it is
easier to push on a door that is being opened from the inside'.[2]

The pressure, of course, is double-edged in its effects: it can provoke heel-digging-in resentment as well as a desire to please. And the desire to please can distort judgement of what happens. The following extract is taken from a magazine-recorded conversation with the chairman of the Japan Association of Corporate Executives:

> Ushio: It will take 40 years to change Japanese culture. But it's clear that if we go on insisting that it takes a long time, we shall only aggravate our relations with foreigners. We have to acknowledge the importance of the market and of the returns on capital.
>
> Dore: To satisfy the Americans?
>
> Ushio: Partly, but we shouldn't be so proud of the Japanese system of management that we fail to make efforts to introduce new ideas.[3]

Long-term value change

One thing about a consensus society is that it produces relatively homogeneous backgrounds for people to grow up in, thus making it more likely that they become consensus-valuing individuals. Japan is still a much more homogeneous society than the United States or Britain, and the median Japanese is still to be found a good deal closer to the groupishness end of any notional individualistic/groupist spectrum than the median American or Briton (assuming 'national character' to be a matter of differently positioned bell-curves on dimensions such as aggressive/conciliatory, affectionate/cold, selfish/altruistic, etc.).

But Japan is becoming a less homogeneous society. An increasing number of middle-class children have had the experience of schooling abroad, often in countries where individualistic standing-apart from the mob is admired rather than seen as a sign of dangerous selfishness. Affluence makes possible a much wider choice of individualistic, non-organization-joining ways of making a living, a far more varied range of lifestyles. And in the matter of economic behaviour, the transpacific migration of MBAs and Ph.D.s already mentioned has succeeded in diffusing widely as principle—if not always principle which determines practice—the doctrines of neoclassical economics which elevate the basic precepts of individualism to the status of axioms.

There can be no doubt about the genuineness with which a minority—still a minority—hold to such convictions and *are* comfortable about putting them into practice in daily life. A lawyer, for instance, writing a book on the cross-shareholding system[4] as a bulwark of the Japanese employee-favouring corporate system, attacks it *inter alia* by quoting Milton Friedman (the management of companies for anything other than the sole purpose of serving the owners' interests 'can undermine the very foundations of a free society'). But he directs his fire chiefly at a late-1980s book on the Japanese firm which describes its 'employee-sovereignty' character as the source of an admirable Human-capital-ism, superior to the material capitalism of the United States.[5]

He writes, he says, 'as someone who makes his living as an independent professional':

> Is Human-capital-ism really so good for humans? In the truly *modern* labour contract a worker sells his work; he doesn't sell his soul, his commitment. The employee-sovereign firm requires Japanese to spend their whole lives, from birth to retirement, in enforced competition, first to enter the firm, then for advancement within it; and for that they have to sacrifice freedom and individuality, human feeling and creativity, cultural pursuits, playing a useful role in the family or community . . . spiritual poverty in return for material riches.

He sees a possibly hopeful sign that the society as a whole is waking up to what it is missing in the fact that the 1989 *People's Livelihood White Paper* has as its subtitle 'Enriching those 600,000 lifetime hours' and concentrates on leisure, choice, and freedom.

To someone who first went to Japan in 1950 and heard all his fellow-students so earnestly discussing the dimensions of modernity —individual integrity, autonomy, sense of self, etc.—this is old hat. And yet there is a difference. In 1950 these were ideas that everybody was supposed to be parroting. Not so any longer. The lawyer is much more likely to be expressing genuine convictions. Still, however, these are convictions strongly and actively held by only a relatively small minority. Most Japanese males gripe about the trammelling restraints imposed by being members of a corporate organization. Some say they are stifled, fantasize about exit options, or even seek to expand their range of options by studying for some marketable certificate, but— even accounting for the effect of the recession in dampening job turnover—there is little evidence of a sustained increase in voluntary quits.

Ambivalence is pervasive. The Japanese businessman who returned to Japan after spending most of his working life running factories abroad, and who remarked how relaxing it was to return to an environment in which one did not get up every morning with the expectation that the day might contain some tense bargaining confrontation, also added: 'But there's a certain blandness, lack of excitement, too.'

In another sphere of 'trammelling restraints' one might look for an indicator of the same growth of the individualism syndrome in divorce rates, though here the change in gender relations, too, is involved. In any case, the increase in divorce rates has been modest: from around 1 per 1,000 population in 1950 to 1.4 in the 1990s.

Gender and the family

The relationship between the sexes, the structure of the family, and the involvement of women in paid work is, of course, another area of change potentially important for the economy. Writing about the family and the world of work in the late 1960s, I noted two main differences between Britain and Japan. In Britain (this was before the days of youth unemployment) there was a sharp difference between middle-class children, who remained dependent on parents into their twenties, and working-class families, where sons and daughters could be earning as much as their parents from their late teens. By contrast, the seniority wage system in Japan meant that even sons who got into a 'good' firm would still be earning much less than their fathers, which made for much greater cross-class similarity, with consequences also for social solidarity. The second difference was in

> the extent to which there is a sharp differentiation between the feminine and masculine spheres . . . [and consequently in] the extent to which the firm can lay claims to a man's time and emotional resources at the expense of his other attachments . . .
>
> To be sure, Britain is far from homogeneous in this respect. [A Durham coal-mining village is very different from Hampstead, but] generally speaking the differentiation between feminine and masculine roles is a good deal more marked in Japan. . . . Husbands and wives tend to have different sets of friends. . . . Feminine speech and masculine speech still remain clearly distinguishable in verb forms and vocabulary . . . the majority of girls go to

special girls' schools and universities. Japan is full of little Roedeans with no particular class associations, designed to ensure that girls can get the kudos of a higher education and so improve their marriage chances without at the same time endangering their femininity. The bringing up of children is primarily a woman's affair . . .

Women are, consequently, rather more prepared than English women to accept the fact that they share very little of their husbands' lives and can lay claim to little of their time. And if it is now the company and the office rather than [as in traditional Japan] the village or the retainer band that claim his primary loyalty, the difference in principle is not so great. When he comes home at midnight from a drunken sales party she will help him to undress and put him to bed, perhaps with not quite the same respectful admiration as her great-great-grandmother helped her husband off with his armour, but at least with almost as little sense of being the victim of an unfortunate marriage.[6]

Victims not only of an unfortunate marriage but of a gross degree of false consciousness? There were already in the late 1960s some Japanese women, exceptions to these generalizations, who would have said so. But they were very few in number—few enough not to make other women feel uncomfortable and inadequate. They made little impact on the media or on politics. Today, however, there is a much more considerable number of women who would prefer the following formulation:

[In both Japan and Germany] there is an institutionalization of a class and gender compromise which embedded a strong male-breadwinner gender contract, compromising women's positions and standardizing employment contracts around the needs, interests and authority of men. . . . Adding to the current weaknesses both societies face, the increase of female integration in paid employment, the growth of marginal work, changing household forms and values, are forcing governments to reconsider how they need to reform existing employment, tax, and welfare arrangements. But, whether this will lead to establishment of a more equal gender contract is questionable . . .[7]

The biggest change in work–family relations since I wrote at the end of the 1960s has been one which has reinforced the male-breadwinner model: namely accentuation of the U-shaped curve of female participation rates. Full-time work in the early twenties is followed by large-scale withdrawal during the child-bearing years (though not for the nearly 20 per cent of women in family businesses, working from home) and return to part-time work when the children can look after themselves (70 per cent participation for ages 40–54, 40 per cent of them part-time workers). Tax arrangements explicitly reinforce this 'secondary worker' status for married women.

At the same time, in certain spheres—health and education, public administration, the media and publishing, corporate research and development, and a wide range of services—there has been a slow increase in the number of women who seek to have (and a smaller increase in the number who succeed in having) careers comparable with men's and involving them in competition with men. (This has happened hardly at all in the corporate sector, except for R&D: the national imperative to mobilize first-class brains overrides other considerations.) This has meant, first, a later average age of first marriage and an even later average age for having a first child for those who marry. (This is a result partly of women finally and somewhat reluctantly giving up careers which could have been extended, and partly of women who never expected to have continuous careers being slow to give up the enjoyments and independence of life as an 'office lady'.) Secondly, it has meant an increase in the number of women who never marry at all, and hence a decline in the birth rate (there being no concomitant change in the acceptability of single motherhood, whatever its sustainability). Ten per cent of women in their late thirties were unmarried in the early 1990s, compared with only 5 per cent in 1980. Marital fertility has dropped only slightly—partly an unintended effect of postponing child-bearing, and partly from a preference for smaller families or childless marriage.

There is widespread (though, compared with the 'ageing problem', muted) concern at the prospect of a declining population which is doubtless due to more than its impact on economic growth, though that could be serious enough to outweigh most other factors in bringing change in the economic system. Memories of discredited 1930s pro-natalism doubtless suppress nationalist reactions, and I have yet to hear alarmists use the eugenics argument that it is the most highly educated women in particular who are failing to reproduce themselves. Even among LDP dinosaurs, at any rate, there seems to be no overt 'get women back to the kitchen' movement. All the talk is of crèches, flexitime for shared parenting, and other ways of allowing women easily to both work and have children.

But while that has become quietly accepted as the universal ideal (by the same processes of internal change and 'globalization'—imitation of admired 'advanced' cultures—as led to the triumph of monogamy and the decline of concubinage at the start of the century[8]), the sort of feminism that makes a crusade out of this ideal is in short supply. The women's magazines do not often reflect the assumption that 'a more equal gender contract' is an urgent necessity and that those women who do not fight for it are traitors to their sex. The Equal Opportunity legislation of the 1980s sprang more from the need to make Japan conform respectably to the resolutions that Western feminists got passed at the UN Conference on Women than from any felt necessity on the part of politicians to make concessions to the small number of home-grown vocal feminists.

There has, to be sure, been some shift of opinion as measured in opinion polls. The number of women who answered 'Fine!' to the question 'What do you think of the idea that men should go out to work and women look after the home?' fell from 83 per cent in 1972 to 70 per cent in 1979 and 56 per cent in 1992 (the percentage of men giving that response fell from 83 to 66).[9] But this could still be an endorsement of the 'wife and mother but later part-time worker' pattern, and the shift in opinion has not been such that women who adopt that latter role are made to feel ashamed of themselves. Only a slowly increasing number of women see the independent-career alternative as manifestly preferable. In an 11-country *Economist* survey (9 October 1999), only 21 per cent of Japanese women thought that they should have the same rights as men (the only other country with fewer than 60 per cent was Switzerland), while 82 per cent said that they were happier than their grandmothers (the only two others with a percentage higher than 50 were Mexico and South Africa). It does seem that the male-breadwinner family model is unlikely to change at anything other than a glacial pace, thus continuing to reinforce the seniority-wage, lifetime-career pattern of male employment.

And, unlike the changes in education and in egalitarian sentiment, changes in relations between the sexes seem relatively unrelated to the key income and power distribution issues of who, among men, controls corporations and in whose interest. It is, though, of some ironic interest that women are quite well represented among the analysts and traders who are the vanguard of the finance industry's attempts to increase its power to milk the rest of the economy. A considerable number of bright women economics graduates from the top Japanese universities end up working for foreign banks and brokerages where they are appreciated, rather than in Japanese firms where they are not.

Class and equality

The other victim of the edging towards more individualistic mores is the egalitarian concern with social inclusion (to put it in the terms of the contemporary European debate); the concern not to let differences in income and lifestyle grow to the point at which the sense of community is endangered—whether the community in question be that of the nation, the neighbourhood, or the firm.

The trend is clear at the political/ideological level, at the level of policy, and in the social substructures of personal relations. Let us look at the political/ideological level, first. At a recent symposium on governments and markets, the point was made that Japanese industrial policy had not been solely growth policy, but also distribution policy with an egalitarian bias. The response of the civil service head of MITI was interesting. Hitherto, he said, with a Socialist Party able to get something like a third of the votes, a system of 'proportionate consensus' had developed. The Socialists were able to get 80 per cent of what they wanted by negotiated compromise. Now, with the Socialist Party practically disintegrated, it was difficult to predict what would happen to egalitarian policies.

In an excellent summary of the contemporary consensus, Masayuki Tadokoro also attributes postwar egalitarianism to the 'historic class compromise' reached in the early 1950s, when the possibilities of left-wing revolution still gave conservatives sleepless nights:

> The only solution was for the conservative government to buy out the forces of social discontent with subsidies and progressive social programs, while corporations adopted policies that deferred to their workers.
>
> With the Cold War behind us, it has become clear that these policies are an impediment to the development of free markets. The redistribution of wealth has created various vested interests and fostered a collusive triangle of pressure groups, politicians and bureaucrats. The protective policy toward banks has led to corruption among bank executives and finance

bureaucrats and discouraged more creative financial activities by banks. Egalitarian employment policies in the big corporations have sapped the competitive spirit, and emphasis on consensus has weakened managerial leadership. In a society where individuals are not allowed to get rich and stockholders' interests are largely ignored, who is going to invest in risky or unorthodox ventures?

In other words, problems with Japanese egalitarianism are now becoming obvious.[10]

Allowing for the fact that this was addressed to an American audience—something which these days almost invariably means that it seeks to assure Americans what excellent pupils of their American teachers the Japanese are—it can fairly be said to represent the dominant consensus. (Note that the touchstone dominant value to which all social arrangements must contribute is described as 'development of free markets'.)

In serious policy terms, one clear manifestation of this trend is the current proposal to abolish the school district system. Japan has hitherto had a national system of public education in which, for the first six primary school years, 98 per cent of the nation's children took part. The catchment areas of each school were delineated by local authorities, and there was little questioning of the principle that which school a child entered depended exclusively on where he or she lived. Unless, that is, the child could pretend to be living with a relative housed in the district of a 'good' (predominantly middle-class-entry) school—a practice which school authorities made every effort to stamp out. There were differences in schools' reputations for quality, grounded doubtless in real differences. But in rural areas certainly, and even in the towns, the relatively weak pattern of residential segregation meant that such quality differences were not all that marked, and primary schools had, and still have, a mixed social character. Not a few men and women over 50, who went to school in the pre-television era when the school was a more exclusive focus of children's lives, still attend primary school class reunions. The tenuous but friendly contacts thus maintained over the years—professors with carpenters, corporation directors with greengrocers—must surely contribute in indefinable ways to social solidarity, to the large amount of voluntary work that still goes into the running of the state social assistance scheme, and to a social climate which still tolerates a, by contemporary international standards, quite progressive scale of income and inheritance tax rates.

The tax reform commission has recommended, and the government has accepted, that the top income tax rate should be lowered from 55 to 50 per cent, and that the bottom-end tax exemption threshold should be lowered. Inheritance taxes are also due to be reduced. At approximately the same time, the Central Commission on Education has recommended that there should be 'flexible administration of the school district system, from the viewpoint of increasing the opportunity for choice of school, with full consideration given to the views of parents and local residents and to equality of educational opportunity'. The recommendation appears to have met with general approval, in which the vague caveat about equality of opportunity never gets a mention. The prospect that parental choice will lead to an increasing polarization between, on the one hand, 'good' schools with a predominance of children from 'educational' homes whose full-time mothers can ferry them by car to distant schools, and, on the other, bad-reputation schools with children from less privileged backgrounds, seems not to have been enough to arouse significant opposition even from the teachers' union. The Japan Productivity Council (now the Social and Economic Productivity Council) organized a working party led by a Kyoto University economist which was so enthusiastic about parental choice and the virtues of competition that it suggested a way of creating them artificially in rural areas with single schools: instead of a single primary and a single secondary school, make two primary/secondary all-through schools. Thus the two can compete and still be of sufficient size to be administratively efficient.

Two other developments in the educational sphere betray the same underlying assumption that the maximum possible, and the most rapid possible, development of the talents of brighter children is more important than getting the less bright up to the maximum of their capabilities or shielding them from the stigma of failure. The first is a drastic reduction in the compulsory core curriculum—in the hours devoted to, and the standards expected to be attained by all children in, Japanese, mathematics, and social studies. This will allow up to a third of the time in middle school to be spent on subjects adapted to children's individual interests—and intellectual abilities. The second is a move, in effect, to shift the point at which the age group is ability-sorted, from age 15 to age 12. At present, only when compulsory mixed-ability schooling ends at age 15 are children sorted out into ability-graded high schools (usually by objective tests which leave little leeway for subjective judgement or favouritism). The proposal is to create all-through schools for ages 12 to 18. This is rarely openly advocated as a means of streaming and thus accelerating the intellectual development of bright children. Instead, the proponents urge obscure pedagogic theories about discontinuities in the process of intellectual maturation, or point to the success of the existing all-through schools, which now admit some 2 per cent of each age group.

That success—as measured by the strikingly superior performance of their graduates in the entrance competitions for the top universities—is not surprising, given the fact that entrance to these schools (either private schools or the 'attached' schools of state university education departments) is fiercely competitive—again through objective entrance examinations. In recent decades a significant number (perhaps the majority) of those who have been recruited into the career tracks that lead to the top of the core ministries, the judiciary, and the major corporations have been graduates of these elite schools. That is to say that they have probably ceased to have school contact with their peers destined for more humble occupations from the age of 11 onwards. And the increasing tendency for students at the top universities to be children of parents who themselves went to top universities means that they probably also have fewer cross-class contacts through family ties than previous generations.

Moreover, not only their formative experiences but also their economic backgrounds are different. Marxists and rational-choice political scientists will have no difficulty in recognizing why it is that the reformers have a fair wind in Japan. The pressures to enlarge the capital share in the national economy are trends which suit very well the interests of that coalition of the high-income middle-class occupational groups which dominates agenda-setting in the main media, the Diet, the ministries, the boardrooms, and even the central trade union councils. Journalists, academics (particularly the politically active academics who get on government committees), politicians, bankers, bureaucrats, businessmen, analysts in business associations and business research organs, accountants, the spokesmen for 'the markets' (i.e. those confident and much-quoted young men and occasionally women who are the chief analysts and chief economists of Salomon Bros., Merrill Lynch, WTBZ, etc.) all have, increasingly, one thing in common. They are, more and more predominantly, what one might call *churyu-nisei*, second-generation middle class. They are the children (and soon increasingly the grandchildren) of first-generation immigrants into the metropolitan middle class. What distinguishes them from the first generation is not just the quality of their historical experience. They also differ in average accumulated wealth.

There are still large numbers of professors at prestigious national universities, and members of corporate boardrooms, who are *churyu-issei*, first-generation migrants to the middle class. They were educated entirely through the public system, often coming from rural schools. They inherited precious little from their parents, with what legacy there was probably divided among five or six siblings. Most of what they own—the mortgaged house in the suburbs at 90 minutes' commuting distance, their libraries—was bought out of their own earnings. But the workings of meritocracy slow down the rates of social mobility, as the composition of the top universities' student bodies shows. Social class status is more likely to be inherited. (For economic, for cultural, or for genetic reasons, who knows? And who is doing the research to find out? Who is bold enough, politically incorrect enough, even to suggest that, because it defines the limits of social engineering, it is an important question?)

For all that inheritance taxes remain high in Japan, there are considerable advantages, not only in being brought up in the top 10 per cent of the income distribution, but also in sharing—probably as one of only two children—in the property it has accumulated. The *churyu-nisei* and third-generation *sansei* are the ones with the threatened insurance policies, liable to despise the Japanese banks and securities companies which cannot offer half of what Merrill Lynch is offering. And if the land and shares they inherit are not going to appreciate in capital value as their parents' experience taught them they had a right to expect, then compensation in the form of higher current returns—higher dividends and rents—seems only fair. They are happy to be convinced that the state earnings-related pension (the *kosei nenkin*) has to be cut back to half its value or else it will involve an 'intolerable' payroll tax, because they are the ones who have the incomes that permit savings and that assure them a good private pension out of, not the labour income, but the capital income of Japan in 2030 and 2040. Hence, more consideration for shareholders and measuring performance by return on equity become for them matters of elementary justice. Memories of their own 'examination hell' hardly prompt frequent reflection on how, in Japan's meritocracy, opportunity is stacked in favour of the top 10 per cent. So 'true equality is equality of opportunity, not equality of outcomes' strikes them as an eminently reasonable slogan. And as for the 'consumer sovereignty' which makes free markets essential, is that not an integral part of the 'democracy' which their parents worked so hard to establish and maintain in postwar Japan?

These symptoms of a diminished social cohesion, the diminished sense of Japanese citizens as constituting a community and of the duty of the most favoured of those citizens to look after the others (*omoiyari* 'extending your thoughts across to others' is the key word), are almost certainly mirrored in corporate communities. Positive assertions of egalitarian, communitarian values are becoming rarer. One would have thought that the introduction of stock options—a direct challenge to the employee-sovereignty firm—would have led to sharp public controversy. A trawl through the references to the 1997 law introducing stock options in the *Nikkei Shimbun*, however, found only one sceptical comment, by the chairman of a steel firm.[11]

It is not individuals so much as group cooperation that makes for success ... at the time of yen appreciation it fell to me to be the main flag-waver for our efforts at restructuring the firm. We didn't do too badly and the firm got back into profit. But that was by group effort. Supposing that my role as flag-waver in the process had been seen as important and I'd been given stock options and exercised them and made a lot of money, I don't think I would have felt too happy about that. And I don't think my colleagues, in the bottom of their hearts, would have accepted the justice of it. In individualistic societies like America and Europe stock option systems may fit in very well, but I really wonder about their suitability for Japan.

Then, secondly, there is the egalitarian approach to human relations of the Japanese firm. As is commonly observed, the difference in pay between managers and other employees is far smaller in Japan than in America. And both managers and workers agree that this should be so. A factory director—a member of the Board usually—wears the same overalls and eats in the same canteen as the shopfloor workers and that is taken for granted.

When I read in the newspapers about CEOs in America who lay off large numbers of workers in a restructuring and earn themselves large sums of money from their stock options as a result, I ask myself how that can be psychologically possible. Japanese managers would have given up a part of their salary before they would get to involuntary lay-offs. My own salary at the moment is subject to a cut of 10 per cent plus. This is not hypocrisy. The saying that sums it up—'Scarcity is tolerable; inequality is not'—is a deeply rooted part of the Japanese ethic.

He excuses himself for setting himself against progress—against a stock option system that, he understands, has 'already been introduced in the advanced countries of America and Europe'—on the grounds that he is only 'an old steel man, drenched in the culture of a historic industry'. And at the end he adds as a further extenuating circumstance that he is an old man and 'people of my generation of Japanese simply cannot free themselves of the feeling that "fishing for people with the bait of money" is just an ignoble thing to do. That may be one reason why I would drag my feet on this issue.'

The voice of a dying generation? The egalitarianism and the appeal to unselfish cooperation within the group come naturally to men like him who are old enough to have vivid memories of the days just after the war when they were struggling to get their factories going again, and their clothes were just as shabby, and their shoes just as leaky, as those of their shopfloor workers. He, like most of his contemporary businessmen in their seventies, was schooled in a Japan whose social cohesion was predicated on the assumption that rich and poor, officers and men, had a good chance of dying on the battlefield together. Their postwar days of shared poverty and shared effort to rebuild the firm mirrored the sort of comradeship that platoon commanders (which many of them had in fact been) develop with their men. They would remember the furious arguments that took place after the war when some of their contemporaries, 20-year-old university graduates who rediscovered their 1930s Marxism, sought to institutionalize this comradeship and led the movement to amalgamate white-collar and blue-collar unions.[12] Such men are unlikely to speak contemptuously of their company's union, or of the blue-collar workers it represents. Their 35-year-old-juniors, affluent products of the elite educational tracks, have no such inhibitions, even if many of them would still hesitate to put on paper anything but ritual affirmations of the admirable way Japanese firms 'look after people'.

There are, then, two complementary ways in which the value-system underpinnings of the Japanese model might be weakening.

Both of them are referred to in popular slang as a shift from 'wet' to 'dry' attitudes. On the one hand is greater individualism, less definitive commitments to loyal lifelong membership in firms or to a trading relationship, a greater insistence on keeping one's options open. On the other is a stronger awareness of society, or of firms, or of the 'society of industry' as being stratified by power, prestige, and 'cultural level', and a diminished sense of the responsibility of upper strata to show consideration for the lower; a diminished sense, in other words, that noblesse—or success, or power, or doing well in entrance exams—should oblige.

These, then, are some of the background factors—over and above the steady drip-drip forces of globalization—which explain both why there is such enthusiasm, almost desperate enthusiasm, for change in Japan, and also the direction in which reformers look for inspiration. Let us start, specifically, with the firm.

Chapter 4

Corporate Governance: From the Employee-Favouring Firm to the Shareholder-Favouring Firm

The context

W OULD the reformers have concentrated so much on corporate governance had not shareholder activism, boardroom salaries, the British Cadbury and Hempel reports, and so on made it such a hot academic and journalistic topic for discussion in the Anglo-Saxon world? Almost certainly not. If it had in fact been some endogenously generated sense of profound dissatisfaction with the way in which Japanese companies are run which had prompted the discussion, one would have expected more explicit concentration on the basic differences between an employee-favouring firm and a shareholder-favouring firm. Instead of which, almost everything to be found in the flurry of what I shall call the 'mainstream' reports on corporate governance—those produced by the major business organizations, Keidanren, the Doyūkai, MITI, the Japan Productivity Council, the Corporate Governance Forum[1]—seems to avoid such a categorization. The reports occasionally admit that Japanese firms have hitherto tended to have other objectives than the simple maximization of shareholder value, but by and large they start from the assumption that the *raison d'être* of business firms is much the same the world over, and that their objectives should therefore be the same. Likewise, since their organs—the Board of Directors, the president, the shareholders' AGM—have the same names, they should function similarly and be measured by the same standards of efficiency. Hence prescriptions drawn from the British Cadbury Report, or the pronouncements of CalPERS (the California State Employees Retirement Scheme), can be quoted as directly relevant to Japan.

There is formal justification for this stance. Japanese company law does not differ much more from the laws of Britain or the American states than those of Britain and the US states differ from each other. That some countries, such as Germany, have different regimes, or that, in diverging from the law, the social reality of Japanese companies may have created a viable alternative form which could well be legitimized by legal change, is suggested in none of these reports.

The one semi-exception to this generalization—a report which explicitly talks of the need to preserve major features of the Japanese system (specifically the 'long-term vision' and 'treating human beings with respect')—is that of Nikkeiren, the Employers' Federation created to deal with industrial relations and labour issues. Its authors, too, claim external authority by quoting the limited 'tolerate diversity: let a hundred flowers bloom' line taken by the OECD's Millstein Commission on corporate governance. But first let us consider the mainstream.

A second stimulus to the reformers' activity, besides the parallel British and American debates, was provided by the Structural Impediment Initiative talks in 1989–90 (the trade negotiations which resulted when, the removal of tariff and non-tariff barriers having made no impression on Japan's perennial trade surplus, a new solution was sought: persuade Japan to change its domestic institutions to more import-friendly, foreign-investor-friendly, less export-prone forms). One complaint was that there was an asymmetry. Japanese firms could, and not infrequently did, acquire American firms by takeover, sometimes even hostile takeover. American firms, however, while they might occasionally acquire Japanese firms by agreement, had no chance of making an acquisition simply by buying up shares in the market.

It did not much help the American cause that the most prominent demonstration of the asymmetry was the thwarting of an attempt to gain control of Koito, a Toyota subsidiary, by the well-known American arbitrageur T. Boone Pickens. (It subsequently transpired that he had been lent the money to acquire Koito's shares by their previous Japanese owner, a professional greenmailer who had bought the stake in the hope of getting the company to buy him out at a profit. The company refused to play and he decided that an American cowboy might be more effective in helping him to turn his honest penny.)

Discussion of the rights of shareholders was never more than a minor theme in the SII talks, but there was one concrete outcome. The

Japanese side agreed that—what with the stage-management of shareholder annual general meetings—shareholders had little influence over their firms. It was equally not in dispute that Japanese company law in principle made shareholders sovereign and that some things could be done to strengthen their rights. An amendment to the company law greatly reduced the risks and the costs to a shareholder of bringing a civil suit for mismanagement against company directors. Henceforth, any David with a hundred dollars or so was entitled to battle any corporate Goliath.

To call this the first stone that caused the landslide is to exaggerate, but the amendment undoubtedly put the question of reinforcing shareholder rights by legal amendment as well as by changes in practice firmly on the agenda.

The arguments for change

It is impossible in the current discussions to separate out arguments for change in management styles and objectives from those explicitly about changes in governance structures, and they are treated together here. One thread runs through them: the patriotic thread. Japanese firms, it is argued, have a duty to the nation to be efficient. So, arguments to the effect that Japanese firms need reform to make them more efficient ('look at the mess we are in and at how well the Americans are doing') far outweigh any explicit arguments about justice, about the rights of ownership, or about giving shareholders their due.

The cost of lifetime employment

One of the central efficiency arguments is, of course, about 'rethinking' (the usual word rather than 'abolishing') lifetime employment. Clearly keeping surplus workers on the books eats into profits, potential dividends, and potential investment funds. Freedom to hire and fire—the famous 'labour flexibility'—requires a change in practice rather than in the law, though the accretion of judicial precedents which in effect establish job rights (heavy compensation for dismissal if the employer cannot show determined efforts to find new markets in order to avoid the need for redundancies, for instance) has brought a certain institutional entrenchment to practice. The grounds on which it is argued that practice must now change are (a) the rapidity of technical and structural change, (b) change in the nature of work and the increasing specialization of skills, and (c) changes in values in two dimensions mentioned earlier: (i) a diminution in both loyalty and the centrality of work in individuals' life-interests and (ii) increasing individualism, manifest in increasing intolerance of wage and promotion systems which give equal rewards for unequal contributions. More performance-related rewards, says the Doyūkai's manifesto,[2] appropriating one of the traditionalists' slogans, is the new way of showing how you *hito o taisetsu ni suru* (respect people)—respect, that is, not the needs they have in common with others, but their unequal contributions.

The fact that the system still shows surprising resilience is attributed mainly to perceptions of (a) a sense of duty on the part of managers (misguided according to the reformers) and (b) the disastrous consequences for morale of unilateral dismissals (since experience has given managers a taste of the difficulties of negotiating even early retirement and worker-outposting schemes.) There is a further argument, not often explicitly made, that the need to find work for redundant idle hands—in the absence of an easy downsizing option—concentrates managerial minds on the possibilities of product diversification. The steel industry is a prime example. The big five set themselves diversification targets (e.g. 30 per cent of output in non-steel products) and have by and large achieved them. Many of their projects proved unviable and a waste of resources. Some took off: Japan Steel has created one of the world's most successful silicon wafer producers, for example. The corporate governance reformers are, however, also for the most part adherents of the current 'stick to your knitting', 'develop core competencies' business school doctrines, and they point to all the failures. What no overall assessment of the profitability of such ventures can hope to measure, however, is their external-internal economies—external to the spun-off enterprises, but internal to the group as a whole—viz. the benefits brought to the morale and efficiency of the core firm by the efforts to maintain the lifetime compact.

The one body which shows rather more awareness of these issues than the others is the Nikkeiren, whose somewhat deviant approach to the corporate governance issue was mentioned earlier.[3] This is the Employers' Federation whose whole *raison d'être* is employment and industrial relations issues. Its report differs clearly from the others and derives a good deal of its inspiration from the OECD's Millstein Report[4]—not surprisingly, since the chairman of the group responsible for its report was one of the six members of Millstein's committee. Unlike any of the other Japanese reports, it acknowledges (following Michel Albert, another member of Millstein's group) a clear difference between the Anglo-Saxon model of the firm, which 'gives priority to the capital market and treats the shareholder's interest as absolute, and the continental European and Japanese model, which respects the interests of a variety of stakeholders, such as the managers and employees, and gives only relative importance to the interests of shareholders'. It goes on to declare that it would be 'somewhat short-sighted' to argue that the Anglo-Saxon model represents the global standard, to which Japan must learn to conform. A lot of people in Britain and the United States are concerned about the inequalities and the consequent social problems which their system produces; and in France and Germany, where there is also a vigorous debate about corporate governance, there are some people who actually argue for a strengthening of the firm's ties with its employees.

Nevertheless, the Nikkeiren has taken the lead in the 'rethink' of lifetime employment, urging a 'third way' of a 'mixed portfolio' of employment contracts (its famous 'Bluebird Plan'), so it is not about to offer a full endorsement of the lifetime employment system. Employees have changing needs; the best way of promoting their interests may be not to give them jobs for life but to help them to acquire skills which they can take into the external market.

But the report does strive towards a certain even-handedness, symbolized in its title by the phrase about making the firm attractive to those in both capital and labour markets. Thus, while the main report talks about 'transparency' in the same sense as all the other organizations' reports—namely, in terms of making data available to shareholders—there is an appendix, 'Supplementary points for further discussion', which points out that transparency is also an essential element in making firms capable of attracting good employees. However, there is a clear asymmetry. Transparency towards employees is not the same as transparency towards investors—it is not a matter of letting employees know where the money goes. Employees, says the report, are not interested in bread alone. Clarity of the firm's ideals and its mission is an essential means of creating an attractive work environment and giving people a sense of doing a worthwhile job. Transparency of personnel evaluation systems is also important.

Nikkeiren's main business is dealing with unions, but there is very little directly about unions in the report, and nothing about wage determination except the following rather strange passage. It follows a paragraph on the way in which greater transparency is necessary because greater 'heterogeneity of values' (which is the current Japanese code for being more single-minded in the pursuit of self-interest) makes both shareholders (increasingly institutional) and employees more interested in the who gets what:

> For example, the division of value-added is a division among all the stakeholders who have taken part in wealth creation, and the proportions devoted to dividends, the wage bill, etc. are an indication of the priorities of individual firms. There are some firms which have declared it to be a matter of policy and principle to make a three-way equal split between shareholders, employees, and the future of the firm.

The interesting thing about this passage is the way it shows the general ignorance of, and lack of interest in, how value-added does in fact get divided—a lack of interest which, indeed, Japan shares with British and American academic and business school analysts of corporation performance. And this in spite of the fact that there are no fewer than eight organizations in Japan publishing value-added analyses for various samples of firms. One of the most comprehensive set of statistics—that of the Ministry of Finance, based on the figures in the (legally required) annual 'Report to Shareholders'—gives the following figures for manufacturing industry as a whole.[5] They are for the boom year of 1990 and the recession year of 1995. First, take away the share of the state, the tax taken out of the value-added, which is omitted in the three-party classification—12 per cent in 1990 and 9 per cent in 1995. Taking the remainder (of gross value-added) as 100 per cent, employees (including the directors, of course) got 64 per cent in 1990 and 70 per cent in 1995; capital (overwhelmingly in the form of interest and rent; less than one-tenth in the form of dividends) got 16 per cent in 1990 and 13 per cent in 1995. The firm, in the form of depreciation and retained earnings, got the remaining 20 per cent, falling to 17 per cent. It stretches belief to imagine that any firm is seriously proposing a three-way equal split, whatever manipulation of the concept of 'value-added' it might contrive.

Nikkeiren makes one other brief gesture towards the interests of employees: the supplementary note also includes the sentences 'There are also recorded cases of firms which have made their trade union leaders outside directors/auditors (*kansayaku*). It is not clear what this means: whether it could be the beginning of a move in the German direction of co-determination or a new form of management–labour consultation.'

These features of the report reflect the fact that—in strong contrast to the dominant assumption of British and American managers that the only good union is a dead one—Japanese managers tend predominantly to believe that enterprise unions are a useful element of the constitutional structure of the firm. But for all that surface evenhandedness, the strongest statements in the Nikkeiren report point in the same direction as those of the 'real reformer' bodies: the world has changed, shareholder-owners will not be gainsaid, and Japanese firms must change to go with the tide. In this it merely follows the lead of its main inspiration, the Millstein Report, which for all that it acknowledges that corporations can have a variety of objectives favouring other stakeholders insists that the essential prerequisite is to make it clear to *investors* what those objectives are. It also preempts a lot of ground by initially defining corporate governance as being about the 'structure of relationships and corresponding responsibilities among a core group consisting of shareholders, board members and managers'.

The insider system: accountability

A central issue behind most proposals for corporate reform is 'insider control'—Boards of Directors exclusively staffed by lifetime employees and not subject to any effective external monitoring. Acton's dictum about unmonitored power corrupting is one of the most universal assumptions of social scientists. Kay and Silberston preface their proposal for making British companies publicly responsible with a passage about the 'insidiously corrupting' consequences of authoritarian company structure:

> Leaders hang on to power too long, and many prefer to undermine those who might seek to replace them than to develop potential successors. Cults of personality develop, and are supported by sycophantic lieutenants . . . inappropriate accretion of privileges . . . excessive fascination with the trappings of office . . . slogans replace analysis, rallies replace debate . . .[6]

Authoritarian abuse of power and personality cults are not the charges which the reformers level against the Japanese system. Rather it is the hugger-mugger tendency of everybody to collude in practices which, in all these reports, are collectively referred to as 'the recent unfortunate incidents' (*fushōji*). These include the New York Daiwa Bank scandal, the Sumitomo copper scandal, the securities firms' illegally making up the stock exchange losses of favoured companies, and numerous criminal prosecutions within Japan of firms which have—often for paltry sums—succumbed to the blackmail of the petty gangsters who threaten to disrupt shareholders' meetings. The following example is from the prosecution's case against one of the more notorious of these *sōkaiya* or 'AGM operators':

> The defendant went along to see Yamaichi's Divisional Manager X in the spring of 1987 to ask that he be given the chance to make profits with a priority allocation of the warrant bonds the firm was about to issue. An account was opened for him at the Shinbashi branch in May under an assumed name and it subsequently received frequent allocations of warrant bonds etc. As a consequence, the defendant undertook before the December shareholders' meeting to make sure that there should be no trouble over allegations that Yamaichi had made priority allocations of MHI shares to certain customers, and himself attended the meeting to cooperate in ensuring the expeditious despatch of the agenda.[7]

None of these 'unfortunate' incidents was primarily about self-enrichment at the firm's expense. They were all unlawful acts committed 'for the sake of the firm'. Indeed, the 'flak-catcher' director who has the job of dealing with the *sōkaiya* and the anonymous telephone calls that come with the job ('We know where your granddaughter goes to school') is an object of sympathy within the firm even before he is indicted and sentenced to six months in jail. Japan does have its buccaneers, its would-be Maxwells and Milkens, and the Jusen mortgage company investigations turned up a few. But these are owner-managers of small, unquoted, mainly financial sector companies, beyond the reach of shareholders, however vigilant and powerful. If one asks about such behaviour in the large corporate sector, the most likely answer is to cite the famed incident of the president of the department store Mitsukoshi who was finally ousted for his blatant abuses of power. But that happened 20 years ago. More recent cases of powerful individuals acting in a factionally partisan way (as at Japan Airlines) seem less clear-cut—they are apparently more about power and status within the enterprise community than about individual self-enrichment.

But the charge that Japan has an 'insider system' over which share-holders exercise little monitoring control remains true. The standard defence of that system by neoclassical economists goes as follows. True, nobody is ever honest and diligent unless subject to external discipline. In well-run societies this is provided by the stock market, but Japan (like many other developing societies too immature to have an efficient stock market) has hitherto found a functional substitute in the main bank system. The bank which sets the pace for other banks in arranging finance and picks up the pieces when firms are in distress has sufficient power over firms to provide effective monitoring.[8]

Other economists allow that it might not be the rational self-interest of owners or creditors but that of employees that counts. One speaks of 'the capacity for self-monitoring of the employees (including managers) [who] know that improvements in productivity and profits will lead to greater rewards for themselves, and this makes for effective internal controls'.[9]

There is clearly, however, something more than rationally calcu-lated self-interest at work, and indeed, the last-quoted author so far deviates from his rationality paradigm as to talk of the 'work ethic'. Other elements of an explanation of why shareholder monitoring may be less necessary to prevent corrupt mismanagement are as follows:

1. The community nature of a Japanese firm—partly predicated on the fact that it is not run primarily for the benefit of shareholders—imposes peer-group moral constraints on those who are selected, as the culmination of their lifelong membership, to be its 'elders'—much like the constraints on permanent secretaries of British ministries.

2. Japanese firms have much more tightly institutionalized gov-ernance structures than Anglo-Saxon firms, whose Boards have free-dom to write almost any kind of contract with the CEO, to whom they give extraordinary powers. Getting to the top in a Japanese company —almost any large company—follows the pattern described at the beginning of Chapter 2—a long process of continuous sifting of those with greater from those with lesser endowments of intellectual and leadership ability. The process begins when managers are in their twenties. In any age cohort, perhaps—in large companies with Boards

of 40 or more—three or four may get to the Board in their early fifties, but only one from two or three adjacent cohorts will make it to the top. Someone likely to abuse power for personal ends is not likely to be that person.

3. The generally conformist nature of Japanese society means that these tight institutional structures are mutually reinforced (another example of the S-curve diffusion effect: when enough company presidents have made 'investor relations' trips to America, every president has to go).

4. The generally conciliar style of decision-making means that a lot of people would have to be persuaded to collude for real abuse to take place.

Are these differences enough to keep Japanese executives honest—with the help perhaps of the regular consultation meetings at which managers have to explain themselves to union executives? (Note that nowadays this frequently means explaining themselves not to bemused shop stewards, but to managers 20 years their junior following the same career track as themselves who just happen to be demonstrating their leadership powers—and strengthening their claim to accelerated promotion—by getting elected to run the union for a while.)

Unfortunately the corporate governance reports, more concerned with ideals than with reality, do not ask this question. All the literature they read tells them to assume the truth of the Acton dictum about corruption: insider control is just bound to be a problem. A slightly more sophisticated version of the argument is that it has recently *become* a problem because the external controls which previously kept wayward directors in check have been eroded. Those exercised by the banks have been eroded by firms' greater financial self-sufficiency and independence, while those exercised by the unions have been eroded as a result of affluence and union members' apathy, and those offered by the government have been weakened by deregulation.[10]

One study by a research institute clearly dominated by reformers recently attempted a statistical demonstration of the negative relationship between efficiency and one feature supposedly fostering insider control, namely cross-shareholding.[11] It took the 'performance' of 910 firms quoted on the Tokyo Stock Exchange for the period 1988 to 1997 and looked at its correlation with (*a*) the proportion of shares in the hands of stable shareholders and (*b*) the proportion in the hands of foreign investors. It found that performance was better for those with fewer stable shareholders and for those with more rather than fewer foreign investors. Unfortunately, the index of 'performance' was dominated by the share price, so there was a more than reasonable doubt as to which way causation runs; the connection between share price and the proportion of the stock available for active trading is clearly complex. In any case, a fragmented share ownership has usually been seen as the prime cause of insider control, not as its cure.

The insider system: efficiency

Although the 'unfortunate incidents' figure in practically every discussion of corporate governance, the more effective arguments about the insider system see the problem as one not so much of outright corruption as of slackness and lack of rigour. Symptomatic of this is the frequency with which one encounters the word 'tension'. It is an irony that, while political economists of the Anglo-American academic world are becoming increasingly preoccupied with the analysis of trust relations (the popularity of Fukuyama's *Trust: The Social Virtues and the Creation of Prosperity* being one manifestation thereof), the Japanese, frequently cited in that literature as exemplars of the virtues of trust, are becoming preoccupied with what they see as the problem of an excess of trust. The following passage occurs in the questionnaire which the Doyūkai's Enterprise Trends Study Group sent to a sample of four-and-a-half thousand businessmen in 1995—the basis of its Twelfth Enterprise White Paper the following year.[12]

> We set out below our basic approach to the problem of corporate governance. Please give us your reaction.
>
> The devising of a new pattern of Japanese corporate governance requires us to rethink relations with stakeholders. In doing so we have in mind the need to introduce an element of tension in the relation of various stakeholders with corporate management, thereby bringing performance closer to perfection. [*Sessa takuma*, the term used, is an old Chinese phrase—'cutting the stone, polishing the gem'—meaning self-improvement through meticulous effort and the rough and tumble of working with others.]
>
> Tension has hitherto been absent in the relations of managers, not only with shareholders, but also with labour unions and with customers. Problems were treated as if they were common problems: that—the

'insiderization' of tension relations—was what counted as good leadership in a manager.

But in this new era of globalization what is required is not merely just conduct towards insiders, but just conduct which can be explained to third parties. We need to shift our focus and appreciate that it is from the tensions of various relations with outsiders that good things can come.

The word 'tension' is frequently used in a context redolent of conflict, destruction, mistrust, and evasion of responsibility, but we wish to understand it, rather, in the context of harmony, creativity, trust, and acceptance of personal responsibility. In that sense it is necessary to build relations with an element of tension not only between managers and stakeholders but mutually among stakeholders themselves.

Tension 1: transparency. There are two main elements in this plea for more tension. One is about checks and balances. Other key words in the reformers' vocabulary are 'disclosure' and 'transparency'. Japanese corporate law requires firms to appoint Auditors who attend Board meetings (without voting rights) and are required to investigate any suspicions they may have about the improper conduct of business in the firm and to give the shareholders a report on their investigations. In practice they are described as 'directors' like any other member of the Board; they are generally men judged to be of directorial calibre but not likely to reach the higher ranks of directors (plus, often, an outsider—a retired chairman of the firm's main bank, for instance), and their reports are notoriously bland and unrevealing. In the most famous case of non-transparency in the 1990s—Yamaichi's collapse under a mountain of off-balance-sheet liabilities—it transpired that one of the main architects of the hoodwinking operations was one of the company's Auditors.[13]

Then there is the independent audit, usually carried out by one of the six firms, all of which have a tie-up with one of the Anglo-Saxon big six. There is nothing particularly Japanese about the universal problem that outside auditing firms, not wishing to upset clients and lose business, sign off accounts too readily and can all too easily turn a blind eye when they discover inadmissible accounting practices or possible evidence of fraud. But, as the infrequency with which approval of accounts is qualified suggests, the problem is clearly much worse in Japan than elsewhere. Accountancy firms are more easily 'insiderized' in a society where the dominant ethic requires trading relations to involve mutual goodwill and consideration. Not so much the corporate governance debate itself as the revelation of the extent to which Yamaichi's auditors had allowed themselves to be hoodwinked led to a good deal of public discussion of the auditing profession at the beginning of 1998. The president of the auditing industry association explained to a reporter that the accountant's job in an audit was to ensure that the presentation of the accounts was fully in conformity with the regulations and that 'if you approach the job in the same spirit as the Tax Office, looking for what's wrong with the accounts, you simply cannot do a good audit. Your job is to be a welcomed advisor, helping in the healthy growth of the firm.'[14]

Currently the auditors of the bankrupt Yamaichi are being sued by shareholders for negligence on the grounds that they could not have failed to discover evidence of the *tobashi*, the accumulation of which caused the firm's downfall. *Tobashi* involves temporarily moving worthless assets off the balance sheet at account-closing time by sale to a firm with a different account-closing date, with a promise of re-purchase—at a 10 per cent premium! The repurchase undertaking should have been noted in the accounts but was not. The only civil law precedent is a case brought against its auditors by Nippon Kop-pasu, a small German-owned firm, alleging negligence in failing to discover that the Finance Director who provided them with all audit-ing facilities was falsifying accounts and robbing the firm blind. The district court found for the firm, but awarded it much smaller damages than claimed on the grounds of extenuating circumstances, notably the exceedingly convincing nature of the fraudulent accounts provided. The appeal court overturned the verdict. Two of the points on which the two courts differed were (a) whether the duty to hunt out possible fraud was implicit in the commission to audit, even though not explicitly specified, and (b) whether failing to examine the actual pass-books for the firm's deposit accounts (and thus failing to discover that some of them were encumbered as collateral) constituted culp-able negligence.[15]

That case—involving an audit commissioned at the owner's dis-cretion—does not necessarily provide a clue as to the courts' treat-ment of the compulsory audits which have been required by law since 1981 for all firms with paid-up capital of more than ¥500mn or in-debtedness of over ¥20bn. Since this is a legal obligation the criminal as well as the civil law can be involved, and it is a major part of the 'greater transparency' case that the regulatory authorities—the

Ministry of Finance and the Stock Exchange—are far less vigilant in following up suspected fraud, and disqualifying negligent or criminally colluding auditors, than the authorities in Anglo-Saxon countries. The fact that to date there have been only two criminal cases brought by the regulators—and both of those a result of revelations made in the course of bankruptcy proceedings—suggests that there is a great deal of truth in the argument.

It does seem likely that the pressure for more probing audits will increase. Most of the discussion is by and for professionals, concerns the legal system and the duties it prescribes, and takes place in the context of the current discussions concerning the internationalization of accounting standards. A summary of the proposed changes by an insurance company research institute (the obligation of firms with subsidiaries to provide consolidated accounts, the treatment of R&D expenditure, and valuation of pension obligations, etc.) stresses the change in orientation.[16] Whereas the public accounts hitherto required by the Commercial Code, the Stock Exchange Law, and the Corporate Tax Laws have been intended to serve three parties—creditors, investors, and the tax authorities—the emphasis now is on investors, on curing the information asymmetry between managers and investors. There is, of course, no mention in this or any other article in the business press that I have seen that, in the standard Japanese employee-favouring firm, the people who have an interest in transparency are equally, if not preeminently, the employees whose livelihoods are at stake. Nor does the report point out what is surely the socially and politically important point—namely, the change in the *purpose* of transparency. The Commercial Code envisages accounts as primarily an assurance to the annual meeting of (presumptively committed, loyal) shareholders that their affairs are being competently managed, whereas now 'investor-orientation' means giving the information to inform buy-and-sell decisions by market players.

Tension 2: Relational contracting and zero-sum games. But the 'tension' manifesto quoted above was not talking only about formal audits. It was also making a more general point about frankness and openness, particularly frank and open acknowledgement of conflicting self-interest. It was criticizing current Japanese practice for, as it were, pretending that all games are positive-sum games and ignoring the zero-sum element.

In a firm's relations with its subcontractors, for example, negotiations about a new contract are, in fact, far from being free from tension, particularly in these recession days when assemblers, in trouble themselves, are pressing their suppliers to cut prices. But neither party is likely to adopt a 'take it or leave it' stance; the assumption is that there is a 'fair' price which can leave both parties satisfied—fair in the light of the history of their relationship and their shared expectation of continuing it in the future.

The same applies to management and labour. In the postwar system, wage negotiations aim to arrive at the level of wage increase which represents a fair, reasonable balance between the workers' wish for more money and the managers' concern with a level of profits which will yield funds for future investment. Both parties acknowledge the justness of the other's concern. The drafters of the questionnaire disquisition on tension probably do not remember the days when there really was tension—when union leaders went into bargaining sessions as leaders of the oppressed working class fighting capital and all it stood for. The situation they wish to see recreated?

Doubtless they would like to see a bit more tension, too, at shareholders' annual general meetings, and given the revelations of the extent of the *sōkaiya* gangsters' operations one can see why. One suspects, also, that there is (for want of a better word) an 'aesthetic' at work in this assertion of the need for more tension, an admiration for what is perceived to be the archetypal American managerial style—cool and courteous, but forceful and frank, unafraid to give offence, if anything enjoying the 'challenge' of tension. And the appeal of this aesthetic is apparent in the replies. More than half say that they agree, though that half includes many who say that they agree 'ideally', or with the basic thrust, the basic direction, in principle—and then go on to qualify, frequently on national character grounds:

> but the historically rooted system of settling everything in discussion will take a lot of time and outside pressure to change. (p. 176) ['Outside pressure' usually means foreign, i.e. American, pressure.]

> but the Japanese habit of fostering warm relations between stakeholders with golf and parties isn't going to change very easily, however much, as we get more and more internationalized, this Westernized, rational style has become more and more necessary for Japanese business. (p. 194)

> but Japanese society is immature and there is always the danger of

prejudiced public opinion, so that at present 'insiderization' is the only way of defending the firm. (p. 178)

Japanese people aren't accustomed to having a fierce debate and then going back to work without any ill feelings. (p. 193)

We've always been a tension-maintaining company from our foundation. However, the problem with that sort of management is that from the employees' point of view it's going to cause a lot of people to fall by the wayside; your suppliers are going to see you as a difficult company to deal with. In the Japanese entrepreneurial climate it's going to be difficult for this to become the general style. (p. 184)

but given how frightfully incompetent we Japanese are at open debate . . . (p. 196)

but when all the rest of society—politics, local government, administration, and especially education—doesn't operate on the principle that relations of tension breed harmony, creativity, and trust . . . (p. 196)

A number of the replies draw a distinction between the 'transparency' question and the 'tension' question—agreeing on the former but not on the latter. Open disclosure of accounts and the need for checks and balances, yes. To underline this, the phrase 'the firm is a public institution in society' occurs frequently. It is perhaps surprising, though, that only seven replies even mention the role of the Audit Committee, only two mention the possibility of non-executive directors, and not one refers to the outside accountants' professional audit. What they do stress is that the emphasis on transparency and accountability by no means has to imply endorsement of the 'tension' notion:

> but given the differences in national character between Japan and the West (groupism versus individualism; valuing harmony versus an aggressive attitude) one has to be careful that introducing Western practices into Japan does not weaken the leadership of Japanese managers. (p. 175)

> but I don't see that treating problems with the union or suppliers as shared problems and trying to resolve them can be called lacking in tension and trying to 'insiderize'. (p. 188)

> but while there are both advantages and disadvantages for competitiveness in such Japanese features as cross-shareholdings and job security for employees, it is lacking in balance to stress the disadvantages. (p. 188)

A few talked about shareholders specifically, reacting also to other questions in the survey. One who sums up and endorses the rationale of the employee-favouring firm says,

> I wouldn't say that shareholders are unimportant, but after all it's only money self-interest that's involved in their case; you cannot put them in the same category as employees who have linked themselves in a 'community of fate' with the company. (p. 192)

Proposals for curing insiderism

Such is the background of ideas and sentiments with which the corporate governance reports set about discussing the concrete governance structures of Japanese firms and what should be done about them. To start with, it is argued, most Boards are too big for effective decision-making. Japan Steel, for instance, has a Board of 50, Hitachi of 38. They are not known for their lively discussions. They are a collection of yes-men who serve to rubber-stamp decisions taken elsewhere.

That is undoubtedly true, but it is an argument for change only if one assumes that the distribution of functions within the firm should conform to the Anglo-Saxon model. Quite other distributions are possible. Why are Japanese Boards so large? Primarily, I suspect, in order to keep the likelihood of appointment to the Board, as an incentive for dedicated managerial performance, at a meaningful percentage probability level. Of all male employees between the ages of 50 and 54, an astonishing 12.6 per cent were directors of their firm in 1997—and 14.4 per cent of those aged 55–59.[17] Among large-corporation employees the ratio is bound to be much smaller, but to maintain a meaningful percentage a big firm has to have a big Board.

And while the hegemony of the Anglo-Saxon model is such that few would admit the fact, argument and decision-making are not the major function of Boards. Instead, through their rubber-stamping, they have the important functions of (a) keeping top managers of various activities informed about the work of other departments and (b) giving them a sense of responsibility for the firm as a whole to temper any 'my division right or wrong' tendencies. The fact that there are a lot of directors, and that they mostly have executive responsibilities, means that they are in personal touch with a very large number of employees.

So if Boards are not places for flying kites, taking initiatives, or reaching decisions either by persuasion or steam-roller tactics, how do decisions get taken? Mostly by interdepartmental discussions at levels below the Board. Ideas may, indeed, start in discussions among the small inner group of president, vice-president, and *semmu*—the top-rank directors of longest standing—and the same inner group may be called on for final arbitration if lower-level discussions reach deadlock, and especially if there are larger strategic implications. There is a fairly close parallel with the workings of Japanese government, with the Board playing the role of the Cabinet. Very rarely do substantive discussions take place in Cabinet. The Cabinet's job is primarily to ratify the decisions already taken in the administrative vice-ministers' meeting which took place earlier in the day; perhaps to get comments on the record—for example, to give notice that having made a concession on the present issue a department feels itself entitled to a fair wind for its own related proposal in the future.

The most common recommendations in the corporate governance reports are (*a*) for smaller, more active Boards to do what is now done by the informal 'nuclear' committees, and (*b*) for the appointment of outside directors, or, more specifically, non-ritual Auditors. It has always been the case that a number of firms appoint a small number of outside directors, most frequently people from banks (often former high officials, disappointed in their hopes of a presidency or vice-presidency in their home bank, who are wished on the firm in order to give them a consolation prize). These people rarely make either trouble or any positive contribution. A minority of firms, however, appoint one or two directors because they think that their experience, looking at the world from a vantage-point that none of the lifetime employee insiders can ever have occupied, would be useful to the firm.

Most of the suggestions in the corporate governance reports for more use of outside directors have precisely this last function in mind. The alternative function of the external director—as a watchdog to prevent abuse of powers—is favoured by others. But here again is a division between those who see the watchdog function as being in the public interest (because the firm is a public institution) and those, the minority, who see external directors as having the American role, specifically as guardians of the interests of shareholders.

Global financial markets and the need for capital

The argument is obvious. Hitherto Japanese savings have stayed at home and provided Japanese firms with a cheap source of capital. With liberalization, that can no longer be counted on. Japanese investors will put their savings abroad, and the facilities for doing so will steadily grow. (Merrill Lynch has taken over the best branches of the defunct Yamaichi Securities.) One of the most frequently cited statistics is that the average return on equity of American firms has recently been of the order of 20 per cent, compared with Japanese firms' average hovering between 5 and 7 per cent.

Not for nothing does the thirteenth Doyūkai Enterprise White Paper have as its subtitle 'Management for capital efficiency'. Equally, the Nikkeiren's report, though the most sympathetic to the claims of employees, tends to equate efficiency exclusively with efficiency in the use of capital. Return-on-equity targets are endorsed but not labour productivity targets. In spite of its even-handed subtitle ('Towards corporations favoured by both capital and labour markets'), the report makes clear that the quality of corporate governance is to be judged by success in capital markets, not in any other market. This is a point of view which the OECD's Millstein Report would seem to endorse. (In spite of Millstein's catholic advocacy of a studied neutrality between the Rhenish and the Anglo-Saxon tendencies represented on his committee, in the end it is the investor who ultimately call the shots. Different countries and different companies can, the report says, have all kinds of social or employee-favouring objectives; the essential thing is that these objectives should be made transparently clear to investors (to investors rather than to potential employees). The message is implicit in the report's very title: *Corporate Governance: Improving Competitiveness and Access to Capital in Global Markets.*)

How far *will* the need for external capital on favourable terms provide a compelling motive for favouring shareholders over employees? First, take a minimal definition of need—not having a cash flow sufficient to cover necessary investment. To take contrasting firms from one industry with high investment levels, neither Toyota, well known for its cash mountain (cash flow, 1996–7, ¥470bn; depreciation ¥270bn; retained earnings ¥200bn; and planned investment ¥320bn), nor Nissan, currently in a bad way (cash flow ¥120bn; depreciation ¥90bn; retained earnings ¥30bn; and planned investment ¥114bn[18]), would have a pressing need for external finance to cover their current investment plans. But define 'need', instead, in terms of (*a*) the maximum investment which the firm's available human and organizational resources in invention, production, marketing, etc. can absorb, and (*b*) the investment necessary to improve its relative ranking in the industry. Then, clearly, Nissan, with its 40,000 employees, could well be investing more than 36 per cent (114/320) of the sum invested by Toyota with its 70,000.

Why is it not planning to do so? How far are financial constraints the determining factor rather than, say, managerial risk-aversion, lack of confidence, the sales prospects justified by its established market position, or whatever? As a result of the banking crisis, loan interest rate spreads were increasing in the summer of 1998. In the bond market there was a 1.5 per cent differential between the yield on five-year bonds of triple-A firms and that of triple-B firms (Toyota and Nissan, respectively, as rated by the Japanese R&I—rating and investment—agency). Suppose that Nissan were to invest on the same scale —i.e. the same sum per employee—as Toyota and to issue bonds (it would be an extra ¥68bn worth) to do so. The extra cost of that 1.5 per cent differential means that it would have to pay a billion yen more for the loan in interest than Toyota would if it were to make a similar issue. That billion represents about 0.03 per cent of 1997's annual sales, and one-tenth of the sum Nissan gains or loses from a 1 per cent shift in the yen–dollar exchange rate. In fact, according to the *Financial Times*, Nissan received a direct loan (so-called indirect financing!) of ¥85bn, at an undisclosed interest rate, from the Japan Development Bank.

Moreover, the extra one billion would be an extra four billion if it were an American competitor issuing triple-B bonds in the United States. The 1.5 per cent spread in Japan is dwarfed by the 4 per cent difference between Japanese and American bond yields (triple A/1.4 per cent versus triple B/3.0 per cent in Japan, 28 August 1998; and triple A/5.4 per cent versus triple B/6.3 per cent in the United States, 4 September). Different inflation rates and inflation expectations, combined with fluctuating exchange rates which are sent this way and that by considerations quite other than inflation rates, plus national differences in the relative attractions of holding bonds, equities, and cash, all add up to flagrant disproof of the proposition that free movement of capital will equalize interest rates throughout the world. Those factors still seemed to be alive and well six months after Japan's

Big Bang, and they still seemed to offer promise that Japan's assiduous savers would ensure that Japanese firms would have a capital cost advantage over their foreign competitors, even if they did not care very much about the creation of value specifically for shareholders.

The salience of the 'satisfy global investors or die' argument is enhanced by the large and increasing role played in the Japanese stock market by foreign, chiefly American, investment funds. By mid-1999 they owned some 14 per cent of the Tokyo Stock Market and were regularly responsible for nearly half the daily trades. One of the ironies, if not absurdities, of the international economy is that as Japanese savings seek fixed-interest securities in the American Treasury bonds which help to maintain American consumption, American savings increasingly take over the equity of loss-making Japanese companies. Some of the American funds, already in Japan as in the United States with holdings too big to exit without loss, and therefore activist exercisers of 'voice', have been very articulate in propagating American notions of the duties of firms towards their shareholders. A notable example is the California Public Employees Retirement Scheme, which in its earlier aggressively confrontational phase sent regular memoranda to the managements of the major Japanese corporations in which it has holdings. It still has close connections with one of the bodies which has issued a set of recommendations on corporate governance—the Corporate Governance Forum.

One consequence of (a) widespread understanding of American investors' preferences and (b) the strength of their hand in the market is that share prices tend to improve for firms which make the right noises. Toshiba, for instance, has a CEO who has declared himself in favour of selling off underperforming subsidiaries and getting rid of cross-shareholdings (see below). Its shares outperformed the average for its industry by a large margin in the autumn of 1998, in spite of not having significantly better 'fundamentals'.[19]

As long as takeovers are ruled out and nobody is thinking of issuing new equity, share prices hardly matter in real terms, but they still affect company presidents' egos. The president of Tokyo Electric (which has not issued new equity for 18 years and whose profits are largely determined by the tariff regulators) recently told his senior managers that the share price was the best consolidated index of how the company was doing, and they should watch its movement as assiduously as they watch their load curves.[20]

Proposals for increasing shareholder leverage

The two requirements for making out in global, 'megacompetition' capital markets, according to the reformers, are, first, transparency, and, second, higher profit levels. The major obstacle to achieving these virtues which the reports identify is the cross-shareholding system.

The cross-shareholding system has never had an altogether good press in Japan. It arouses all those suspicions about the evils of concentration of power which have lain behind anti-trust movements since the end of the last century. It is equally a deviation from sound sense to the theorists of corporate governance, for whom shareholder power is an essential discipline without which managers will never be honest and diligent—whether that power be exercised by 'voice' in shareholders' meetings or by non-executive directors on the Board, or else by exit or the threat of exit, especially mass exit in response to takeover bids in the market for corporate control (what might better be called 'mass transit', i.e. transference of support from an existing to a new management). Cross-shareholders do not discipline each other; 'don't scratch my face and I won't scratch yours' becomes the prevailing principle. And a major purpose of the whole system is to thwart takeovers. In both ways, the reformers' argument runs, the interests of the minority shareholder, of the small punter who buys shares in a supposedly public company, are bound to suffer. The whole system, therefore, militates against the public interest in investor protection. And this, in turn, by scaring off potential investors, makes for an impoverished stock exchange. And that means that the economy as a whole suffers from the inefficiency of capital markets.

The authors of the most authoritative annual survey of the state of cross-holdings (the Nippon Life Insurance Institute) leave no doubt where their sentiments and their inspiration lie:

> Recently there has been a great deal of discussion of cross-holdings in the context of the corporate governance debate, and it is surely obvious that unless management stability can be shown to have some relation to shareholder value by improving performance or raising the share price, it is impossible to explain to shareholders the rationale for cross-holdings. CalPERS, the American public pension fund, in its *Principles of Corporate Governance for Japan*, published this spring, speaks of the long-term desirability of eliminating such holdings.[21]

In any case, it is argued by optimistic reformers, the cross-shareholding system is slowly dissolving by a natural and wholly beneficial process. Firms no longer rely much on banks for their finance and are happy to realize a bit of cash by selling off their shares. Moreover, with the depressed state of the stock market, the banks themselves no longer derive much benefit from the Bank of International Settlement's special dispensation which allows them to value 40 per cent of their equity holdings at current market price rather than acquisition price for calculation of the capital adequacy rule that own capital should equal at least 8 per cent of loan liabilities. They would rather be shot of these low-yielding, low-value equities and hold their capital in a more profitable form.

The reformers recognize a difficulty, however, which has to do not at all with matters of long-term structure, but with the present cyclical impasse.

The Nikkei index may be close to a third of its 1990 peak, but Japanese stocks at the end of 1998 were still overvalued by any rate-of-return standard. Dividend yields hovered below the 1 per cent level, and because of low profitability price–earnings ratios were still higher than in America, for all the American bubble and the mythical p/e ratios achieved by Microsoft and its ilk. Equilibrium would be attained, in the sense that stock market prices could be justified by dividend returns plus reasonable growth prospects, if the recession ended with the index standing at 9,000–10,000 rather than the 17,500–18,000 mark around which it was hovering at the end of 1999. Nevertheless, the consequences for firms' balance sheets of tearing up so much paper wealth are such that the whole business, political, and bureaucratic community conspires to keep stock prices up. The government has used some of its huge social security fund reserves in PKOs (price- rather than peace-keeping operations). Foreign investors, the pension and mutual funds mentioned earlier, are treated with disproportionate respect, because they have been net buyers at a time when the Japanese public has by and large turned its back on the stock market. (They buy partly from the prospect of exchange rate gains, partly to get a balanced weighting in all the world's major markets.)

There are two compelling reasons for this policy of bolstering stock market prices. First, a serious fall would hit the balance sheets of all those companies which hold substantial equity, most notably the banks (some of which would consequently fail to meet the 8 per cent capital adequacy rule). Secondly, Japan's economic managers, with their big spending packages, are hoping not just to create real demand, but also to boost spending, credit, and investment, by boosting confidence in any way possible (though the lacklustre way they present their spending packages almost seems calculated to destroy any benign announcement effects they might have). They cannot therefore ignore the fact that watching the Nikkei index has become a national pastime, and its vagaries one important ingredient determining the state of consumers' and investors' confidence, their willingness to spend and to invest.

The discussion of cross-shareholdings in 1998 and early 1999 was dominated, therefore, less by the intrinsic (de)merits of the system than by the fear that the unloading of cross-holdings on the market might have a disastrous effect on market prices. One solution proposed was to set up a government fund to buy up cross-held shares, but this was in the end abandoned in favour of a plan to give tax incentives for companies to transfer such shares to their corporate pension funds, which, with low interest rates, are increasingly underfunded. This is one of three plans actively promoted by the Keidanren business federation.[22] It was notable that the initiative in all these matters came not from the bureaucracy but from the Liberal Democratic Party itself, where the interest in share prices is intense. (Ramping up prices of particular stocks for the benefit of favoured MPs has long been thought to be a condition of survival for securities companies. One MP whose bullying of the securities companies went seriously wrong committed suicide in the spring of 1998.)

To be sure, the cross-shareholding system has its defenders: some would say that it promotes cooperation between firms and joint-ventures; that it reduces the transaction costs of information asymmetry and encourages long-term, stable relational contracting; that it reduces the overwhelming importance of return on equity as a management objective; and above all, that it releases the energies of managers for long-term planning and the thoughtful collection of information the better to improve business decisions. Above all, cross-shareholdings are the main bulwark against the hostile takeover; and whether those who want to dissolve them actually want to facilitate such takeovers is unclear. If they really mean to get shareholders taken seriously, that ought to be their objective, since manifestly, in Anglo-Saxon societies, managers' preoccupation with pleasing shareholders and keeping up share prices depends a great deal on the fact that a falling share price intensifies the danger of a takeover threat.

But here, it seems, the reformers' courage fails them; takeovers do not get a mention in the reports. There is silence on takeovers, as there is on the other key institution of Anglo-Saxon capitalism most obviously responsible for the creation of the 'winner-take-all' society —an active labour market for executive talent.[23]

By the autumn of 1999, it seemed also that the reformers' enthusiasm, as well as their courage, was beginning to fail them. The 1999 survey of the Nippon Life Insurance Research Institute, whose ebullient 1998 introductory paragraph was quoted above, is notably more restrained. It notes that 'it is unclear whether recent trends actually mean an unwinding of the system' and goes on to report that less than 5 per cent of the two-and-a-half thousand companies it surveyed had no discernible cross-shareholdings at all.

Legislative changes

So much for the reformers' agenda and the reasons behind it. How far have there been legal changes to promote their cause? Clearly, no substantial changes are required for a shift towards the shareholder-favouring firm. The Japanese Commercial Code is little different from that of Britain and the United States in the dominant powers it gives to shareholders, though the practice has so diverged from the legal prescriptions that, significantly, the only amending legislation on the table at the end of 1999—a bill drafted by the Liberal Democratic Party[24]—began originally with a resounding declaration. Two formulations were offered:

Basic principle 1.

Shareholder sovereignty:
The company belongs to the shareholders; sovereignty in the firm is theirs. OR

The maximization of shareholder profit:
The firm must be governed in such a way as to maximize the interests of the shareholders.

In the third draft, of June 1998, however, this had been replaced by a long and very explicit statement of 'the purposes of the proposed bill':

> For the past ten years the dominant mood on the Japanese stock market has been one of dark confusion. At bottom this is the result of what might be called the chronic complaint of Japanese corporations—their long-standing tendency to treat their shareholders lightly, as is manifest in low dividend propensities, the concentration of ownership in cross-shareholdings, the overissue of shares, and favouritism of certain shareholders. [Efforts at legal reform have been made—shareholder suits, stock options, etc.] but in spite of these efforts, there are no signs that the disregard for shareholders is on the way to improvement. At the same time there have been moves to unwind cross-holdings, and the danger is that the stock market will become a place of anarchy. This is therefore an appropriate moment to reaffirm the importance of taking shareholders seriously, and to introduce global standards of corporate governance, taking as model the United States, in which so much has been done to strengthen the functions of outside directors.

Class action suits over mismanagement

The first major change of company law was the outcome of the Structural Impediments Initiative already mentioned—an amendment to reduce the risks and the costs to a shareholder of bringing a civil suit for mismanagement against company directors. This had a two-edged effect. It struck fear into the hearts of some corporate executives. By 1996 half of Japan's quoted companies had taken out insurance to protect their directors against loss from shareholders' suits.[25] Japan's lawyer/population ratio may be 1 to 8,000-plus rather than the American 1 to every 330 or so, and total tort costs may be a tiny fraction of the American 2.5 per cent of GNP, but there are still some litigious people about, and there were good reasons for expecting, if not capricious judgements, at least the time-wasting and bad-publicity-creating experience of dealing with frivolous suits. There was a more general fear that the spirit of corporate enterprise would be dampened; that already overcautious management styles would be made even more timid. As it turned out, the number of 'cases pending' in the courts increased only modestly, from 74 at the end of 1993, when the law was passed, to 203 four years later.[26] Most of these cases seem still to be of the traditional kind—that is to say, small-time squabbles among the shareholders (often relatives of the owners) of small to medium-sized firms. Although there was some talk in a MITI report of the possibility of single-issue environmentalists, say, mischievously using the system, it appears that no such cases have materialized, and it is not clear that courts would entertain the plaint of someone who claimed that he had been hurt, not in his pocket but in his social conscience.[27] What one does not know is how many cases were settled out of court, or how many of those were brought by blackmailing *sokaiya*. The lawyers who wrote the only book on the subject—that just quoted—are content to point out that if such out-of-court payments were made to induce withdrawal of a suit, it would constitute the offence of favouring a particular shareholder.

Stock options

The next significant change concerned the use of stock options as a form of payment and was quietly slipped into legislation in the summer of 1997. It was not a government measure—that is to say, it was not initiated in the bureaucracy like most legislation in Japan—but a Diet member's bill, worked out in a committee of the Liberal Democratic Party under the chairmanship of Ota Seiichi (who, at the time of writing, had become Director of the General Affairs Agency).

The Labour Standards Law had originally ruled out payment by stock options, but a relaxation had been passed into law in 1988, as part of a package of measures designed to promote the formation of entrepreneurial firms funded by venture capital. The 1997 law made the practice legal for all firms.

The measure did not get a great deal of publicity. A trawl through the main business newspaper for that year revealed, in the reports about the law and about this or that firm adopting it, no hint that the specific intent of the law was to give directors reasons for identifying their interests with those of shareholders, though this was clear in the minds of the law's drafters.

It is not so apparent that it was clear in the minds of businessmen, however. The Toyota annual general meeting passed a resolution adopting the payment of stock options to directors within a few weeks of the law's enactment. I asked a senior Toyota official why.

—— The idea is to give an incentive to the directors.

Dore: Was there some thought that they needed the extra incentive, that they were getting slack, say?
—— God heavens no. It was also—well, our chairman as you know is also the chairman of Keidanren—to do our bit to help the new system to take root in Japan.

A new twist on the 'social responsibility' theme, perhaps: all Japanese bear a responsibility to do their bit to deflect endemic American criticism. It is not only Americans who speak about Japan having 'promised' to reform its system and abide by 'global' practices. It was reported that at the Davos World Forum in 1997, Mr Toyoda, the chairman in question, made a speech in which he set out some of the measures being taken in Japan to bring about the 'shareholder sovereignty firm'. Used to being congratulated by Americans, he was astonished to find Europeans in his audience asking why, since Japan was blessed with Rhine-model corporations, it should be seeking to throw away its advantage.

Of the 3,000 quoted firms, 150 had introduced stock option schemes within the first year, according to a Daiwa Securities survey, and the Ministry of Finance announced a tax concession; tax is incurred not when the option is exercised but only when the shares are subsequently sold.[28] Schemes are not always confined to Board members. Sony, once again a pioneer in the 'Westernizing' of formal structures, and a company with half its stock in the hands of non-Japanese, has announced a scheme for giving stock options to 200 of its senior executives.

Share buy-backs

The same statute that introduced stock options also amended the law to facilitate share buy-backs. This appears to have been prompted not just by the popularity of this practice in the United States, but also partly as a method of acquiring the stock needed for directors who take up options, and probably more importantly to counter the tendency of the stock market to depress everybody's spirits by falling continuously. The legislation was aimed at one feature of Japanese company law which clearly modified the rights of shareholders, but primarily in the interests of creditors rather than employees. In principle, payments to shareholders, whether of dividends or by the repurchase of shares, can only be from profits or accumulated retained earnings. Payment out of paid-up capital requires a complex process of approval not only by shareholders but by major creditors (deemed to have a right to prevent any attempts by shareholders to get their money out first when bankruptcy looms). The 1997 legislation made this process easier, but confined the concession to the 'stated capital' not to the 'capital reserve'. (All money paid into the company for share issues has to be divided in two: at least half into stated capital, and the rest into a capital reserve fund. Companies have chosen close to a 50:50 division: for large companies capitalized at over a billion yen, the totals at the end of 1996 were ¥47tr for stated capital and ¥43tr for reserves—accumulated retained earnings stood at ¥75tr.)

Vanguard reformers in 1998 were proposing to make not only the stated capital, but also the capital reserve available for the purpose of share buy-backs, thereby substantially increasing the resources available. One advocate of such a move acknowledges that the reduction in net worth and worsening of debt–equity ratios could affect credit ratings and threaten the integrity of loan contracts already entered into, but suggests that this could be dealt with by restrictions on the volume of buy-back transactions in any one year.[29] His advocacy of the practice rests on a good neoclassical marketist argument: much better that spare cash be returned to the market, which can be relied on to allocate it efficiently to its most profitable uses, than that it be used by the firm for dubious, un-market-tested, investments.

As for current use of these provisions, the Nomura Research Institute found that 40 out of 100 firms surveyed had already bought back shares, and about a third were preparing changes in their incorporating charter to permit it. The explanation, however, seems to lie not in preparations for unwinding cross-shareholdings, nor in any enthusiasm for enriching shareholders, much less any principled 'public interest' belief that capital returned to the market will be allocated more efficiently than they can allocate it themselves. It lies, rather, in the currently fashionable ROE talk which is sweeping the Japanese management world. 'The number of firms which give raising profits in order to boost the return of capital as the major financial criterion they use has increased (since 1995) from 42 to 70 per cent, and 60 per cent of firms have set themselves ROE objectives.'[30] Reducing the denominator, by cutting back shareholders' funds, offers firms a seemingly quick way of moving from their present single-digit ROE figure to the 21 per cent they are always being told the average American firm achieves.

Holding companies

The ban on holding companies in the 1950 Commercial Code was originally intended as a measure to stop the re-creation of the *zaibatsu* conglomerates. It was a combined product of deep-rooted American anti-trust sentiment and the belief that the *zaibatsu* shared responsibility for aggression and should be eliminated once and for all. The lobby for its relaxation has grown over the years, but in a desultory sort of way, since the major firms—Hitachi, for instance, with its 300-odd subsidiaries making its consolidated balance sheet 125 per cent bigger than that of the main company—do a lot of 'holding' already. There may be financial advantages in having the central control exercised by a legally separate company which produces nothing except decisions and financial allocations, but the main advantage envisaged seems to be the greater fragmentation of wage bargaining and consequently greater differentiation of wage levels depending on the profitability of different divisions. A good many firms achieve this already, their union taking the form of a federation which coordinates the bargaining of constituent units but leaves them with ultimate autonomy.

The relevance of this change to the 'rise of the shareholder' movement lies indirectly in its institutionalization, as it were, of the dominance of the finance function over the engineering, marketing, research, etc. divisions, and the greater consequent weighting of 'rate-of-return' calculations over other considerations in strategic planning. It could thus accelerate a creeping evolution which is already a couple of decades old.

Reform of audit committees

The most recent proposal for a change in the Commercial Code—the draft bill with the declamatory preamble quoted earlier—is ostensibly aimed at the 'insiderism' problem. There is no intention of making appointment of external directors compulsory; firms can do so or not as they wish. The current proposals concern, instead, the role of the *Kansayaku* or Auditors. The current law refers to them only as individuals, but they in effect act as a committee. They are a relic of the original 1890 Commercial Code and its 1899 revision, which adopted the German notion of a Supervisory Board. (*Kansayakkai* is the standard translation for the modern German *Aufsichtsrat*.) They survived the American-inspired revision of the code in 1950, but with much reduced powers—largely confined to certifying the accuracy of the external audit of the accounts.

They began an intended come-back in two revisions of the law, in 1974 and 1982, prompted by a number of scandals and the growing perception that it was not enough for the law to lay on the Board of Directors the duty of mutual supervision and self-regulation. The point of these earlier revisions was, on the one hand, to strengthen the powers of the shareholders' annual meeting (and at the same time try to deal with the *sōkaiya* gangster problem) and, on the other, to give the Audit Committee the duty of overseeing the general conduct of business as well as the auditing of accounts. Auditors attend, as non-voting members, all meetings of the Board and are required to give their own report to the shareholders' meeting. In many companies the chairman of the Audit Committee is someone (often a retired bank president) from outside. In the firms of the 700 respondents to the Doyūkai questionnaire quoted earlier, the average size of the committee was 3.5 persons, of whom 1.8 were from outside the firm. They had their own staff of 2.1 persons, less than a secretary each.

There clearly is not much 'tension' in the relation between the Audit Committee and the Board of Directors. Audit Committee members are listed in reports as officers of the company in the same way as other Board members, and they are popularly referred to by the same term, *juyaku* (though the general image of the *kansayaku* is of someone who is just about of Board stature but not in the running for the top jobs). Their ineffectiveness seems apparent from the answers to the same Doyūkai survey. 'Who provides the necessary checks and balance [on the propriety and good faith of decisions taken] on the following issues?' asked one question, and listed 14 issues ranging from the dismissal of a president to dividend levels and investment decisions. Respondents were offered 17 possible 'exercisers of control checks' ranging from presidents and vice-presidents to government, the main bank, major shareholders, and the Audit Committee. The last was chosen as an effective agent by less than 1 per cent of respondents on all the personnel questions such as dismissal of the president, and by a maximum 5 per cent only for 'Adoption of the financial strategy'. When a second question asked 'not who does but who ought to check', the Audit Committee got rather more votes, but still only to a maximum of 11 per cent on financial strategy; 4 per cent for a president's dismissal (p. 159).

Clearly the current plan to strengthen the Audit Committee's powers, without much changing structures, is not going to make a serious difference to the way firms are run. This is particularly true given that a major intention of the amending legislation appears to be to defend the Board from 'frivolous' malpractice suits by giving the Audit Committee powers to examine such suits, and requiring them either to accept them and join the plaintiffs against their directors, or to reject the justice of the suit and join the accused directors as defendants. Alternatively they can mediate. (The steely-eyed, knife-in-the-back-pocket *sōkaiya* consider themselves rather good at dealing with mediators.)

Changes in labour law

The other area of legislation with some impact on the 'for whom is the firm run?' issue is labour law. The lifetime employment system in itself is not in contention, since it is a matter of convention not of law. There is a good deal of case law which indirectly supports that convention—findings, for example, that dismissal of redundant employees without strenuous efforts to find alternative ways of using their services (new products, etc.) amounts to unfair dismissal and merits substantial compensation. But there have been no moves to override such precedents with a statute reinforcing the employers' right to hire and fire.

The culmination of much guarded talk about the need to 'modernize' labour law was a revision of the Labour Standards Law in 1998, which did little more than nibble at the edges of the worker-protection measures enacted with the blessing of New Dealers in the American occupation army in the later 1940s—probably in sum less than the previous amendment of 1987, which introduced flexitime and reduced to 40 hours (from 48) the standard working week beyond which overtime pay is required. The scope of short-term contract hiring (which does not give rise to the implicit lifetime commitment enjoyed by 'regular employees') has been increased to a wider range of professional and semi-professional workers (and all workers over 60), and the contractual period extended from one to three years. There has also been some relaxation of the regulations governing 'agency despatch'; but here again the amendment only enlarges slightly the list of the occupations (home help, secretaries, software writers, etc.) who may be sent on daily or weekly hire by an employment agency, rather than switching, as the reformers advocated, to blanket permission plus a negative list of a few occupations where the system might be open to abuse. There has also been an enactment of a new form of labour contract for 'discretion-exercising work' for a restricted list of occupations such as research, information systems development, design, and production and programme research in the mass media, but not business strategy planning, sales, finance, and public relations as the Nikkeiren Employers' Federation had advocated. Essentially, the employer does not specify the hours to be worked but the nature of the job to be done, how and when to do it being left to the worker's discretion. This has the advantage of greater freedom for the worker, but also obviates the need for overtime pay by the company.

The debates on these measures in the various Deliberation Councils and Diet committees, although arousing little passion and little comment outside the specialist press, were protracted (six years from the Ministry's appointing a revision working group to final enactment). And even after an initial draft reached the Diet, several final amendments were made to get an all-party agreement which included the Socialist Party, now more than ever a party of ex-trade unionists, and the Democratic Party, to which the main trade union centre has transferred its allegiance and vote bank.[31]

Labour law is, in fact, one area in which the trade unions still have a voice to be heard. And, in striking contrast to, say, British legislation of the 1980s quite deliberately designed to reduce union power, a number of provisions in the new amendment serve, instead, to reinforce the notion of the firm as a consensual community. Where 'discretion-exercising work' is introduced, for example, there must be created a supervisory committee, half of whose members are appointed by the union, or, if there is no union, by agreement with a representative employee. In the latter case, both that employee's representativeness and employees' approval of his choice of committee members are to be tested in a formal supervised ballot. This is a statutory reinforcement—like similar provisions in earlier 'declining industry' legislation for the closing of establishments—for well-established legal precedents which make consultation with the union a criterion for judging unfair dismissal cases. The new amendment also strengthens the employee's position in unfair dismissal cases by requiring employers to issue a written statement of the reason for dismissal whenever the employee requests it.

Changing pressures: changing practices

We have looked at length at the advocacy shifts—the movement of opinion and how this has been reflected in legislation. What effect has all this—and the dramatic shifts in the market environment—had on what firms do in practice?

Changing management structures

Some of the bolder firms, well known for their adoption of 'non-Japanese' practices, have sought to give their Boards a real decision-making role and cut down their size. Sony has a Board of 15. The president of Orix makes a point of his boldness in reducing his Board to 21. Others have sought to change Board practices. A newly appointed, energetic president of Toray decreed on taking office some years ago that rubber-stamping should stop. Henceforth, directors bringing to the Board proposals from the divisions with which they were concerned should refrain from the usual *nemawashi* practice of getting the agreement of other departments which would be affected. The first round of discussion should be open, frank, and unrehearsed. Only after that should refinement of the proposal—negotiation, compromise, horse-trading—begin. He retired earlier from the job than had been generally expected.

The employment relation

For some years, a favourite story of the Western financial press, reporting with barely concealed delight evidence that the Japanese system was coming apart at the seams, has been of wholesale dismissals of staff, particularly managerial staff, and the development in self-defence of a Managerial Staff Union—a real transenterprise union on Western lines.[32]

True, there is such a union with about a couple of hundred members, mostly contract workers for small firms. True, there have been cases where plans for 'voluntary' early retirement have been announced with such unmistakable 'taps on the shoulder' as to cause open rebellion, or where the mere announcement of such plans has been handled without consultation with the union, or in such a maladroit way that open conflict has led the aggrieved parties to call the newspapers. But, although all the talk in mid-1999 was of a recession worse than any since the war, and although bankruptcy and the fall in vacancies had brought the unemployment rate to its highest point for decades (over 4.5 per cent), the conventions of the lifetime employment guarantee seemed pretty much intact. The Ministry of Labour has been running an 'Employment Adjustment Survey' since the 1970s. The proportion of manufacturing establishments which were undertaking so-called labour adjustment measures in the third quarter of 1998 was 38 per cent, compared with 71 per cent at the peak of the oil-shock adjustment crisis of 1975. In most cases, these measures were restriction of overtime and redeployment of workers (redeployment, in 8 per cent of establishments, to other firms—several years ago New Japan Steel had 15,000 workers 'leased out' to other firms at a lower rental than the wage the company continued to pay them). Only 3 per cent of firms—compared with 5 per cent of firms in 1975—were planning dismissals or voluntary early retirement schemes. The pattern was much the same—the actual figures slightly lower—in the wholesale and retail commerce, and eating establishments sector.[33]

The figures for job turnover tell much the same story. The proportion of separations which were not regular retirements, deaths, or voluntary quits was running at around 13 per cent in 1993–7 (about 8 per cent 'at the employer's convenience', which includes bankruptcy and early retirement, and 5 per cent 'dismissal for cause'). This compares with the lowest figure of 8 per cent in 1991, at the height of the boom period (4.5 per cent employer's convenience and 3.3 per cent for cause). It is still lower than the 15 per cent registered in the post-oil-shock recession of 1975 (10.5 per cent for employer's convenience, 4 per cent for cause). The spread of these figures between firms of different size-groups is not great for 'employer's convenience'—7.0 per cent for firms with over 1,000 workers, 8.6 per cent for the 30–99 size-group. It is larger for 'dismissal with cause'—1.5 and 6.4 per cent, respectively (1995 figures). In 1975 the difference between size-groups was more marked—smaller firms dismissed more for convenience. This is another indication of convergence, of the way in which the employment patterns which are standard in the large unionized firm sector have formed expectations and consequently affected practice in smaller firms without unions.

And as for the strength of the normative sense of a 'right' to job security, the *Nihon Keizai* newspaper recently carried a telling item. It had come to light that after one of the first bank failures—that of Hanna Bank in 1996—the union, threatening to go on strike and to refuse to do the work of cleaning up the residual mess (mainly assessing the claims of depositors to money from the remaining assets and the deposit insurance fund), had negotiated with management a considerable enhancement to the established contractual retirement gratuities —amounting to some ¥11mn (about $80,000) per person. This considerable sum became an additional charge on the Deposit Insurance Fund. Under the mediation of the Receiver Court, the Ministry of Finance and the Bank of Japan had given their approval. The tone of the article suggests that the reporter thought the affair scandalous, but it apparently did not seem so to the officials concerned.

The legislative changes mentioned earlier marginally facilitated the use of non-standard employment contracts. Their actual use, however, seems limited. Of the total employee population in 1990, 10.6 per cent were classified as something other than 'regular employees'— temporary or daily workers: the former predominantly housewives who worked part time, the latter chiefly students working irregularly and part time—doing *arubaito* as it has been know since the 1920s, when German was the favourite foreign language. In 1996 the proportion had risen by half a percentage point, to 11.0 per cent.

There is much advocacy, in the context of these non-standard forms of employment, of a brave new world of labour 'flexibility'—the pattern being the active external labour markets of the Anglo-Saxon model, in which independent self-reliant workers, masters of their certified skills, are in a position to make their choice of the firms in which they will, from time to time, make their careers. Seeking ever to be in the vanguard of change, over the last five years the Vocational Training Division of the Ministry of Labour has shifted its attention from the old skill tests with which it used (with considerable success) to encourage the development of manual skills, to a new Business Career Scheme with the emphasis on professional-level and sub-professional-level qualifications. There has certainly been a great proliferation of courses—mostly correspondence courses—for the national certificates in tax accountancy, labour law and personnel administration, small-firm management consultancy, etc. It seems that the main clients of these courses are (a) university students doing *daburu-sukuuru* (taking a certificate course parallel to their degree, mostly with the idea of enhancing their chance of getting a good lifetime job) and (b) middle managers, not destined for the commanding heights of their firm, who foresee that they might be 'tapped on the shoulder'—or might, though untapped, find it a good ploy to take advantage of a voluntary retirement scheme to find a small-firm niche with a later retirement age. A preference for 'the self-reliant confidence of the independent worker' ideal, as opposed to the 'security in slavery' of Corporation Man, may be responsible for only part of the increase in these enrolments in certificate courses.

The other area of change, much discussed in the personnel management literature, is that sometimes summed up in English as basing pay and promotion on 'performance, not seniority'. In fact, however, the Japanese words *noryokushugi* and *nenko-joretsu* mean, respectively, something more like 'rewarding ability' rather than performance, and 'seniority and achievement', not just seniority. Perhaps the most common version of the traditional system worked as follows. For the first x years (often as many as ten) wages did rise uniformly by seniority—both for blue-collar workers and for university graduates. Thereafter there was increasing differentiation, faster and greater in some firms than in others. This might be brought about by tying a large percentage of the wage to rank or job function. Hence, it was the speed of promotion that counted most. But promotion speeds were conventionally highly constrained by seniority—the universal device of bureaucracies to give career incentives but at the same time minimize unrealizable expectations and interpersonal friction. It might be established convention, say, that it was only after 13 years' service that the *issenbatsu* —the 'premier cru' of any year's entry group—got to be section chief, which might be two or three years ahead of the average for that entry group, though most would get there in the end.

How far has this changed? Very little, it would seem, in most firms, except perhaps for reducing the x years of initial purely seniority increments from ten to five. But as for changing the promotion system, the 'brave new world' literature is full of stories of firms which have thrown away all seniority rules and promoted solely according to ability. The effect does not appear in the statistics, however. The wage census has for many years given the age breakdown of managers of different ranks. In 1980, in firms with more than 1,000 employees, 13 per cent of male division chiefs were in the youngest, 40–44, age group. By 1995, the figure was only 4 per cent. In smaller firms with 100 to 499 employees, the figure had gone from 19 to 10 per cent.

In other firms, differentiation was effected by allocating part of the wage bill to merit pay or performance pay, which allowed for variation around the median depending on a merit assessment by line superiors in consultation with the personnel office. A great deal has been made of a widespread shift, for managerial workers, to an annual salary system, replacing the traditional monthly wage plus midsummer and year-end bonuses. This is one of the changes hailed as bringing Japan closer to a genuinely modern personnel system on American lines. American consulting firms such as Hays have prospered mightily from contracts with firms determined to be in the advance guard. As for its modernity, ostensibly the system does involve annual negotiations over individual contracts, though the independent bargaining position of managers in a lifetime employment system is hardly strong; exit options are limited unless they have worked abroad, have a good foreign language, and have contacts with American firms in Japan— of which there are a growing number.

What no individual firm can do, however, is to create an external market which would give some real meaning to the notion of a 'going rate' for individual skills, or put a manager's worth to a market test. Whether the traditional monthly wage or the new annual salary, the criterion for an appropriate wage can be based only on internal performance evaluation or job-evaluation schemes involving a large element of subjectivity. It is therefore not surprising that, for all the changes in form, the actual dispersion of wages and salaries seems to have changed relatively little. It is not surprising because the basic factors which determine it have not changed. They are, first, the relative ability-homogeneity of intakes: top firms take from top universities and from among high-scorers in high school. The individual variations in performance, therefore, are mostly in energy, initiative, strength of character, leadership powers, degree of dedication to work, rather than in the intellectual ability to handle problems (although this is increasingly important with the growing complexity of production systems). The other factor is the sense of fairness: prevalent ideas about the relative deservingness of effort and natural endowments, and about the degree of inequality deemed compatible with community-like comradeship. A wide-ranging survey of employees' opinions found, indeed, a broad measure of support for the merit principle, the idea that performance should be rewarded.[34] Over 4,000 respondents were then asked, 'All right, how much? How much more should the "top group" of high-flyers get, and how much less the "bottom group"?' At the same time the personnel managers of some 500 firms from which the employee sample was drawn were asked about current ability/performance differentials. There was a remarkable convergence between the gap deemed fair and desirable and the gap in current practice at age 50: the top should be and was 27 or 28 per cent above average, and the bottom 19 or 20 per cent below. The younger the respondent the wider, by a very slight margin, the gap thought desirable (30/21 according to the average 30-year-old rather than the 50-year-olds' 28/19). In actual practice, however, the spread is much narrower at the lower ages—+13/−11 at age 30.

So why all the fuss about revolutions in pay systems? Partly it is just another manifestation of the whole pattern of inflated rhetoric about revolutionary change, but there is also another factor at work. Thirty years ago Hitachi was introducing 'job-related pay' for manual workers as a great innovation—and one which would bring Hitachi closer to American/Western modernity. It was in practice having very little effect on the correlation of pay with seniority, while adding to the complexity of an already complex wage system. I noted at the time that one reason was the premium on initiative and innovation in Japanese firms.[35] The personnel division had to prove itself *vis-à-vis* the other divisions by doing something new, some innovation which could be hailed as the best thing since rice cookers. Within the division, the young graduate workers had to prove themselves by being the original proposers of a scheme which could fit the 'something new' bill. Doubtless, much the same factors are at work today.

But to say that there is no revolution in pay systems is not to say that the creeping changes which are occurring are insignificant. As the survey just quoted showed, the sense of fairness of the younger generations seems to have fewer egalitarian ingredients than that of their elders; they are more ready to accept interpersonal competition for differential rewards. And one factor in the situation which is of increasing significance is the growing number of foreign (mainly American) firms with rate-for-the-job pay and ability-not-seniority promotion systems—or some hybrid mixture of Japanese and American patterns. A prominent reformer-economist writes that his best students are increasingly looking to foreign firms for their careers. Genuinely meteoric careers are, however, hardly available outside a relatively small financial sector, and the favoured candidates are predominantly young Japanese who have had enough education abroad to be quasi-native speakers of a foreign language. Long-established foreign firms—IBM, Macdonalds, etc.—tend to follow Japanese practices in all essentials. At Mazda, since control shifted to Ford, there have been a good many changes in management practice, but in personnel management they seem to have been not much less marginal than elsewhere. That someone has been appointed to the Board not at the usual age of 52–53 but at 47 is instanced as a great innovation.

Enterprise unions

It is remarkable how infrequently, in discussions of corporate governance, the role of trade unions in the enterprise is mentioned. Asserting 'managerial prerogatives', the right to manage without interference from hostile, uncooperative unions (so much a preoccupation of the Thatcher counter-revolution and, if by a smaller minority, seen as the major problem of German industry), does not preoccupy either managers or management theorists in Japan. The 'constitutional settlement' of the 1950s has stuck.

The annual wage-bargaining sessions are framed by the assumption that payments to capital are pretty much fixed, and the argument is primarily about how much seed corn and how much eating corn. When managers persuade the union to take a 2 per cent rather than a 4 per cent increase, they are almost certainly condemning themselves to a 2 per cent rise too.

Equally stable are the Workplace Consultation Committees, generally established by contract with the union with a specified range of items for joint decision, items for consultation, and items on which management provides information on its unilateral decisions—categories which run from long-term product strategies to training, with the decision/consultation/information categorization often getting blurred in practice.

As the strike becomes seen as more and more 'unusual behaviour' for which a union leader would find it difficult to work up enthusiasm, and with generational change in union leadership, the extent to which these consultation mechanisms actually constrain managerial decision-making probably becomes increasingly limited. But in a consensual society, where the managerial culture is such that managers attach considerable importance to employees' commitment, they are none the less important parts of the system.

How far unions can be effective in defending the system against a shift to the shareholder-favouring firm is a question for later. Here the important thing to stress is that there seems to be (a) only a slight decline in union density in manufacturing, a greater decline in the economy as a whole (35 to 24 per cent 1970–95) largely a function of the shift to a service economy,[36] (b) a stable pattern of both bargaining and consultation mechanisms,[37] and (c) a not inconsiderable spread of elected employee-consultation institutions (some more, some less of the nature of 'white unions') among smaller firms with no formally registered union.[38]

Cross-shareholdings

A question with far-reaching implications is how far firms are dissolving their mutual shareholding arrangements. The most reliable estimate, an annual survey (since 1987) drawn from company reports and share registers,[39] uses two definitions: 'mutual shareholdings' (two firms holding each other's shares) and 'stable shareholdings' (those, plus all other holdings of bank (excluding trust bank) and insurance company shares by other companies and all holdings of other companies by those banks and insurance companies). It finds that cross-holdings, which had accounted for 21 per cent of all shares from 1987 to 1992, had fallen to 16 per cent in March 1999. Stable holdings had also been falling for six years, to stand at 41 per cent.

As to the who and whom, it is difficult to discern a consistent pattern. Non-financial companies had been the major sellers in 1996, but in 1998 it was clearly the troubled banks and life insurance companies which were disposing of shares. Non-financial companies, in fact, had a *higher* proportion of cross-held shares in March 1999 than in 1987.

Not yet any signs of a general sell-off, then, but certainly a declining trend, somewhat accelerated since 1997. The interpretations on offer are as follows:

1. Evolution moves in mysterious ways, but economic logic is slowly bringing Japan to modernity, to a proper form of shareholder-value-driven capitalism. Take the following conversation with the retiring president of a large trading company:

> —— Our cross-holdings are running down and I've been encouraging the tendency.
> Dore: Why?
> —— Well, when I go to your country or to America and meet our foreign investors they all ask me: why do you keep such unprofitable assets on your balance sheet? Look at the miserable returns. Why don't you get rid of them. And I don't know how to answer.
> Dore: But why do you need foreign investors anyway, when Japan is awash with savings?
> —— I think a global company should have global investors.

2. The second interpretation is a more sophisticated form of the above. The trend to securitization is based on the economic logic of firms which need the cheapest capital. There is a secular trend for the ratio of bank debt to equity and other securities to decline, especially for large firms that can issue their own bonds and commercial paper at reasonable rates. Those firms have less need of banks and will be less keen to hold bank shares. Also, for the banks' part, they have become more than ever conscious of the risks involved in owning Japanese shares, given the difficulty they have in meeting the BIS capital adequacy rules every time the market value of the shares they hold drops. The need for better risk management—a lesser concentration of risks—will, Fukao Mitsuhiro argues, force them to disgorge their holdings.[40] At its most convincing his argument involves not only economic logic, but also generational cultures:

> A majority of firms look towards their main bank or a group of core banks for emergency financial help in times of crisis. And they are prepared, in return, to hold 'cooperative deposits', to pay heavy underwriting fees for their bond issues, and to encourage their employees to have accounts in those banks to pay their wages into.

These 'wet' attitudes on the part of the older generation of managers are often based on recollections of incidents when the banks did indeed help them out of a tight corner. But today, firms have much greater freedom to raise money in the market, and if the credit ratings of some of the major firms continue to be better than those of most of the banks, one can expect a much 'drier' evaluation of the relationship with change in the generations.

'Challenge to Japan's Traditional Corporate Culture' and 'Japan Inc. Unravels' were the *Financial Times*'s headlines[41] reporting that Toyota had refused to join 21 other major Mitsui firms in contributing to an injection of fresh capital for the main Mitsui bank, Sakura. Toyota, with 2.6 per cent, is Sakura's fifth biggest shareholder, and 5 per cent of its own shares are owned by Sakura. But its president denied that Toyota had ever had Sakura help them out of a tight corner, and said that even if they had, it was economic rationality that would shape their decisions not sentiment. So Fukao may be right. However, few firms are as cash-rich as Toyota. Even those doing so well out of exports thanks to the weak yen, and with credit ratings that make bond issues profitable, still need banks, even for long-term finance. The trend away from bank loans should not be exaggerated.

The banks for their part seem reluctant to let their partners go, even if at the height of their troubles in 1998 they did reduce their holdings. Insofar as direct market finance threatens to cut them out of straight lending, they have good reason to hold on to their shares, and thereby their claim to handle 'their' companies' bond issues and commercial paper. Similarly, although the life insurance companies have been responsible for a larger share of the decline, they too are anxious to keep the pension fund management business and the special group insurance business which they do with firms, and have good reason not to offend their managers by dumping their shares.

3. The obvious alternative explanation is that the decline is more a cyclical phenomenon than a long-term trend. As the recession deepens, more firms really do need the cash. Some firms are selling equities to fill holes in their pension fund accounts.[42] Moreover, there was, so goes this argument, an unreasonable proliferation of cross-holdings at the time of the bubble, when inflated stock market prices made the issue of equity a favourite form of finance. Cross-holding partners were offered/asked to take a share of new issues. Some of this

excess is being liquidated. Also, some of the sales may represent a restoration of balance. Bank shares have fallen far more than the shares of some of the more prosperous manufacturers. A Bank and B Electronics may have bought equal amounts of each other's shares at a roughly equal price. If A's shares now stand at 200 and B's at 1,000, A could sell some of B's shares and thereby equalize the value of their mutual holding and profit from B's buoyancy.[43]

Again, mutual holdings always were shifting depending on the development of a firm's business. When trading and joint-venture patterns change, shareholdings change too. In a period of expansion, there are more new connections made than old ones broken. In a recession vice versa.

In any case, it is argued, when firms sell off the whole or part of a mutual holding, they would always consult with their partner and give it the chance to arrange for some other firm to take over the share package in order not to depress the market price. There may be a promise to buy back later when times improve. In one very enlightening survey of finance managers' 'opinions and declared intentions',[44] the question was asked: 'When reviewing your cross-holdings, how many and which of the following criteria do you use when deciding whether to keep them or not?' Sixty-four per cent said 'the business we do with the other firm' and 23 per cent gave the related reason 'the effect of amalgamations and restructuring of banks and other financial companies'. Only 10 per cent and 21 per cent, respectively, gave the true 'market' reasons: the dividend returns and the capital value of the shares.

The 100 respondents were also asked for their general views on the cross-holding system. Thirty-nine firms said that it was essential, and 56 that it was not essential but had advantages (*meritto*). Only one firm said that the demerits outweighed the merits.

So far, then, of the alternative explanations, the most convincing is the claim that cyclical factors alone are a good enough explanation of the statistical trends discerned, without recourse to structural trends. And one should not forget the reasons why the stable-shareholder system was built up by cross-shareholdings in the first place—very specifically to defend firms against shareholders who might sell out to marauding raiders. Those raiders were, in the early days, the somewhat peripheral nuisance greenmailers; later, in the 1960s, as Japan was moving towards capital liberalization, when the system was being most completely institutionalized, they were the much-feared powerful Americans. There is a clear realization not only that cross-shareholdings are a collective good which prevents the culture of the takeover society from developing in Japan, but also that for each single firm its stable shareholders represent security from attack—as was demonstrated in the thwarting of T. Boone Pickens' bid for Koito.

The imponderable is the future of the other non-rational-maximizing factor, namely a sense of reciprocal obligation between firms. One measure of the force of this factor is the differences among the major enterprise groups (the *keiretsu*), the presidents of whose member firms still have their monthly lunches and a variety of lower-level liaison, information-exchange, and cooperation arrangements. Three of the four former *zaibatsu* groups—Mitsubishi, Sumitomo, and Mitsui—have almost as high a ratio of cross-holdings as they had in 1992 and higher ratios than in 1987 (about a half being cross-holdings within the group and a half outside). The fourth, the Fuyo group, the Fuji Bank's assemblage of the firms of the old Yasuda *zaibatsu*, has been showing a sharper decline; its ratios in March 1998 were similar to those of the other two *keiretsu*—the two formed around the Daiichi Kangin and the Sanwa banks which did not grow out of a prewar *zaibatsu*. Fuji always did have the reputation of being less solidary than the other three ex-*zaibatsu*, held together more by the main bank's ties with member firms than by ties among member firms themselves—a star pattern rather than a fishing-net network. It also had a higher proportion of second-rank firms (Nissan not Toyota), and some of its most powerful firms seemed semi-detached—like Hitachi, which belonged also to the Daiichi Kangin group. At the end of 1998 a good deal of (credit-destroying, situation-worsening) journalistic attention was given to the problems of the Fuyo group in general and of the Fuji and Yasuda Trust banks in particular, but (perhaps as a result of fire-fighting measures for firms in difficulty—and the recapitalization of Fuji itself) in the following year it was the only one of the groups to show an increase in cross-holdings—by 3 percentage points.

As the difference between the more and the less solidary groups suggests, sentiment, managers' sense of their firm's obligations *qua* organizational actor, does count. Even outside such enterprise groups a long-standing relationship may be broken only with difficulty. A senior finance official of Hitachi said, not about its shareholdings, but about its borrowings (in carefully graded amounts) from some ten banks, 'We could do without most of those loans, but if we try to reduce borrowing from any one bank, they say, "only if you make the same all-round reduction to all your banks", which makes things difficult in terms of varying maturities.' In a really severe crisis Hitachi might let such considerations go by the board, but it is hard to say how severe the crisis would have to be.

But Fukao may be right: his more 'dry' successor 20 years hence may have no such inhibitions.

Risutora

There is no clearer sign of the 'cultural hegemony' exercised by the American business school than the frequency with which the word 'restructuring' occurs in the Japanese business press and the speeches of business leaders. In 1998 and at the beginning of 1999, the major electronics industry firms—Toshiba, Sony, and Hitachi—all announced what sounded like extensive plans for internal reorganization, always accompanied by announcements of substantial cutbacks in their employee headcount—the feature which made the headlines in the foreign business press. 'An aggressive restructuring plan that would see the loss of 17,000 jobs, 10 per cent of its worldwide workforce and the closure of 15 of its 70 factories', the *Financial Times* called the Sony plan, reporting that the good news had caused a 9 per cent jump in Sony's share price.[45] At a time when foreigners were the major net buyers on the Tokyo Stock Exchange, it is a safe bet that they were primarily responsible for the jump in price.

Sony's restructuring is worth looking at closely since it has long been regarded as the leader, and is certainly the biggest, of the handful of Japanese manufacturing firms which have explicitly adopted American business practices—declaring decades ago that it was abolishing the seniority system (though not yet having personnel practices markedly different from its competitors'), having an outside director on the Board (a former official of the American Department of Commerce), adopting stock options for 200 senior managers as soon as the law was changed, and so on. It is clear from some of its leaders' pronouncements that it was the example of General Electric getting 40 per cent of its profits from GE Capital which prompted it to be the first major manufacturing firm to develop its finance subsidiary as a growth business rather than as simply an internal service division. It does a great deal of business in the United States, of course, and the New York Stock Market is as important to it as Tokyo's; already 40 per cent of the firm's shares are owned outside Japan.

So it is not surprising that the first paragraph of the English-language press release announcing the restructuring ran: 'Sony corporation today announced plans to realign and strengthen its Group architecture. The objective of this change is to enhance shareholder value through what it calls "Value Creation Management".' The Japanese version does not mention shareholders, but talks instead about enhancing the 'value of the company'. (In an interview the year before the CEO had said, 'In America they say that the company belongs to the shareholders and creating shareholder value should come before anything else. But that is wrong. The Japanese idea that the company belongs to the employees is also mistaken. Management should be about finding the path that is right for all three elements in its environment—shareholders, employees, and customers.'[46])

As for the drastic surgery, it turns out that the bulk of the cuts will be overseas and that the run-down of the labour force is a matter of 'reducing the headcount by about 10 per cent by the end of March 2003', well within what natural wastage can take care of, while the emphasis is on retraining and reallocating employees from analog to digital businesses and from hardware to software. One major element of the restructuring is taking private three separately quoted subsidiaries—i.e. incorporating them into Sony proper—a move which does seem to indicate an acute concern with the share price, but which also seems in danger of running counter to one of the dominant doctrines of restructuring, namely that one should not allow profitable divisions to cross-subsidize weak ones.

It is not entirely clear whether its oxymoronic label 'unified dispersion' (which is its press office's preferred translation: 'coordinated polarization' is more what the original sounds like) represents any really new answers to the centralization/decentralization problem that every organization has to wrestle with and for which every management consultant has his or her own branded, but not necessarily different, solution. The statement does, however, talk specifically about making accounting, human resources, and general affairs into separate units within a future holding company which will compete in the outside market; though the only concrete proposal—for a Sony

Human Capital Inc. drawing personnel from its Human Resources department—looks as if it will primarily be marketing training services. Some laboratories are to be transferred from headquarters to divisional control, but it is not clear that the Central Research labs will cease to exist.

As for management structure, in 1997 Sony had already, like a number of other firms, demoted most of the members of its standard Japanese-size Board (i.e. large enough to give a substantial number of managers the incentivizing prospect of being promoted to it) and made them *shikkō-yakuin*—corporate executive officers—a move billed as being to create an American-style small, tight, strategy-controlling Board (which in fact existed already within the old Boards) but which is more cynically reputed to be a move to save the costly insurance premiums covering directors against shareholder class action suits.

What might, however, represent a substantial edging towards the shareholder-sovereignty firm is the announced change in performance measurement. Sony has been sold the EVA formula for calculating the enhancement of shareholder value—economic value-added, which equals post-tax profits minus the cost of capital, with the latter being calculated in bizarre and subjective ways known only to the firm of management consultants (Sterns-Stewart) which has branded the formula. Managers' bonuses are to be based on this calculation, though how the notional attribution of shareholder capital to each business unit will be made remains obscure. There are enough arbitrary elements in the calculation to make it entirely possible that bonus differentials will depend on much the same assessment by organizational superiors as before; but even if the change is only symbolic, symbols can have long-range effects on attitudes and practice.

What Sony shows is that there is a general syndrome:

- adoption of the 'caring above all for shareholders' rhetoric;
- use of EVA calculations;
- considerable expenditure of effort on management accounting to assess the performance of internal profit centres;
- decentralization of authority to these profit centres and the linking of managerial rewards to measured performance;
- having a sizeable part of the equity in foreign hands; and
- having a higher than average share price.

An extreme example is HOYA, a manufacturer of spectacles, hearing aids, and photomasks (about 2,000 employees) and one of a tiny handful of Japanese firms which writes its name in Roman rather than Japanese characters. It describes itself in the stock exchange handbook[47] as 'promoting management practices which give importance to shareholders, with its EVA index base' and was written up in the *Financial Times*[48] as an admirably efficient firm whose 'shareholder-friendly management practices' had paid off with a record share price —outperforming the TOPIX index by 350 per cent. By the time the *Financial Times* reporter got to the president, EVA had been renamed SVA (shareholders' value-added) and he admitted that he did not understand how it was calculated. But he was sure that the principle was right: 'shareholders are not at the bottom of our priorities as they are in some Japanese companies'. The company has invested heavily in German software to enable it to give investors quarterly reports (still very rare in Japan) which include details of the sales and operating profits of its individual divisions.

How far these firms are swallows that herald the arrival of a shareholder summer is hard to predict. Clearly the link between a company's share price and its president's self-esteem is growing. The 'moral authority' of the stock exchange is increasing. It is not clear, though, what the disadvantages of a low stock price, or the advantages of a high stock price, actually are. HOYA, for example, has not issued any new equity since 1991, at the height of the bubble. Its president did, however, declare an interest in making acquisitions, and for that, presumably, the possibility of paying for an acquisition with the company's own shares would represent a real financial advantage.

Nor is it entirely clear how far the firms which have made the greatest efforts to woo shareholders have done so at the expense of the traditional community characteristics of the firm. Much depends, clearly, on the degree to which objectively rated performance pay induces an intensification of interpersonal competition within the firm, and on how far the objective-index-linked rewards are seen as a product of real excellence of performance or merely as profiting from the hard work of subordinates. So far at least, even in Sony, any such possible impact is modified by the relatively marginal nature of stock options and performance bonuses compared with the base pay determined by more traditional criteria.

What would change that would be the growth of a real external labour market for executive talent—and of that, even at Sony or HOYA, there seems little sign as yet.

Dividends and payout ratios

Better returns for shareholders are not just a matter of raising payout ratios, which are not particularly low in Japan compared with, say, the United States—though hitherto they have tended to fluctuate far more because they have been treated as a more or less fixed charge at *x* per cent of the par value. (For Japanese quoted companies as a whole, the payout ratio was 24 per cent in 1991, 101 per cent in 1993—i.e. an actual drawing-down of reserves to pay dividends—and back to 54 per cent when things got better in 1995.[49]) What has been lower is not the proportion of profits given to the shareholders but the profit ratio itself. It is a tougher profit drive which is called for, it being left to the imagination whether that can be achieved by greater efficiency in the use of resources or by more rigorous treatment of all those expenditures—wage and bonus increases, their maintenance through bad times, welfare expenditures, avoidance of lay-offs—which have hitherto justified the designation 'employee-favouring firm'.

The favourite measure of success in achieving a tougher profit drive is the return on equity, which has replaced market share or profit margin on sales as the most frequently cited performance indicator. The quarterly company handbooks have added 'ROE ranking' to their performance lists along with traditional measures such as profit margins on sales.

One change has certainly taken place. Top managers talk to large investors more often. It used to be common practice for firms to call meetings of all their major 'stable' shareholders to explain their future plans, outline their investment needs, and give forecasts of out-turns. The fact that minor shareholders were excluded from such meetings used to worry nobody. Now it does, and firms are forced to visit their stable shareholders in turn, at the much resented cost of a great deal of managerial time. Now that American and British pension funds have become substantial holders—either by unilateral purchase or by invitation—an annual presidential or vice-presidential pilgrimage to funds in the United States is becoming *de rigueur*. An American firm which arranges such visits was reported to have done so for 150 firms in 1997, compared with only 35 two years earlier.

This is in itself evidence, perhaps, that keeping up their firm's share price has acquired higher priority among managers' objectives. I have already quoted the New Year message to senior staff of the president of Tokyo Electric, in which he told them that whereas they used to be preoccupied with such indicators as profit margins on sales, it was their share price which was the best, the most comprehensive, crystal-lized measure of the firm's performance. This was in an industry, moreover, where the stability of the relative share price rankings of the nine generating companies shows the extent to which convention competes with calculative performance evaluation in the setting of share prices.

One place to look for evidence of change is in firms' 'Statement of dividend policy', which since 1994 (reflecting the 'take shareholders seriously' trend) they have been statutorily required to make in their annual reports to the Ministry of Finance. A random (haphazard) sample of three years' reports by seven companies shows very little change from year to year, and a rather bland uniformity, particularly in the insistence on 'stability' in dividend level. These are not, after all, propitious times for raising returns to shareholders, and even stability seems a lot to promise. Take Japan Steel, for example, in 1994 (at a time when it had some 15,000 workers kept on its books but 'leased out', at some considerable cost, to other firms):

> Our dividend policy has been fundamentally based on the principle of stability, but taking into account also the need for funds to strengthen the firm's foundation, current trading results, and prospects for the future.
>
> This year, however, although we tried, in accordance with this policy, to do our best to meet our shareholders' expectations, it is with deep regret that, faced with losses on a far greater scale than expected and having had to draw down reserves, we have been forced to reduce our dividend from 6 to 2.5 per cent. We have drawn down the Special Reserve Fund to find the funds to do so.
>
> It is our intention, with our Third Reconstruction Plan starting in March of this year, to strengthen our competitiveness in steel, to raise our earn-ings from engineering, and to put our new businesses on a more solid foundation, and thus we hope to resume our accustomed dividend level at the earliest possible moment.

That 2.5 per cent dividend put the yield back to 0.7 per cent of the share price (mean between highest and lowest price of the year), close to the 0.85 per cent which the earlier 6 per cent dividend had represented when share prices were at their peak in 1990.

Not much different is the report of Ushio Denki, the company headed by Ushio Jiro, the son of the company's founder and owner of 2.4 per cent of its shares, who, as president of Doyūkai, has become one of the most vigorous exponents of shareholder-oriented management. The company had cut back its standard 11 per cent dividend to 8 per cent in 1992–3. The next year its statement said:

> We are always conscious, as an enterprise, of having the return of value to our shareholders as one of our major objectives, and, bearing in mind the need to retain earnings, current performance, and the trading environment, it is our fundamental policy to pay a stable dividend.
>
> In accordance with the above policy we have decided to pay a dividend of 8 per cent this year as last, but with the addition of one yen to commemorate the firm's thirtieth anniversary. This makes the dividend propensity 59 per cent; the profit return on shareholder capital being 3.6 per cent and the dividend return 2.1 per cent.
>
> As for our retained earnings we shall use them for investment to strengthen R&D and to raise productivity and improve our competitiveness.

While there is no difference in substance between Toyota and Nissan, the language perhaps reflects differences in enterprise cultures: Nissan somewhat cooler and business-like, Toyota 'wetter', 'doing our best for you our shareholders' (*kabunushi no minasan*). Toyota pays a dividend of 19 per cent, however, compared with Nissan's 14 per cent at the time of the bubble and 7 per cent after it got into serious difficulties. But Toyota describes its dividend as a 'basic dividend' of 12 per cent, a 'special dividend' of 6 per cent, plus 1 per cent to celebrate something or other—the 80 millionth car, the 5 millionth produced overseas, etc. Stock prices equate both companies' dividends to an approximate 1 per cent yield.

Of the seven firms in my sample, the only one not to talk of stability, but to claim to treat shareholders as the residual risk-bearers and profit-takers they are supposed to be, is Matsuda, now under Ford majority ownership: 'It is our policy to decide the dividend level each year in accordance with performance and the business environment.'

In sum, neither the prescriptive rhetoric about giving shareholders their due, nor the predictions about the way in which capital market pressures will force firms to change the level of the rewards they give their shareholders, seems yet to be reflected in the way firms decide dividend levels or even, in concrete terms, talk about them.

The managerial labour market

There is still only one market for managerial talent which counts—the market for new graduates, somewhat supplemented by a supply of graduates in their twenties who decide that they made a mistake first time and want to change career.

Two questions need to be asked which are relevant to the future shape of the firm. First, what are the relative pulling powers of the financial and the non-financial sectors? A capitalist society gives power to the providers of capital, and that power is normally translated into higher incomes for those most closely engaged in allocating capital, which in turn serves to recruit the best and brightest into finance, which further serves to enhance the dominance of the finance industry over the economy. How far has this happened in Japan?

In postwar Japan, too, the banks have on the whole been in the stronger power position. Non-financial firms have been anxious to borrow to a greater degree, and more often, than banks have been anxious to lend. And, when a main bank has to come to the rescue of the firm, it is often a senior bank manager who takes control of the restructuring, whereas one has never heard of a manufacturing manager called in to knock a bank into shape. Bank salaries have traditionally been higher than manufacturing salaries, and banks have probably had a lion's share of the intellectually gifted coming out of faculties of law, humanities, and the social sciences, but to a far lesser degree than in Britain, for example. And what applied to the banks did not, as it did in Britain, apply also to the stockbroking companies; they paid high salaries, but their shady-dealing image severely limited their power to recruit from the top universities.

The bubble widened the salary gap in the late 1980s—for 40–44-year-old graduates salaries were 28 per cent higher in banking than in manufacturing in 1990, according to the Ministry's earnings survey—and this increased the pulling power of the banks. There was a good deal of comment at the end of the decade on the fact that not only was the financial sector creaming off the law etc. departments, but they were also—quite unprecedentedly—beginning to do what British merchant banks had been doing for decades, namely to recruit from the science and engineering departments, partly for technology appraisal, but more often simply for the quality of their brains.

The bursting of the bubble stopped that, and though the salary differential narrowed only slowly, the much publicized problems of the banks in the latter half of the 1990s greatly reduced their recruiting power. There seems no great likelihood, then, that increasingly sharper wits in the financial sector than in the rest of the economy will aid the trend towards the shareholder-favouring firm.

That is about the dividing-up of the pool of law, social science, and humanities graduates. The other question relevant to the future shape of the firm is about the balance between them and those with scientific and engineering backgrounds. Science and engineering still have high prestige: you have to be academically brighter to get into a top science faculty than into a top law faculty. A bright 17-year-old, coming up to the last year of his or her comprehensive senior secondary curriculum, might well be influenced to choose the science route because the challenge is greater and the honour of 'making it' therefore the greater. There is no 'two cultures: men of letters are gentlemen, engineers are philistines' tradition to counterbalance that effect. It has long been argued that one element in the strength of Japanese manufacturing has been the fact that top management has had a large share of science and engineering graduates—people who are (a) fully aware of all, including the technical, aspects of their business and (b) (because of those selection processes in schools) among the brightest of their generation. Is this changing? One does, indeed, read assertions that the route to the top is increasingly likely to lie in experience in the finance function rather than in R&D or production. However, a brief check on the Boards of Directors of nine large firms, each a leader in its industry segment, found no evidence that this is the case. In 1975 they had 256 directors, of whom 43 per cent were graduates of science or engineering faculties. In 1995, by which time they had 329 directors, the proportion was 47 per cent.[50]

International operations

It may be objected: yes, all that may be true about Japanese firms producing in Japan and connecting with the outside world only through trade, but an increasing proportion of Japanese firms are indeed global;

producing—more and more as the Japanese manufacturing sector 'hollows out'—overseas as well as selling overseas, in the context of very different financial climates where the shareholder holds sway.

Though they may be locally incorporated and conform to local accounting rules, the vast bulk of Japanese overseas operations are, however, 100 per cent owned by their parent Japanese company. The 'shareholders' to whom the managers of those companies answer are their contemporaries and seniors on the same management tracks as themselves. These overseas subsidiaries often do raise capital locally, but predominantly in the form of bond issues and bank borrowings. Indeed, the issue of bonds by an overseas subsidiary, and the transfer of the cash raised to Japan, can be a way for the Japanese parent company to raise capital more cheaply abroad than at home.

The form of internationalization which can bring about pressures to raise dividends and to switch to more shareholder-friendly forms of management is the joint-venture, of which there have lately been an increasing number, particularly in the financial sector of banking and insurance, where Japanese firms have been most threatened by the onset of foreign competition in domestic markets. An American Board member, arguing with all the assurance and self-righteousness of one who has never for a moment doubted that firms ought to be run for the sake of their shareholders, can have a powerful effect on enterprise behaviour, even if he represents only 20 per cent of the equity voting power. In a study of strategic investment decisions, and the extent to which they were governed by financial calculations which privileged the short-term, the one Japanese company (out of ten) which used discounted cashflow analysis was a joint-venture with an American firm.[51]

Pensions and shareholder pressure

One major source of pressure to give greater consideration to shareholders comes from those concerned with the pension futures of Japan's ageing population.

Take, first, the pension funds run by many companies in partial alliance with the state Kosei Nenkin fund. Companies were allowed to opt for reduced participation in the state fund, in return for managing part of the statutory contributions plus supplementary contributions in accordance with certain rules. One of these was that the contributions to these funds should be calculated to meet the (defined-benefit) retirement liabilities on the assumption of a 5.5 per cent return on investments. In recent years yields have been woefully short of that figure, and in 1998 the rule was changed to require calculation on a 4.5 per cent return basis. This means, in effect, enhanced contributions by firms to their funds. In 1996 Hitachi spent ¥29bn—about 0.7 per cent of gross sales—on filling the accumulated deficit in its fund.

The typical large corporation apportions out its funds to a variety of fund managers, traditionally in Japan the trust banks as well as the life insurance companies. With the recent drastic decline in earnings, the competition from foreign fund managers has become intense, and most of the large firms have diversified their choice of investment managers. In typically Japanese fashion the shift has been handled collectively. In the autumn of 1997 agreement was reached between the life insurance industry association and a group of major firms that the firms would shift management of x per cent of their pension funds to foreign managers, and the insurance companies, realizing that they were in no position to compete with foreigners in exploiting the profit opportunities offered by the buoyant American equity market, agreed to accept the shift and not to retaliate by reducing their stable shareholdings.

Firms' increased involvement with the foreign financial community will undoubtedly be one further route by which the shift to Anglo-Saxon notions of economic rationality comes to permeate Japanese management. Another lies in the defensive reaction of the Japanese life insurance companies, the creation of joint fund-management ventures with foreign firms—Toho Life Insurance with GE Capital, for instance, Meiji Mutual Life with the Dresdner Bank, Mitsui Trust Bank with Prudential, and so on. The purchase by the American International Group of Aoba Life raised a few eyebrows, since the company, the successor to the failed Nissan Life, had been nursed back to health with the help of capital contributions from all the other life insurance companies

The problems of the state pension system raise different issues. As elsewhere, the calculations of the future tax and social security contributions required to keep pensions (both the basic and the earnings-related) at their current levels show the need for what are generally agreed to be alarming increases—from 29 per cent of pay to 36 per cent over 40 years, according to the Ministry of Welfare. (The degree of alarm is increased by the fact that the possibility of economic growth is not brought into the calculation. If there is growth of 1.5 per cent per annum, the '29 to 36 per cent' figure means, in effect, that to give the old people a pension with the same relation to the average post-tax wage as now would mean that everyone would have not the full 100 per cent but 'only' 90 per cent more disposable income than now.)

This impacts on the 'more for shareholders' question in two ways. First, Japan's system is still partly funded; it is not entirely hand-to-mouth, pay-as-you-go. Having had a relatively young population paying high premiums over a fairly long period, Japan still has a sizeable surplus on its pension account—such that, depending on the interest rate used, the fund can contribute as much as some 3 per cent of GNP to public finances. Clearly, the returns to that fund are of some importance for the welfare system's future. Those returns are intimately linked, through the intricacies of FILP (the Fiscal Investment and Loan Plan), to the yield on Japanese government securities. And those in turn are linked to the yield on equities. (Moreover, as a result of the Price-Keeping Operations mentioned earlier, the link to equity yields is currently becoming more direct.) Here, then, is a good public interest reason for bureaucrats to be interested in raising equity yields, to add weight to the traditional interest of LDP politicians.

(As for the politicians, they do not need any public interest reasons. Their costly electoral machines have traditionally been financed partly by donations and partly by earnings on equities and land. Hitherto most of those earnings have come, not from dividends but from stock trading—often on the basis of advice from one of the broker firms which has not been above the odd bit of ramping to please its friends. There developed during Japan's nineteenth-century Wild West phase of capitalism—as in the similar Russian phase today—a complex politician/stock market operator/ gangster/ultra-nationalist nexus: the gangsters doubling as *sōkaiya* used to intimidate awkward shareholders, and 'patriotic' *ingaidan* used to intimidate political opponents. It has still not entirely disappeared. I mentioned above the unusually flamboyant politician who became too overbearingly demanding of his stockbroker friends and committed suicide the night before the Diet voted to remove his immunity to investigation.)

The other consequence of the pressure on the social security system is the growing talk of switching a substantial proportion of pension provision to personal initiative, and shifting as much as possible of the non-statutory pension system from a defined-benefit to a defined-contribution form—i.e. making the eventual pension received dependent on the capital income from invested savings. 'Taking individual responsibility' is the ethical gloss the financial industry's spokespeople put on the matter when they extol the virtues of America's 401(k) tax incentives, the boost they give to the flow of mutual funds into the equity market, and the high returns thus provided in capital gains. (The disillusion of post-bubble Japan turned, not to caution about all bubbles, but to an urge to share in America's.) The Social Security Deliberation Committee has already recommended following the British example set by Mrs Thatcher in the early 1980s of linking pension levels to prices and not to average earnings. Books on the virtues of 401(k) private pension funds abound, as do advertisements for the certificate courses of the Institute of Financial Planners, which is one of the fastest growing professional bodies—its membership grew from 4,000 in 1992 to 14,000 in 1997 and 28,000 in 1998.

On present reckoning this trend will further accelerate, and it will receive further feedback boost from the increasing proportion of the cleverest Japanese who choose to earn their living out of the administration fees subtracted from the earnings of pensioners' savings before they are handed over to them. Whether it will really take off—i.e. be consolidated by institutional changes (a cutback in public pensions and tax advantages for the investment of savings in equities)—probably depends, more than on anything else, on the ability of the American stock market to avoid a spectacular crash.

Defence of the employee-favouring firm?

The extent to which the reformers have command of the ideological airspace in Japan is astonishing, given the contrasting fact that, through all the crisis years of the 1990s, when firms were under great pressure from bad debts, unpredictable and unpredicted exchange rate shifts, and stagnant domestic demand, very little actually changed either in the way they were governed or in the way they treated their employees. But if the reformers do begin to chip away at the edges and seem likely to succeed in transforming the large Japanese corporation, what political forces are there which might succeed in mounting an effective defence?

The egalitarian characteristics of the Japanese system—the compressed reward differentials, the strong redistributive element in the
welfare system and the health service, the emphasis on universal
schooling—have all rested, not only on the benevolent sentiments of
the elite, but also on the power to make trouble possessed by unions
and opposition parties. I quoted above the civil service head of MITI
who attributed to the voting power of the Socialist Party in the Diet
the egalitarian bias in industrial policy—a power now almost entirely
vanished.

As for the unions, the steady decline in strike activity tells its
own story about the ability of unions to make trouble for managers
who might choose to take firms in an Anglo-Saxon, shareholder-
sovereignty direction complete with downsizing, fabulous stock options, and all the rest. What it does not tell, however, is the why and
how of the change. A full account would have to include:

1. The driving-force of earlier militancy. The leaders of the spring
struggle, from the formation of the system in the mid-1950s to the
mid-1970s, worked with a straightforward Marxist model of capitalism
as a system in which capitalists extract surplus value from workers.
Yearly wage negotiations were about wresting as much as possible of
that surplus back. But, especially when the oil shock produced a
national sense of crisis, the perception grew that capitalists were not
getting an awful lot out of the system, and that the managers with
whom they negotiated were as much concerned with workers' welfare
as with that of their shareholders.

That reality perception gradually took the fire out of the belly of
union organizers as it reduced their capacity to inspire indignation in
their members against the bosses. What that perception has not done,
however, is to create a new and adequate rationale for the unions'
existence. They clearly have one. They still can perform, and often do
perform, a very real function as watchdogs of the managers' concern
for the interests of their workforce, able to block or delay decisions
taken without due consideration of their effects on the work and non-
work lives of the lower ranks of the hierarchy. But they are frozen in
the rhetoric of the earlier era. Wage negotiations are still described by
union leaders in the now-empty terms of 'struggle', 'victory', and
'defeat'. And that is one reason why neither the industrial nor the
national federations seem at all disposed to see the present structure of

the typical corporation as something that operates to the workers' benefit, nor to react to moves to restore shareholder sovereignty as a threat.

2. A second factor lies in the change in union leadership. The postwar generation included a large number of highly able shopfloor workers who had left school at 14. With the rapid and nationwide expansion of higher education, men and women of comparable ability levels were, by the 1960s, almost without fail entering the labour market as graduates from 'good' universities. In the 1960s some of these with a history of student activism became union leaders and injected new blood into traditional militancy. (The closed-shop enterprise union encompasses graduate future managers until they reach positions of line responsibility—usually in their early to mid-thirties.) More recently, however, a position in an enterprise union has come to be seen, rather, as a means of demonstrating the leadership qualities which get a manager early promotion. A bright young man might even find the personnel manager inquiring over a beer, 'Have you ever thought of standing in the union elections?' It will not be held against him that he might take a tough line in wage negotiations or in defence of members who have been unfairly treated—provided the consensus within the firm is that the line he takes is 'reasonable'. And, of course, what he and the managerial consensus deem reasonable is highly coloured by his prospective career track.

The major union federation, Rengo, is on record as supporting many of the reformers' plans for a revamping of the Japanese employment system—for example, drastic modification of the seniority system to give more rapid promotion to the most able. That is why business federations are frequently heard to praise Rengo for its 'realism'. There is, however, one organization of older union leaders which is seeking to entrench union power. These are people who have moved out of the enterprise union orbit to make a union rather than a company career and hold office at the industrial federation level, but who have not moved on to the 'political' level of the central Rengo federation. They have recently been undertaking the serious work of drafting a law to establish legally required works councils, with (as in Germany) legally defined powers. They have in mind an entrenchment of the management–union consultation committees which are part of the institutionalized structure of most unionized firms—governed by a variety of arrangements set by local union contracts.[52] Their bill also proposes that the union should appoint one of the auditors of the company. The chances of their getting the backing of the cautious politicos at Rengo, much less of getting enough political support to enact their draft bill, seem slim, however.

3. And where else might one look for an organized defence of the Japanese model? There remains a party of protest—the Japan Communist Party—which can be sure of at least 10 per cent of the vote in a general election and which in a recent governorship contest scored almost as much as the main Conservative opposition party. It too has an affiliated union federation, which is still very much wedded to traditional Marxist militancy but which is almost wholly confined to the public sector, where the capitalists against whom its literature rages are not very much in evidence.

It was characteristic of the JCP's position as an 'anti-system party' that through all the endless shuffling which produced the most improbable succession of coalition alignments in the first half of the 1990s, there was never any suggestion that the JCP might become a member of a governing coalition. But that may change. The party's media prominence has certainly changed. The party political debates on the main national television channel now regularly include a JCP spokesman who is usually able to run rings round the poor unhappy Socialist who appears as a member of the governing coalition and defender of government policy.

The JCP's relevance to attempts to preserve a characteristically Japanese form of capitalism is, however, in doubt. It is still dedicated to the battle against capitalism in general and the local manifestation thereof in particular. In spite of the fact that it has recently published an analysis of the Japanese economy[53] which makes graphic and telling use of national income statistics to show the different 'reproduction cycles' of the UK, the US, the Swedish, and the Japanese economies, and the resultant 'who gets what', there is no disposition to draw from these calculations the conclusion that Japan might have a more benign form of capitalism which the party might make its business to defend. Among its Marxist academic sympathizers, in fact, there is rather a disposition to welcome the reassertion of shareholder rights. The world is easier to deal with when you can make it conform to your theory.

Eventually, one would guess, generational change within the party and the need to win elections will put the JCP through the same sort of transition as its Italian counterpart began 20 years ago. But there are few signs of this yet. And whether, when it does so, it will transform itself into a defender of employee sovereignty and the egalitarianism of the Japanese model remains to be seen—as it remains to be seen whether, by then, there is any longer a Japanese model to be defended.

Perhaps the most important determinant of the outcome will be what happens to executive pay. If stock options find wide acceptance and grow in importance (in spite of the mounting criticism they receive in the United States and Britain; see Chapter 1), they will break the links between top salaries and bottom wages which assumptions about the community nature of the firm, and the bureaucratic pay system in which those assumptions are embodied, at present provide. (Those links in 1997 caused an average pay rise of 2.0 per cent for top executives while average workers' pay rose 2.1 per cent.) The fact that those assumptions still hold was made clear in the outcry over retirement allowances in the Long-Term Credit Bank. When the bank was nationalized to prevent its failure, former executives who had been responsible for getting it into a mess were asked to return their lump-sum retirement allowances. It was thus discovered that a former president, then chairman, then special counsellor, had, on his final retirement from the last post, received an allowance of what was considered outrageous proportions. It was approximately $8mn.[54]

Chapter 5

Trading Relations

T HE advocacy by reformers of 'drier', more arm's-length, more contractual, more market-driven, less committed, less option-foreclosing employment relations within the firm is clear and sometimes vociferous. The second of our four ways in which Japanese capitalism differs markedly from the Anglo-Saxon variety—relational trading between firms, relational banking, and the solidarity within mutually trading *keiretsu*; long-term relationships with elements of mutual consideration modifying the pursuit of one's own or one's own firm's interest—is much less often the target of 'dryness preference', of advocacy as a matter of principle. The exception, perhaps, is in trade talks: the 'xenophobically closed' supplier networks of Japanese automobile firms which kept out American suppliers who offered better prices and quality was a central issue in Japanese–American trade negotiations in the mid-1990s, and the Americans did have some support from Japanese economist advocates of market rationality.

Even if there is not much strong advocacy, predictions of impending and inevitable change abound. What Whittaker calls the 'paradigm shift'-school talks of a new world, 'a more fluid, open system with entrepreneurial firms, quick to adapt to new or fragmented markets and technology shifts'.[1] Evidence of actual change is not lacking either, albeit of dimensions much less dramatic than are often reported in the Western financial press.

One basis for such predictions is identical to that for employment relations—a change in modal personalities. Younger generations are closer than their predecessors to Anglo-Saxons in the degree to which they approximate the rational maximizer postulated by economic theorists. They are more bottom-line-ist, keener to keep their options open and to avoid possibly costly commitments, both in their own personal affairs and when they are acting on behalf of the organizations they work for.

Factors likely to erode relational trading practices

But there are other, more specific factors. Consider, first, the supplier–assembler relations, about which so much has been written—particularly about those in the automobile industry.

1. The competitive advantage Japanese manufacturing gained from superior quality and faster product development was conferred by a combination of (*a*) clever production organization, (*b*) own workforce commitment, and (*c*) supplier commitment. That competitive edge has been eroded as Japanese firms' American and European competitors have improved product quality by adopting the production organization and, to some degree, also, the means of evoking supplier commitment which they have learned from the Japanese. When quality comes to be taken for granted, price competition becomes more important; and higher Japanese wages and a (periodically) overvalued yen make that price competition formidable. When they are under such intensified competitive pressure, the short-term cost of paying a committed supplier more than the price offered by a cheaper newcomer may well come to loom larger in managers' eyes than the longer-term advantages of always being able to cash in the loyal supplier's commitment. This effect is much discussed in Germany, where the level of hourly wages which superior quality used to guarantee is under threat. 'We used to be able to sell at a 20 per cent premium because of our quality reputation. Now we're lucky to get away with a 3–5 per cent premium,' one German manager in the pump industry is reported as saying.[2]

2. The recession, reduced revenues in domestic markets, and the consequent increased competition have the same effect in inducing short-termism.

3. 'Hollowing out'—the increasing location of production overseas in response to high domestic labour costs—can obviously disrupt supplier relations, especially when firms are subject to pressure (sometimes formal local-content rules) to source locally. This effect is reduced, of course, when the overseas production (in 1996 already close to 10 per cent of Japanese total manufacturing output and around one-quarter of the output of those firms which have any overseas plant at all[3]) is incremental to production at home, or—as often happens—when assemblers induce their suppliers to accompany them overseas.

4. The effects of technological change, especially in cheapening transport and communications, are also, possibly, a factor. Thus, *The Economist*, which may have a point, even after a heavy discount for e-hype:[4]

> Computers also undermine the advantage of Japanese firms' much-praised relations with a core group of subcontractors. These links ensure that manufacturers obtain faultless parts at short notice. But now technology offers a new way of securing reliable supplies; manufacturers will soon be sending three-dimensional drawings down modem links to subcontractors. The assiduous purchasing officer, who visits subcontractors to explain what parts are needed and even how they might be made, will soon be redundant.
>
> Once communication moves on-line, having a core group of sub-contractors turns from strength to weakness. It is as quick and easy to send out a parts order to 50 subcontractors as to five; to Arkansas as to Aichi prefecture. Having placed an order on-line, the purchaser can wait to see which supplier offers to fulfil it most efficiently. By scouring the world for the best deal technology favours on-line opportunists. The tight family of subcontractors traditional in Japan will become uncompetitive.

5. A more problematic issue is suggested by the following comment made by a British parts supplier describing how his firm developed a warm and lasting relationship with Honda:[5] he spoke of an emphasis on 'not so much technical ability, but the right attitude and commitment'. In the early days, when Honda engineers were inspecting and making improvement specifications for the parts Unipart offered to supply, 'Some of the rejections might have mystified European vehicle makers.' 'For instance,' recalls Unipart's MD, 'they wouldn't tolerate weld splatter on a silencer, even though it has no bearing whatever on the part's performance. A Western company simply wouldn't care . . .'.

It is arguable, in other words, that a key element in the strength of these supplier ties—what hitherto has kept them going—has been a shared commitment to what one might call 'quality-fetishism', perfectionism carried to what are essentially bottom-line-irrational limits—overengineering. Not one customer in a thousand ever looks for weld splatter. And even that thousandth customer is not likely to let her purchasing decision depend on what she sees. Hitherto, the

Japanese car makers have had the profit margins which enabled them to indulge their perfectionist whims, but no longer. Toyota's sharp cutting-back on its baroque variety of model variations is a case in point. Economizing is the order of the day; and one of the first things to go will be the self-indulgence of perfectionism unrelated to profitability.

The argument, then, is this: the extra-economic element in relational trading—the moral commitment—was not just mutual consideration based on the recognition of mutual dependency, but also a shared commitment to a perfectionist version of the productivist ethic. And if that has to go in the interests of the bottom line, these relationships will be weakened.

Not wholly convincing, perhaps. The counter-argument takes two forms. First, to take weld splatter as an example, it is simply myopic to dismiss the Honda concern as quality fetishism. Weigh the wasted solder in the splatter for a start. Multiply that by the hundreds of thousands produced a year. Work out its cost. Experiment in all sorts of conditions to see whether the time and equipment cost of producing an unsplattered weld is greater than that for a splattered one. Do your sums and you will see that it is bottom-line-rational after all. Perhaps.

Secondly, factory cultures are wholes. Call it fetishism, if you like, but maintaining a concern for quality is not something you can do in one corner of a factory while sloppiness reigns elsewhere. It is by maintaining that determination to think of every possible contingency, to do the best job humanly possible, *even* when it comes to weld splatter, that produces those improvements in quality which lead to the trouble-free engines and the low warranty-period repair ratios which without any doubt affect customer decisions and determine your bottom line.

Reinforcement?

Against all these reasons for expecting change, there are, on the other hand, some developments which one might think of as reinforcing the traditional pattern of relationships. First is the increasing technological complexity, on average, of manufacturing products. Suppliers have expertise which has moved out beyond what the assembler could easily duplicate. In a 1996 questionnaire sent out by the Small and Medium Enterprise Agency (hereafter SMEA), 38 per cent of firms answered the 'Why outsource?' question 'because the supplier has technological capacity which we lack', compared with 72 per cent which cited lower costs.[6] It may be that greater equality of bargaining clout within the relationship compensates for any diminution of *noblesse oblige* considerateness on the part of the formerly stronger party. Secondly, as Japanese firms move abroad and develop the same sort of relationships with non-Japanese local suppliers, they may become confirmed in their habits—cease to see them as subject to the general rule 'Japanese = bad; Western = good'. The *Financial Times* interview with Unipart's MD is relevant. Recall that he attributed Honda's choice of Unipart to Unipart's having 'the right attitude and commitment. When we got the business, we knew they had a lower quote from elsewhere'.

'Now,' says Neill, 'I go once a year to see Honda in Japan to maintain our good relationship and say, "We promised to do things; we've done them—now what can we do for the future?"'

The deepening relationship, says Neill, means that 'we don't have to look at a one-year horizon. We can make capital and people investments, and we've now got young engineers we are training so that we can provide them [Honda and Rover] with high-quality research and development and production expertise.

'If all their Japanese suppliers work in that climate, is it any wonder the Japanese are winning?' ponders Neill. 'They eliminate all useless argument, instead putting all their efforts into improving. This is so much more efficient than the West, it's hard to see how Western companies can catch up.'

The manager of the Toyota plant in Britain also testified to the strength of the relationships the firm had built with its suppliers, assuring them in a speech at the opening of a new plant that it would not copy Rover and Vauxhall and switch component purchases to continental Europe. 'The high value of sterling is very difficult for us, but we will not allow short-term situations to affect our long-term view.'

Observed trends in behaviour

The general story about the impact of these secular changes and the prolonged recession on subcontracting relationships is best summed

up in a 1998 study of developments at Toyota, Honda, and Nissan.[7] (a)
There is an increasing distinction between a core group of essential
long-term suppliers and an outer group with whom trade relationships are certainly not arm's-length but to whom the commitment is
weaker. (b) For the core group, there is, if anything, an intensification
of supplier-development activity on the part of the assemblers—not
just advice on production methods through hands-on, labour-intensive
transmission of tacit knowledge by engineers, but also help in management organization, financial management, and business planning.
Toyota has a consultancy service separate from the purchasing department with some 20 members, one of whose main jobs is to
organize the 9 'self-study groups' into which 56 of the main supplier
factories are grouped—a sort of Quality Circle for enterprises which,
like the QCs, set themselves annual 'improvement themes' for investigation and experimentation. There seems to have been no greater
tendency than before for these intensified services to be meticulously
costed; the assemblers are still 'casting their bread upon the waters'.
Nor is there evidence that financial control—by increased capital
participation—has anything to do with the increasing control by
assemblers over suppliers which these relations imply. (Getting help
with business plans means exposing details of a firm's affairs normally
counted as commercial secrets.)

Other automobile makers seem to be altering their suppliers' organization on similar lines. The top headline in the Nikkei newspaper
one Sunday in March 1998 spoke of a big shake-up in the Nissan
supplier system.[8] Firms in the Nissan *keiretsu* (i.e. those in which it
had capital invested) were no longer to be given priority. Nissan
would in future be more willing to buy from foreign firms and from
firms in the Toyota 'family' with whom it had hitherto hesitated to
deal. But its suppliers association, though purged of 'exclusive family
club' elements, was to be consolidated and expanded. There was no
suggestion that the supplier relationship would in future be any less
close.[9]

The best relevant statistical information about manufacturing as a
whole not just automobiles comes from two surveys conducted by the
SMEA, one of 1,500 large enterprises and one of 20,000 smaller enterprises (fewer than 300 employees). The response rates—35 per cent and
22 per cent, respectively—mean that what follows has to be treated
with caution.

Just over a quarter of the large enterprises which responded said that over the last three years they had concentrated and consolidated their supplier relations; 37 per cent of those simply 'to increase efficiency'. More precise reasons, each given by 10–15 per cent of the firms, were greater standardization of parts, more ordering of complete subassemblies, lower production levels (presumably meaning lesser resort to non-regular peripheral suppliers), and trying to equalize suppliers' technological levels. Five per cent said (or chose the offered questionnaire response) that it came from their having greater confidence in some suppliers.[10]

On the density of subcontracting in general and the effect of 'hollowing out', half of the firms with more than 50 per cent of their production overseas said that they had decreased their procurement expenditure in Japan in the three years to December 1997, while 9 per cent said they had increased it. Among firms which produced some but less than 10 per cent of their output overseas, more had increased than decreased their procurement expenditure in Japan (31 per cent as against 17 per cent).

Looked at from the other side, the SMEA survey reported that, over the same three years, 44 per cent of subcontracting firms had seen a decline in the total value of supply orders received, 15 per cent 'a severe decline'. Slightly more said that they had had to cut prices, 9 per cent 'drastically'. Only 6 per cent of those who reported a decline said, though, that the cut was due to the ending of a trading relationship, compared with 64 per cent who attributed it to a contraction of markets and the size of orders.

The three years in question, or at least the first two of them, were years in which the economy seemed to be pulling out of the post-bubble recession, but the overall picture is not one of a drastic break-up of relationships. Nor were there drastic changes in the enterprise-size structure of Japanese manufacturing. The main industrial survey suggests that firms with fewer than 100 workers produced 36 per cent of total value-added in 1996, little different from the 37 per cent in 1985. In terms of relative productivity (value-added per employee relative to that of firms with over 1,000 employees), the 32 per cent for the 4–9-employee category for 1995–6 compares with 1985–91 figures fluctuating between 32 and 35 per cent. The recession has taken its toll in bankruptcies to be sure, but the increase in bankruptcies for small and medium-sized enterprises (under 300 workers) from 1992 to 1997 was only from a 0.34 per cent to a 0.45 per cent annual death rate.

In short, there is no evidence of substantial change in subcontracting patterns. Their efficiency advantages were quite spectacularly demonstrated in the spring of 1997, when a fire practically destroyed the factory of one of Toyota's main suppliers—an affiliated company, Aisin Seishi, which was responsible for the group's whole production of proportioning valves, a complex part which goes into the brakes of all Toyota cars. It was a period of maximum production for the sales rush preceding a hefty rise in the consumption tax. Just-in-time production meant that there were only two days' stocks. Complete shutdown of production was inevitable, but lasted only two days, thanks to rapid improvization by associated firms to make the valves (formerly made on dedicated machines which had been destroyed) on ordinary machining centres. They were delivered through Aisin Seishi, which carried out the 70-step inspection process before sending them on—a 'collaboration effort involving over 200 firms [of which approximately 70 took a direct part in producing the valves] . . . orchestrated with very little direct control from Toyota, and without any haggling over issues of technical proprietary rights or financial compensation.'[11]

This is an elite segment of Japanese industry. Toyota is famously successful. Nothing keeps up the moral tone like a high reputation, and nothing makes loyalty and consideration for others less costly than a steady flow of profits. In sectors where life is tougher, it may well also be rougher. Nevertheless, there is no reason to think that the following conclusions from a large questionnaire survey of 675 automotive component suppliers in the United States and 472 in Japan do not point to real and continuing differences in economic behaviour.[12] In both countries the trust/distrust balance was affected by the length of trading relations, the degree to which information and technical assistance were exchanged, and so on. But there was a large Japan effect, not only in the level of trust (measured by questions such as 'What would you expect your customer to do if a competitor undercut you?' and 'How would your customer react to an unexpected rise in your raw materials cost?'), but also in its determinants. The longer American suppliers had had a supply relation with a particular customer, the more likely they were to expect it to take opportunistic advantage of any weakness. Also, in the United States the expectations of being kept on as a supplier were significantly increased by having promises in a written contract, but having or not having a written contract was irrelevant to such expectations in Japan.

Enterprise groups

Once upon a time economists used to make a distinction between *keiretsu* proper—like that of Nissan referred to above: a single dominant firm and its subsidiaries, affiliates, and suppliers—and the six major inter-industry 'enterprise groups' which account for about 16 per cent of total corporate output and 18 per cent of manufacturing output. These latter are the three largely derived from the old *zaibatsu* conglomerates (Mitsui, Mitsubishi, and Sumitomo) and the less solidary groups put together by banks, Fuyo (also a partial reconstruction of the old Yasuda *zaibatsu*), Daiichi Kangin, and Sanwa. Today, even Japanese have given in to foreigners' sloppy habits and started calling these six *keiretsu*, too.

Here again there is little evidence of much change in the extent to which extra-economic ties of loyalty, reinforced by personal ties built up as fellow-members of, say, the London Mitsui Golf Club, induce a preference for fellow-group member firms as trading or joint-venture partners, a willingness to rally round when a fellow-group member firm needs a subscription of extra capital or a large number of excess workers taking off its hands.

The importance of these ties always was limited in any case. The Fair Trade Commission keeps track, and it appears that it is a rare group firm which does as much as a third of its business with other members of its own group. The figure was about 20 out of a total of 167 firms in 1989. In the same year the average group firm got almost exactly as much of its loan finance—short and long term—from the banks of other groups as from its own (about one-quarter each, with the other half coming from sources outside all the groups).[13] Joint-venture partnerships, too, much more often cross group boundaries than not. Cross-shareholdings are perhaps more likely to be intra-group, but cross-group ties are almost as common: most large companies exchange shares with a number of banks, for instance, not just with their own group's main bank and trust bank.

Much was made by the press of Toyota's refusal, noted earlier, to join all the other members of the Mitsui group in providing a capital infusion for the group's bank.[14] It is doubtful, though, whether one departing swallow makes a winter. Toyota has always been somewhat semi-detached from the group, most of whose firms were founded within, and bear the name of, the old *zaibatsu*; and it was not clear that its refusal was definitive anyway. The best indicator of group solidarity is probably the extent to which cross-shareholding arrangements have held up. As the earlier discussion indicated, there seems to have been little erosion except in the Fuyo group, with its particular difficulties, and even there the latest figures suggest that cross-shareholdings are being rebuilt.

Chapter 6

The Industry as Community: The Competition/Cooperation Balance among Competitors

O N THE third of the four features which mark Japanese economic structure and behaviour off from the classical Anglo-Saxon model—a greater tilt towards cooperation in the competition/co-operation balance among market competitors—there is rather more sign of change, much of it traceable to deregulation, the removal or weakening of regulatory arrangements which put limits on competition.

Cooperation and conspiracy: public contracting

'People of the same trade seldom meet together even for merriment and diversion, but the conversation ends in a conspiracy against the public, or in some contrivance to raise prices.' The most direct recent expression of Adam Smith's scepticism has been in the sphere of public works contracting, where the conspiracy has been very directly aimed at public bodies. At the beginning of the 1990s, media attacks on the *dangō* system—bid-rigging and Buggins-turn sharing of con-tracts among contractors—intensified. So did the frequency of stories about local government corruption—boondoggling by local council-lors on 'study trips' at the taxpayer's expense, and lavish entertain-ment of central government officials by local officials seeking subsidies. A new 'rate-payers' association' type of grass-roots democracy, Om-budsman's Associations sprang up. By 1997 they had formed a national league with prefectural associations and were giving many local governments a hard time. Early in 1999, for example, they brought a successful suit against the Tokyo metropolitan government and its three suppliers of steel sewage pipes, who were shown to have rigged the bidding—with official connivance—for years.

The *dangō* system for public works contracts had long been a well-known feature of Japanese life, a prime example of the complex intermeshing of the on-the-whole uncorrupt bureaucracy and the on-the-whole corrupt world of politics. The ability of politicians to lean on the administrators whose discretionary powers were crucial to the system was a major source of the funds which made Japan's expensive style of politics possible, and a major sphere for the exchange of favouritism and support which linked local and central government politicians. The traditional, conservative politician's ties with the two industries which chiefly provided the funds with which elections were fought—the securities industry and construction—had their roots in the Tokugawa period. Men of strong physique and an aggressive disposition—the ancestors of the contemporary *yakuza* gangsters—often combined the roles of construction worker, fire-fighter, and gambling organizer. The *sōkaiya*, who provide a contemporary link between politics and finance, represent one branch of their descendants, and the master-carpenters turned construction-company giants (who were occasionally helped to clear existing owners out of development sites by thuggish wielders of persuasive power, the *jiageya*) are another.

Dangō means 'coming to a conclusion through discussion'. Public works were in principle conducted by a bidding process. It was customary, however, to name, for each contract, a set of designated bidders drawn from a register of qualified contractors. It was also customary to give them an idea of what the official engineers had calculated as the anticipated price, and to let them in effect decide whose 'turn' it was and rig the bids accordingly. It was effectively a system of negotiated contracts on very much the same lines as defence contracting in any modern industrial society. It was a system which clearly economized greatly on estimation costs, avoiding wasted duplication. It required, within each of the multiplicity of groups of designated contractors, a sense of distributive justice, which, as in the subcontracting system, took the form of assuring everyone a place in an established hierarchy—making sure that the little firm got its little share (the market shares of major contractors were remarkably stable over the years), and making sure that everybody took the rough with the smooth. (The contractor which got, because it was its turn, the job of building a controversial pipeline to Narita airport, a prime target for terrorist attacks, had enormous difficulty shedding it to someone else.) In addition, the system gave some assurance of quality: contractors whose bridges fell down had a hard job getting back to designated status, however powerful their political friends.

The problem was that the whole system conferred great discretion on officials, first in setting (together with politicians, through the budgeting process) the list of project priorities, secondly in designating potential bidders, and thirdly in setting the price. The conspiracy against the public was not usually, by the 1980s, a matter of crude bribery—this much payment for that favourable decision. It was just taken for granted that politicians leaned on officials to favour their friends. And the conventional tariff of charges for becoming and staying friends with politicians was sufficiently high to everybody in the business for the cost of public works to be considerably inflated. When the prosecutor service's attempts at a clean-up got going in the 1990s (especially in districts where the factional in-fighting in the Liberal Democratic Party led to a change in local political power, rendering particular friends of the losing politicians vulnerable), some idea of the scale of these donations became publicly available. Shimizu, one of the big five construction companies, for instance, made regular New Year and midsummer cash gifts to 54 Liberal Democrat politicians, the amount depending on a scale ranking them A to D: the two faction leaders, Takeshita and Kanemaru, were ranked 'special A' and got ¥10mn a time (about $100,000).[1]

All this became a major public issue only when American trade negotiators made the exclusion of American construction firms a central negotiating point—particularly over the new Osaka airport—and when the arrival of the Hosokawa Government in 1993 suddenly seemed to suggest that many things hitherto seen as parts of an unalterable 'system' could be changed.

The system evolved considerably in the 1990s. Construction firms have become more careful about political contributions (certainly at the national level), and the system of public funding of political parties has made construction industry contributions less crucial, though the new small-constituency system may have had the opposite effect at the local level. The designated-bidding system has been replaced by a qualified open-bidding system—qualified in the sense that there is a general ranking of contractors by size and financial strength, and some contracts may be reserved for smaller firms or confined to firms above a certain rank, while the tender specifications may confine bids to firms with certain types of previous experience. The local citizen ombudsman groups have had a considerable impact in increasing transparency at the local level; it was a suit against the Osaka government which led to what is rapidly becoming the standard practice of publishing the official, secret, 'anticipated price' after the award of a contract.

In short, the system is, albeit slowly, being cleaned up and made more transparent. It is not clear, however, that the process has much shifted the balance between cooperation and competition among competing contractors. There is a general recognition that this is not an industry like the car industry where quality and price can be judged simultaneously. Excessive emphasis on price competition can lead firms to cut their margins to the bone and rely for their profits on change orders, holding the client up to ransom with an army of litigious lawyers. In the end, since quality has to be anticipated, it is reputation 'in the industry community'—among one's peers and the engineers of corporations and public bodies who share the same culture—that brings success. The impression one gets from dipping into the extensive array of industry newspapers and magazines is that the industry retains a good deal of solidarity and that one source of that solidarity is a culture which truly values technical competence, innovation, and conscientious craftsmanship and not just the state of balance sheets or profit-and-loss accounts.

'My firm first'

It is undeniable that there has been a weakening of the sense that each industry constitutes a community whose member firms have some kind of minimal duty to help each other. When MITI, in the early 1980s, organized a recession cartel in the spinning industry—a 15 per cent cut in production until inventories were cleared and the price rose again, thus preventing the weaker firms from going under in a price war—officials said that the declining willingness of the stronger firms to go along with the scheme, plus the increasing difficulty of controlling imports through mere 'administrative guidance', meant that this was probably the last time such a cartel would be feasible. And so it proved.

Which is not at all to say that industry solidarity, the persistence of traditional ethical constraints quite unrelated to regulation, has entirely disappeared. The fire at the Aisin Seishi factory mentioned in Chapter 5 is a case in point. Toyota owns 20 per cent of Aisin Seishi; its president is a member of the Toyota founding family. The whole Toyota production machine had to close down as a result of the fire, to be resuscitated only as the supply of proportioning valves could be restored. Toyota could have put pressure on the firm to favour it and to restore supplies more slowly to its competitor Mitsubishi motors, which also bought its valves from Aisin Seishi (and remember that the factories of both firms were working overtime to meet the demand boost prompted by the impending increase in the consumption tax: lost production was serious.) Nevertheless, Toyota is said to have exerted no such pressure.[2]

When Kobe Steel had a couple of blast furnaces put out of action by the earthquake, the other four major steel producers took over its regular orders and gave the customers back when the blast furnaces were repaired.

Such decent, gentlemanly constraints, which maximizers would scorn as a foolish squandering of opportunities (a lack of normal opportunism[3]), are not so difficult to maintain in good times, among 'satisficers' who are making normal acceptable profits. Even satisficers may begin to question these limitations on behaviour, however, when the going gets tough and there is serious talk about the possibility of bankruptcy.

As, for instance, in the ferrous foundry industry, which in late 1998 was under considerable pressure. To a secular decline in the output of user industries, a continuing shift to non-ferrous alternatives, and a growth in imports were added the effects of the renewed recession. It is a small-firm industry par excellence (only seven firms are not classified as small or medium, all of them subsidiaries of an automobile maker). Most of the firms are family firms, many of postwar foundation; and though about half of the founders had sons with university degrees, they were not all inclined to commit themselves to an ailing industry. The average age of the workforce was 48. Of the 740 firms with more than 20 workers which existed in 1990, 126 had disappeared by 1997. Output over that period declined by 15 per cent.

Most firms were members of one of 31 prefectural ferrous foundry cooperatives and paid an annual $8,000–$9,000 fee to support their activities and those of the four-man federation office in Tokyo which did most of the lobbying. (Once a wartime organization with mandatory membership, its informal successor was dissolved by fiat in 1948; but, like most of the industry associations, it was made respectable (and tax-privileged), by a 1952 law, after the Americans had gone.) Drop-outs had increased in recent years. According to the federation officials, it was very often when a 'drier' son took over from a loyal long-standing-member father that a firm decided to go free-rider. The concessions the industry received from government—equipment modernization grants, partial exemption from local taxes on 'modernized' sections of the factory, enhanced first-year depreciation allowances, reduced-cost loan guarantees—were granted to members and non-members alike.

Harder to measure, but no less important, were the less formal patterns of inter-competitor cooperation. Such patterns were most pronounced in the more or less concentrated industrial districts. Fellow-firms were nearly all potentially direct competitors, but in practice they mostly had some very special capacity, perhaps some special equipment, developed for particular customers and called on each other's help when they had a job which entailed work they were unused to doing. (Many of them were asked to do quite a lot of prototype work.) In this, as in most industries in Japan, in a context in which long-term relational trading was taken for granted, it was considered the path of wisdom for no firm to be dependent for more than 30 per cent of its sales on a single customer. Likewise, most customers tried to double- or triple-source. This meant that any firm might have as actual direct competitors only two or three other firms, and they might not be in the same district. When a customer described how the dire state of the market was bringing it close to bankruptcy and asked for a 5 per cent cut in supplier prices, which firm would suffer most from a cut in orders? Not necessarily the one which showed least willingness on that occasion to comply. Customers would be more likely to be swayed by the whole history of their relations with the supplier: quality, delivery reliability, response to one-off prototype requests, willingness to take the initiative in new developments (the successful firms were undertaking finishing and subassembly as well as the founding), frankness and reasonableness in negotiation.

This meant that the pay-off for undercutting a competitor on price was limited, which raises two points. First, our second and third 'Japaneseness' characteristics are systematically interrelated. The 'moralization' of trading relations affects the character of market competition. Secondly, there is, once again, an analogy with the employment system. The bureaucratic promotion structure within firms rewards consistent cooperative performance over time; one does not get ahead by claiming the credit for particular achievements at others' expense.

It would be surprising, however, if sometimes the handful of suppliers for a particular part, under pressure for a price cut from the same customer, did not phone each other to try to coordinate a response. It would be equally surprising if many did not refrain from phoning, or answered guardedly, from fear of losing their 'good supplier' reputation if the customer got to hear of such attempts to gang up against it.

All the federation officials of the ferrous foundry industry could say when asked how the intensification of competitive pressure was manifesting itself in actual behaviour was, 'The speeches of prefectural cooperative chairmen more often talk of the need for competition to be "kept within bounds" [*Setsudo no aru kyoso*].' What would count as beyond the bounds? Sneaking tales to the customer about competitors. Trying to muscle in on existing customer–supplier relationships by offering loss-leader prices, especially if this was done by imitating the existing supplier's technology.

Whether or not such behaviour is increasing is a subject which deserves systematic research, not just the anecdotal journalism which is all there is on offer at the moment.

Another industry under pressure, also with an average age over 40, is coastal shipping. Small operators (10,000 ships, 3,500—predominantly family-enterprise—owners, and 733 operators in 1996) have small clout in a recession when they bargain with the large corporations whose cargo they carry. It is a highly regulated industry, however, segmented into five industry associations by cargo type, all brought together under an umbrella federation which has the job of negotiating, and plays a large part also in administering, the Ministry of Transport's regulations designed to control capacity. Licence to build ships has always been on a 'scrap and build' basis, with the ratio of scrapped tonnage to built tonnage varying with demand forecasts. In the expansionist euphoria of bubble boom, having any kind of a ship to scrap—and hence a right to build—was a source of wealth. Licences were marketed at prices sometimes greater than the cost of building the ship. With the current overcapacity, the federation is try-ing to cut back capacity and offers to buy up licences at a price which is higher than the licences are likely to fetch on the market. Deregu-lation, a removal of all capacity limits and free competition, has been demanded by government committees and decreed by the government to be a Good Thing. The date for deregulation was, however, set a safe five years hence at the time of writing.

Other industries have experienced much more dramatic change. Petrol retail, for example, used to be the subject of a joke: in the United States, petrol costs $5 a gallon and as soon as you leave the gas station three or four youths hold up your car and steal the tyres. In Europe it costs $50 a gallon and the three or four youths, ostensibly on some socially useful work scheme, can be seen round the corner having a quiet smoke. In Japan it also costs $50, but the three or four youths swarm all over your car polishing every inch of it. No longer; recent years have seen the removal of the control over refined gasoline imports and of the ban (formerly justified on safety grounds) on self-service petrol stations, and this at a time when the falling price of crude would anyway have brought price cuts as well as fatter profits for the oil companies and the wholesalers. Price competition became the order of the day—a far cry from the solidarity with which local dis-tributors collectively tried to harass an upstart price-slashing outsider and drive him to bankruptcy in the 1970s, as graphically described by the victim.[4] (This was the man who subsequently became the hero of the famous attempt to import gasoline from Singapore which MITI succeeded in blocking and which led to the translation of informal administrative guidance into the 'transparent' import control law of 1986. The law was a flagrant piece of anti-competitive legislation but never figured in trade talks with the United States, since the American majors did too well out of it.) By the summer of 1998 the oil companies, suffering sharply reduced profits, had announced plans to close one-sixth of the nation's 60,000 petrol stations, thus adding some 30,000 to the unemployment rolls. They expected that it would be some time before a slimmer, wiser industry would settle down to a stable pattern of 'normal profit' competition.

The domestic airline industry is another recently opened to com-petition, with one small cut-price operator on one of the most popular routes starting before the end of 1998, others planning to follow, and the Ministry of Transport announcing regulations for the allocation of landing-slots which would favour such newcomers. How far the three existing operators will succeed in buying or freezing them out remains to be seen, but meanwhile travellers on some routes are getting greatly reduced prices.

By contrast, price competition remains alien to other industries. Beer, for instance, has its unacknowledged price cartel effectively protected by its regulator, the National Tax Agency, which obviously wants the revenue and so permits brewers to set a recommended retail price. There has been trouble leading to litigation about secret discounts on posted wholesale prices, but so far only from retailers complaining about the favouring of rivals, not among the five members of the industry association themselves. The industry has survived the liberalization of imports with a loss so far of only 2.5 per cent of the market, in spite of the fact that a Budweiser retails 15 per cent cheaper than a Japanese beer. It has equally survived the appearance of local 'real beer' brewers, who have so far gained less than a fifth of one per cent of the market. Its industry association, in marked contrast to the foundry association, can afford 15 employees at its well-appointed headquarters, at the cost of a mere 0.006 per cent of factory gate sales. One of the things it busied itself with in 1998 was drawing up a revised set of guidelines to regulate the use of sales gimmicks—favours, competitions, stamps, prizes—as a means of competition: 10 clauses and 33 subclauses elaborating in great detail a basic general code promulgated by the Fair Trade Commission in 1977.

The effective elimination of price competition does not mean, however, that the beer industry is a cosy complacent oligopoly. Competition is for real. Thanks, primarily, to its success in leading the part-technological, part-advertising innovation game, Asahi, which once had a 9 per cent market share to Kirin's 63 per cent, finally, in 1998, became the market leader.

Fire and accident insurance is an interesting industry in that its structure tells one something about the position of a society on the individualism/collectivism scale. The individualistic assumption is that everyone is responsible for assessing his or her own risks and providing for them by buying insurance:; a free competitive market will produce the best match between price and risk. The collectivist alternative is based on 'there but for the grace of God' solidarity—disastrous things can happen to anybody, and the decent thing for any community to do is to arrange for the maximum sharing of those risks between the lucky and the unlucky.[5] The industry, formerly highly regulated, was a major target of the Clinton Administration's attempt to open the world up to American financial services in general and to the (individualism-based) American insurance industry in particular.

Japanese regulation took the form of a common, quasi-official ratings agency which set standard rates, thus eliminating price competition. New insurance products required ministry approval—generally negotiated with 'the industry' (i.e. the industry association). The number of firms was stable (around 25) and their market shares shifted only slowly. The ranking of the top five was unchanged for decades, the top four being each the main insurer of one of the four big enterprise groups. The lengthy and tough negotiations with the Americans centred on car insurance and ended in a compromise whereby third-party insurance remained a matter of regulated rates (with a system of state reinsurance, the accumulated fund of which adds an astonishingly large sum to the money which the Trust Fund Bureau can invest). The Ratings Agency will continue to set guideline rates for comprehensive insurance, but any operator can undercut them—as, in 1997–8, the first years of deregulation, telephone direct-selling foreign firms, rapidly imitated by some of the smaller Japanese firms, were already beginning to do.

The industry association, housed in the same building as the ratings agency, is of formidable size: some 300 employees. Every year it donates a dozen fire engines to deserving local governments which have shown the most zeal in fire prevention. Its budget amounts to nearly 0.1 per cent of the industry's premium income. It has 33 member firms, which now include 4 foreign firms, but there is a rival industry association of 26 firms, all foreign. Association officials were fairly sanguine about direct telephone sales: they expected them not to go beyond the 10 per cent level of France and Germany, rather than reaching the 30 per cent level of Britain. In the marine field, transborder cargo insurance has long since been a stable unregulated oligopoly, with the Mitsubishi group's Tokyo Marine being the price-setter. Hulls have been deregulated recently, and the price dropped 20 per cent over two years. In answer to a questionnaire survey,[6] officials said that, though the new competition for premiums and to introduce new products had weakened the industry's cohesion, 'change in the environment' had increased the need for collective representation of the industry's interests, and 'if anything has made more important our task of educating and dialoguing with consumers'.

The results of the questionnaire survey of 311 industry associations just mentioned will serve to give an indication of general trends. Its key question asked whether, over the last ten years, there had been any change in the *kessoku*—cohesion, solidarity—of the industry association members. Of the 99 responses, a majority of 55 said there had been no overall change in cohesion, 22 said that cohesion had in fact strengthened (sometimes giving plausible reasons, but most especially the need to negotiate the deregulation process), and 22 said there had been a decline. (It is hard to say what inherent bias there might be—how far an unwillingness on the part of association officials to admit to their own increasing irrelevance might be balanced by the despairing jeremiads of officials on the verge of retirement.) Many of the associations said to be losing their cohesion were in clearly declining—import-competing—industries from which protection had recently been withdrawn or was in the process of being withdrawn (various kinds of textiles, cattle-rearers, butchers, etc.). But there were also chain stores, securities firms, foundries, etc. where increased domestic and foreign competition was the reason.

The questionnaire asked all respondents whether information was exchanged more or less frequently (compared with ten years earlier) in a number of specific areas. The area in which there was the greatest decline in the frequency or willingness to exchange information was investment plans (15 associations), then came sales coordination (14), R&D (11), personnel matters (10), and wages (10). There were more claims to have strengthened cooperation—by 28 associations in R&D, 23 in sales and marketing, 9 in personnel matters, 7 in investment, and 5 in wages. (A number said that they had never been involved in some areas, notably wages, personnel, and investment.)

The questionnaire listed ten factors which might affect the work of an industry organization and asked whether they had become more or less marked in the last ten years, or whether there was no change. There was the greatest unanimity about change in two factors: that competition among the firms in the industry had increased, and that so had the number of firms undertaking a restructuring. There were 64 organizations making each statement. The next most common observation (49 replies) was that there had been a relaxation of regulations (only 3 said that regulatory pressure had increased), while 32 said that there was greater pressure on firms from shareholders. The other factors said to have an increasing impact were new entrants from other industries (29 replies), competition from foreign firms (28), the willingness of big firms to give leadership (21), pressure from foreign shareholders (17), and interference from the Fair Trade Commission (16).

As for the factors of weakening significance, apart from government regulations as already mentioned, 16 organizations said that there was a diminishing willingness of big firms to give leadership, and 22 (with a great deal of overlap with the last) a diminishing willingness of small firms to accept big firms' leadership. Ten thought that the ratio of new entrants from other industries had declined, and 5 saw a reduction in the Fair Trade Commission's interventions.

Here are a few of the more illuminating comments which respondents added:

(The recording industry) Our membership has gone up from 23 to 29 in the last ten years (10 of them foreign firms), and there are no outsiders. Competition has intensified in an industry in which brand names count for little and the quality of the product counts for 90 per cent of the variance in sales success—which means signing up famous artists and creating hits. But for working out the legal changes made necessary by digitalization and networkization the industry is tackling the problems with one voice.

(Plastics machinery: 133 members) We formerly did a lot of work getting favourable tax treatment, subsidies, R&D grants, and so on. Now, there is much less of that and much more concern with machinery safety, international standards, environmental problems, and product liability matters.

(Oxygen production: 81 firms) We still have a lot to do. Our major concerns at present are: (1) to induce firms to get proper written contracts (a lot have on-site plants supplying steel firms and very loose contractual arrangements); (2) to persuade the government to remove safety regulations now outdated by changes in technology; (3) to take part in international standards regulation.

(Metal sheeting (roofing) in construction: 16,367 mostly small-scale, often one-man, operators) There is bound to be a decrease in number of establishments, but we hope to keep up output and employment by flexible networks. We need to move from being a mere 'labour-providing service' to 'fully responsible project execution', and change the association from being one of skilled tradesmen to an association of businessmen.

(Paper products: 108 members and an estimated 30 firms outside) There are big changes going on, both in the industry associations and in the ministry. I was astonished the other day at a meeting at the Small and Medium Industries Bureau to hear an academic member of the Shingikai ask 'Do we really need industry associations in an age of deregulation?' It made me think. Originally, I suppose, the policy towards small and medium industry was started to provide compensation for the fact that the strategic investment policy favoured the basic heavy industries. It may be the same with other associations, but I sometimes get the feeling that the only things that keep up our membership are the 'exit barriers': 'I shan't be able to go playing golf with the others'; 'I'd have a bad conscience about leaving'.

(Department stores: 109 members, no outsiders) History of the association: 1960s—for creating friendly ties among competitors ('merriment and diversion' as Adam Smith called it); 1970s information exchange; 1980s deregulation—the fight over the Large Retail Store Law and designation as special category under the Fair Trade Law; 1990s collaboration—common gift certificates, uniform hangers, standardization of information systems software, common delivery systems, etc.

(Railway truck exporters: 27 firms, down from 35 ten years earlier) Weakened solidarity because of an increasing unwillingness to respect regional spheres of influence.

As many of these replies show, the functioning of the industry associations was intimately linked to the role played by the ministries which had jurisdiction over the legal framework within which they operated. The questionnaire just quoted was carried out at the beginning of 1998, at a time when the economy was in dire straits, when deregulation was the Law of the Prophet, and when the bureaucracy's confidence in its authority and its ability to give its traditional 'guidance' was at an all-time low. By the autumn of 1999, however, there were some signs of a recovery of bureaucratic self-confidence and a renewal of the ambition to lead. At any rate, it is clear that future trends in the coordinating power of industry associations depend greatly on the future role of the bureaucracy, and it is to that question that we now turn.

Chapter 7

The Role of Government in the Economy

THE notion that government is a necessary evil, the ideal of the nightwatchman state, was never a strain of any consequence in Chinese or Japanese political thought. That government should, and in the proper hands could, be a repository of virtuous and benevolent leadership was an almost universal assumption among rulers and rebels alike. It was the justification, in fact, for rebellion against tyrants who failed in benevolence. There were no Japanese John Balls leading peasant revolts which questioned the very need for governments. The anarchists of the 1920s and the neoliberals of the 1980s all derived their inspiration from foreign not traditional sources.

The background to the deregulation drive

The drive to cut down the functions of the state began in the early 1980s, when 'small government' became the slogan of the day. The spread to Japan of Reagan and Thatcher radicalism coincided with the need to cut back budget deficits and reduce a national debt swollen by the reflationary policies adopted to deal with the oil crises. Deregulation—or rather 'the easing of regulations'—became the slogan par excellence after the arrival, in 1993, of the first coalition government of Prime Minister Hosokawa, who was famous for the complaint that, as governor of Kumamoto, he couldn't move a bus-stop a hundred yards down the road without permission from the Ministry of Transport. For a year or so it became almost impossible to open a newspaper without finding some reference to the deregulation drive, until, in 1996, the Hashimoto Government's preoccupation with rehabilitating the public finances and with reforming the structure of the administration displaced it.

The declining role of industrial policy as an engine of growth is much discussed and well documented. MITI (and the other ministries involved, such as Communications and Transport) lost a major interventionist instrument at the beginning of the 1970s when the liberalization of foreign exchange removed licensing controls on the import of technology. The maturing of the industrial structure meant that 'more advanced countries' could no longer provide clear catch-up agendas to set priorities for the next industry to receive subsidies and cheap credit. The increasing internationalization of production made it more difficult to coordinate investment plans in the process industries to avoid creating excess capacity. The increasing heterogeneity and diminishing solidarity of industry 'communities' weakened the power of 'administrative guidance', which had always worked primarily *vis-à-vis* whole industries through their associations rather than *vis-à-vis* individual firms—witness the disappearance of the recession cartel already mentioned. The pursuit of growth through industrial policy became more and more a matter of organizing research clubs for 'pre-commercial' R&D.

But that still left a good deal of industrial policy, some embodied in formal regulations, some exercised by administrative guidance, which was not so much about growth as about distribution—about preventing those with strong market power from swallowing, or displacing, the less efficient; about keeping niches for the more labour-intensive, lower-productivity, lower-wage enterprises. All the credit facilities, machinery modernization grants, and tax concessions offered to small and medium enterprises were one way this was done. Another— which often involved licensing control over entry—is illustrated by the way the capital-intensive whisky firms were kept out of the market for sake rice-wine, or by the Large Retail Store Law, which inhibited the growth of supermarkets and department stores in the interest of Japan's vast army of ageing small retailers.

It was regulation of this type—mostly statutory, sometimes, as in the case of whisky and sake, through administrative guidance— which, together with some safety/consumer protection measures like the ban on self-service petrol stations (manifestations of what Mrs Thatcher called the 'nanny state'), was the target of the deregulation drive of the mid-1990s.

The deregulators could point to quite enough clear examples of regulations which served to preserve a comfortable level of profits for established firms. And there were plenty of examples, too, of regulations whose effect had changed beyond their original intentions with the evolution of economic structures. The Large Retail Store Law, for example, operated to protect not just the surviving small shopkeeper, but also the chain stores and department stores which had worked their way painfully through all the licensing hurdles and were not keen to make the process easier for new competitors. Deregulators driven by an ideological commitment to competition and anti-statism could expect to draw on the support of many who lost out from the system. Among the latter, for example, one might have expected to find all those urban consumers with no family ties in the countryside who have to pay for the heavy subsidies which keep controlled prices five times the international level. It appears, however, that Japanese consumer groups, though often vigorous in their pursuit of big corporations suspected of rigging prices, have been more influenced by a 'fellow-underdog' sympathy with protected groups like small retailers and farmers than by a 'rational' concern with the lower prices which the abolition of protective controls and greater competition might bring.[1]

An equally important background factor in the deregulation drive is the growing unpopularity of civil servants. They are increasingly the target, on the one hand of populist media attacks in which all the newspapers have joined, and on the other of attempts by a new generation of politicians to rule as well as to reign. A central target has been the Ministry of Finance. It is accused, on the one hand, of incompetence in allowing the bubble to happen in the first place, and then in failing to deal with the bad debt problem and the disarray in the banks. At the same time its claim to elite incorruptibility has been badly dented, in part by one or two spectacular revelations of personal corruption on the part of senior officials—clear examples of personal enrichment, or the enrichment of friends, through the abuse of power. Whether there has in fact been a secular decline in the moral quality of civil servants (quite plausibly a response to the decline of their power to shape, and their sense of the responsibility to shape, Japan's place in the modern world), or whether it is just that more attention is now paid to the few bad apples in every barrel which were always there, is a matter of dispute.

But such clear cases of secretive corruption are to be distinguished from the second aspect to which the media have directed attention: the long-established conventions of entertainment of the regulators

by the regulated—'relational regulation', as it were, paralleling relational banking and relational trading. Newspapers report the size of
the restaurant bills turned up by the prosecutors investigating cases of
bank fraud, but rarely relay the bureaucrat's defence: 'Our decisions
are not swayed by feasting and golf course treats, which we receive in
moderation from all participants about equally; but they are essential
ways in which we get to learn informally the problems of the industry;
they serve to establish the relations of trust which enable Japan to
have reasonably honest banking with only 400 bank inspectors, a
tenth of the number in the United States. And all those geisha parties
with karaoke are hard work, anyway.'

Likewise under attack are the established patterns of *amakudari*, the
'descent from Heaven' of bureaucrats in their fifties who move to jobs
in the private sector, more or less onerous, and more or less lucrative
depending on how close they got to the top in their ministry career
and how well they were regarded by the ministry personnel office
which is in charge of such 'second career' placements. Although the
prospect of such placements, at salaries a good deal higher than their
modest civil servant pay, doubtless helps the public service to go on
recruiting from the best and the brightest, these are not mere sinecure
rewards. Finance Ministry and Bank of Japan officials go to the banks
which are not Japan's most profitable, and performance seems to improve after they arrive.[2]

The relevance of these media attacks to the deregulation debate is
clear. There is a greater tendency than used to be the case to see
officials as selfish and corrupt rather than public-spirited. Hence, any
opposition to deregulation proposals on the grounds of public health
or safety or the interests of the environment is likely to be interpreted
as simply an attempt by the bureaucrats to hold on to their power. In
all democracies the dividing-line between the demand for public and
transparent accountability and knee-jerk populist distrust of all authority is a thin one, and in Japan today it is much more frequently
blurred than it used to be.

The arguments

Whereas privatization in the 1980s was controversial—at that time
the Socialist Party still counted for something and opposed it—the

principle of deregulation came to be like motherhood and apple pie. Everybody is in favour. It was a major commitment of the Socialist Prime Minister Murayama when he took office in 1994. Even the *Asahi* newspaper joined what was often semi-deprecatingly referred to as 'the great chorus'. The standard arguments of this consensus are well set out in a report of the Deregulation Subcommittee of the Administrative Reform Committee, published in December 1996 under a crusading title that translates as *Creativity Builds a New Japan*.[3] The report covers a highly diverse range of topics. It recommends, for instance, freer entry into the domestic airline industry, a simplification of the wheat price system and the milk marketing system, clearer rules for the licensing of gas subcontractors, and the abolition of the plot-building ratios for urban factories (which are designed to preserve open green spaces) on the grounds that they are public goods the expense of which should not be thrust on individual businessmen. Many of the recommendations seem eminently sensible responses to changed circumstances; others, like the last, a good deal more controversial.

But more revealing than the individual recommendations is the committee's general crusading stance. It included a number of businessmen, but none from the traditional manufacturing sector: there are the heads of a supermarket chain and of a research consultancy, the Japanese chairman of an American firm called Polyfibron Technologies Inc., and the French chairman of the Tokyo subsidiary of Louis Vuitton Moet Hennessy. The committee also included one trade union official, one journalist, one novelist (who doubled as the token woman), and a sprinkling of academic economists. It was doubtless the latter, together with a few hand-picked modernists from the bureaucracy in the committee's secretariat, who were the main authors of the report.

The arguments are of two kinds. First, there is the purely individualistic argument from consumer sovereignty:

> The first fundamental principle is consumer sovereignty. What gets produced, and how, should be decided not by producers and producer associations and bureaucrats but by the choices that citizens make in the marketplace and the responses of creative entrepreneurs to those choices. Our existing system is based on the false premise that the interests of citizens are best served if bureaucrats regulate; that they should take the lead in balancing demand and supply in order to protect and monitor es-

tablished producers and ensure stable and orderly markets. That is wrong. The aim should be to promote healthy competition through appropriate and transparent rules, such as product liability rules written from the consumer's point of view, thus avoiding the feather-bedding of inefficient existing producers and encouraging vigorous new entrants . . .

Beware those who say that deregulation will lead to the law of the jungle [Jakuniku kyōshoku, literally, the strong eating the flesh of the weak]. First one has to ask, who are the weak? Because people are involved in a particular [declining] industry is no reason for considering them as weak [i.e. treating them like the disabled, widows, and orphans] and deserving of protection. What competition produces is not 'the weak', but losers. No matter whether they are big firms or small, those who cannot adapt to the needs of the market are losers. It is no use saying that competition should be curbed because it produces losers; the interests of the consumer should come first.

But there is also a powerful appeal to collectivist sentiments. Japan's competitiveness as a nation is at stake:

We live in a new age of intensified world competition thanks to the rise of Asia and the arrival of the post-cold war world. Unless Japan can reform its high cost structure and create a new, transparent, and open economic system, we shall be quite unable to compete.

The 'high cost structure' argument was repeated ad nauseam in reports by the major business federations in 1995 and 1996. The facts with which they illustrated it—that at 103 yen to the dollar, Japanese manufacturers had to pay 30 per cent more for their electricity than Americans, for instance—may have seemed compelling when they were made in 1997; less so a year later, when the yen had lost 40 per cent of its dollar exchange value. And in any case, as an eloquent economist critic pointed out,[4] suppose it is true that the non-tradables sector is inefficient and through greater competition could be made less so. A powerful factor making the yen exchange rate so much higher than its overall purchasing power parity rate is precisely the competitive productivity of the tradables sector. So you cure the famous 'high cost structure', and thereby improve that competitive productivity. That could drive the yen even higher, thus making domestic costs just as much above those of competitors (in dollar terms) as they were before.

The other part of the argument is about entrepreneurship. Silicon Valley is at the heart of America's rip-roaring success. The whole Japanese system, particularly the barriers to entry and entrepreneurship posed by government regulation, is responsible for Japan's failure to produce anything of similar vigour. Instead of protecting people from failure, we must let the market rule, accept failures as inevitable, and help people to pick themselves up and start all over again.

Actual changes

The attention of the business federation/think-tank apocalypse-nearly-upon-us industry shifted, around 1997, from deregulation to corporate governance. Changes, some marginal, some of consequence, continue—as anyone in the big cities, observing the combined results of licence deregulation and recession in the long lines of fare-seeking taxis, can observe. The 1997 Deregulation White Paper[5] begins its 530 pages with an illustrative list of deregulation achievements:

1. Primarily to enrich the comforts of daily life:
    (a) changes in building regulations to improve land use allow taller apartment blocks, with more generous common facilities but more densely packed;
    (b) a simplified licensing system for mobile phones, allowing growth from 1 million to 18 million subscribers, 1992–7;
    (c) simplification of the rice distribution system;
    (d) taxi deregulation;
    (e) revision of the prescription/off-prescription categorization of drugs;
    (f) relaxation of domestic boiler regulations to take account of universally used new technologies;
    (g) introduction of the 'comparative efficiency yardstick' system for setting electricity and gas tariffs;
    (h) self-service petrol stations;
    (i) greater flexibility in curriculum choice in schools.

2. Primarily to revitalize the economy:
    (a) liberalization of telecommunications;
    (b) ending of enforced specialization of function for firms in the financial industry;

(c) liberalization of foreign exchange transactions;

(d) freer entry into electricity generation (for steel firms and the like);

(e) greater flexibility of labour and employment regulation;

(f) permission for the creation of holding companies.

3. Primarily to achieve international compatibility:

(a) promoting mutual-recognition rules for building standards;

(b) adjustment of the Japan Industrial Standards system to international standards;

(c) licensing private firms, at home and abroad, to certify conformity to Japan Industrial Standards;

(d) allowing an increased role for foreign lawyers in international arbitration cases.

4. Primarily to reduce the burdens on the public:

(a) allowing wider scope for paperless electronic record-keeping, making of applications, etc.;

(b) relaxation of the vehicle inspection system;

(c) reduction (as yet not finalized) of the compulsory 66 hours of instruction required in driving schools;

(d) acceleration of the customs procedure;

(e) simplification of procedures for company mergers;

(f) passport validity extended from five to ten years;

Many eminently worthy developments, many of much more controversial import. In addition, many developments likely to lead, paradoxically, as in the financial sectors of post-Big Bang Britain, to an extension of regulations in order to protect the public from the increased incidence of fraudulent dealing, as competition intensifies and less reliance can be placed on trust and the constraining crust of convention. The new Financial Services Supervisory Agency has begun to show its teeth. It may come to need, not the 400 bank regulators it has now, but the 4,000 employed in the United States.

The outlook for the active state

But how will all this affect the characterization of the Japanese economy as one in which civil servants play a more important role than in the Anglo-Saxon economies, both in promoting growth and in arbitrating between private interests?

Their role in growth promotion is increasingly confined to adjustment of the macroeconomic framework and the minutiae of fiscal incentives—as in all the other OECD economies. There is still more direct intervention in the promotion of *civilian* R&D than elsewhere—bringing private firms together in research clubs, etc.—but the increasing complexity of the economy and increasing heterogeneity of the firms in any particular industry probably serve to reduce the effectiveness of such efforts.

Three factors affect civil servants' role in the hands-on regulation of competition, primarily in the interests of distributive justice (on the one hand achieving a balance between consumer and producer interests, and on the other fairness among producers). The first is the ideological climate, about which much has already been said. There is no doubt about the dominance of neoliberal ideas today, but in Japan's consensus society climatic change can be very rapid. The second is possible change in the tendency, elaborated above, for individuals and firms to regard themselves as part of an industry 'community', to be likely to consider the presidency of their industry association an honour not an imposition, and to draw a sense of security from their membership but accept that this imposes restraints on modes of competition and especially (*noblesse oblige*) on the bigger firms. Though attenuated, this is still an important element of Japanese economic life, as Ulrike Schaede, in a new book,[6] amply documents in convincing detail. And she sees little sign of anything but the most gradual attenuation. At the intersection of the 'industry as community' and the bureaucracy is the whole apparatus of the *shingikai*, the 'deliberation committees' for nearly every industry, great and small, which still have their importance—a system which Britain tried to copy in its Little Neddies in the 1970s and which Mrs Thatcher swept away. Schaede counted 252 of them in 1952, not including vast numbers of standing subcommittees. It is a safe bet that all the changes in regulations listed above received their final endorsement in the recommendation of some *shingikai* or other.

The third, imponderable factor is the quality and prestige of the civil service. For all the present attacks, and for all the reshuffling of ministries through the much-vaunted Administrative Reform, there is little sign of any fundamental change in the system, though it is too early to tell whether there will be long-term effects from the new parliamentary rule, introduced in the autumn of 1999, which tries, in the name of democracy, to allow—nay, compel—politicians to rule as well as reign. The new rule abolishes the age-old practice of allowing senior bureaucrats to answer for their ministry's policies in the committees where the real work of the Diet is done: eventually, perhaps, the electoral system, which at the moment produces a ruling party half of whom are the sons and nephews of defunct MPs who have used the family 'vote bank' to get elected,[7] will produce enough politicians intelligent enough to master their ministry briefs, but for the moment few will be likely to deviate far from the briefs their bureaucrats write for them.

As for the Administrative Reform, it resulted in bitterly resisted amalgamations of ministries; but what might really have changed the system—common recruitment to a unified civil service—was never on the cards. Long after the merger of the two ministries of Labour and Health and Welfare had been decided, but before it actually took place, it was only with difficulty that they were persuaded to adopt a joint recruitment round. Civil servants will still loyally belong to, and battle for the interests of, the particular ministry which recruits them. Pay levels in relation to the private sector and the internal pay and promotion system—including the *amakudari* moving on to second jobs, quangos, and the private sector—show no sign of changing.

The big question is whether the ministries, and in particular the elite ministries of Finance and Industry, will continue to be able to attract the best and the brightest as they have throughout most of the postwar period. The recruitment rounds of 1997–9 suggest that, so far, they can. One should not exaggerate the importance of what the newspaper headlines say. Students at the elite universities note that their professors are still only too flattered to be asked by civil servants to sit on some government *shingikai*. They note that in serious policy discussions in, say, the Nikkei, the positions reportedly taken by the various ministries are treated with some respect. They note that a politician minister who tries heavy-handed intervention in civil service appointments gets a bad press rather than congratulations. The prestige capital built up by a mandarinate whose origins lie two millennia back in Han China is not easily dissipated in the course of half a decade.

And indeed, just as there seemed in the autumn of 1999 to be something of a revival of national self-confidence, so there were signs that the bureaucracy was beginning to reassert itself. The Nikkei newspaper has, of course, been a stalwart source of support for the free marketeers, and one of its editorial writers professed himself a little alarmed by recent initiatives of the economic bureaucracy. In an article with the headlines 'Revival of interference in *gyokai* [industrial sectors]' and 'The economic bureaucracy unable to shed its bad habits' he wrote as follows:[8]

> Last week the head of the Shipbuilding Section of the Ministry of Transport published proposals for the restructuring of the shipbuilding industry pro-duced by a study group he personally had set up. The notion is that the seven major firms should consolidate into three . . . [Comment by a MITI section chief: 'Well it's good news that nowadays you don't have to be a Bureau Chief to set up private study groups: even section chiefs can do it.']
>
> The shipbuilding section chief grinned when I met him and, to disarm expected attack, started off 'I'm an anachronism [*anakuro*], would you say?' The idea is that to compete with the Korean industry, retain the capability of producing a wide variety of ships, and protect all the dependent supplier industries, the big builders have got to seek economies by combining their sales and design functions. But they seem slow in getting off their butts. Mitsubishi Heavy is probably viable on its own, but the others should double up. That is the blue-print he is going to take to the firms, and if they do insist on going it alone, they might find, should they apply for tax bene-fits for restructuring under the new Industrial Revitalization Law, that they are asked to 'think again'. Tough talk.

He goes on to quote the chairman of the Shipbuilding Association for the view that firms are in no mood to respond to bureaucratic calls to 'work together for the prosperity of the Japanese shipbuilding indus-try'. He points out that in these days, when 'it is the markets, chiefly the stock market, which determine the fate of firms', the ministries are playing a risky game, because if firms which follow their lead go under they will be blamed—as the Ministry of Finance is being blamed for the fate of the long-term credit banks. So why do the ministries persist? According to one official, because 'of course we are moving to market-oriented administration, deregulation, and all that. I understand that. But firms don't seem fully to understand the reality of the intensi-fication of competition and the transition to global oligopoly, and we think we can help them.'

The truth is, says the writer, that they chafe under 'market-oriented administration'. They can't give up. But in fact, firms aren't that dumb. So why don't officials get on with market liberalization—reform of the tax system and of regulatory law—and let the market work?

It is notable, however, that not even this Nikkei editorial writer, anti-bureaucracy marketeer though he be, recommends, or even mentions, the hostile takeover as a means of consolidating industries. His preference for an economy in which it is the stock market which decides the fate of firms does not take him that far.

— PART III

German Parallels

Chapter 8

Finanzplatz Deutschland

J APAN's post-Confucian neighbours apart, Germany is the country
which most obviously resembles Japan both in being at the beginning of the financialization/liberalization process and in starting, like
Japan, with more deeply institutionalized, uncertainty-eliminating
structures and a much more 'productivist' culture than either Britain
or the United States. The two countries are the two in which manufacturing's share of GDP has been least eroded; the two countries
whose citizens were shown by a recent poll to share gloomy fore-
bodings about the future sharply contrasting with the optimism
of respondents in the United States and Britain. They are also, as the
same poll showed, the two countries where, when asked the question
'Which in your view is the more important: to have an egalitarian
society without too big a gap between rich and poor, or to have an
open competitive society rewarding drive and ability?', more people
chose the former option, unlike in Britain and the United States.[1] A
look at the major similarities and differences between the two countries might illuminate the prospects that either or both will follow, or
resist, or modify the marketization/financialization process.

The public debate in the two countries shows many similarities.
Proof of the failure of *Modell Deutschland* is found in Germany's unemployment rate (which only in the summer of 1999 came to be as
prominently a matter of public concern in Japan) and in its failure to
match American or Japanese progress in the new information industries or biotechnology. The source of 'lessons'—as was made clear by
a series of articles on *Modell Amerika* in the main German business
weekly *Wirtschaftswoche* in 1996[2]—is, as in Japan, the United States.
And in addition to a transatlantic backflow of MBAs and economics
Ph.D.s comparable to the transpacific flow to Japan, the carriers of
American practice and ideology include a number of businessmen
once prominent in America now in influential positions in German
industry—Sommer of Deutsche Telekom for example.

As in Japan, deregulation and privatization occupy a prominent place among those lessons. And so, crucially, does the notion that high returns on capital—*to shareholders* and not just to all stakeholder sharers in value-added—are a crucial condition for survival in global markets. The major differences between the two countries lie in two things. First, in Germany integration into Europe provides an extra and important dimension to debates about institutional reform, particularly about financial regulation and corporate governance. This has ambiguous effects as far as financialization is concerned, since it means accommodation to the more or less equally 'continental' France and Italy, as well as to the Anglo-Saxon United Kingdom. Secondly, whereas in Japan those who advocate more attention to shareholders only rarely admit that this might mean less attention to employees, in Germany the battle between reformers and defenders of the employee-favouring firm is clearly joined and fought in class terms: business interests versus the workers and their unions. The major concern of those who call for reform is to reduce high wages, change the rigidity of the wage-bargaining system, abolish the 'industrial democracy' impediments to speedy decision-taking, and lower the generous levels of social security benefits, all of which (together with high business taxes) are seen as responsible for a serious loss of competitiveness. Such changes are called for, in Germany as in Japan, as necessary measures to improve competitiveness for the benefit of the whole nation; but their implications for the redistribution of income, wealth, and power are more overtly recognized and fought over in Germany.

These open German debates are debates—conflicts—over institutional changes which can only be brought about by political decision and legislation. Meanwhile a variety of evolutionary changes are also taking place, some of which are not much the subject of debate in themselves but may cumulatively have a profound effect on outcomes. The financial field is one of the most important sources of such changes.

German finance

First, something about the pattern of financial flows in the two economies. To start with, a smaller proportion of German than Japanese firms are quoted on the stock market: total market valuation of equities was, respectively, 23 per cent (Frankfurt only) and 78 per cent (Tokyo only) of GDP at the end of 1995 (it had climbed to well over 100 per cent in Japan at the peak of the boom). Germany has a bigger fixed-interest bond market, however: 88 per cent of GDP compared with 42 per cent in Japan. Total bank lending in both countries (end 1996) was 97 per cent of GDP, with manufacturing taking 15 per cent in Japan and 9 per cent in Germany. (Thirty per cent in both countries goes to housing, construction, and real estate, though with a much higher proportion going to the last in Japan—the source of the banks' bubble trouble.) Of new securities issues (excluding government debt instruments), in the first half of the 1990s equity accounted for less than 1 per cent in Japan and 2–3 per cent in Germany. Corporate bonds were around 15–20 per cent in Japan but close to zero in Germany; the bulk of the issues in both countries—65–70 per cent in Japan and 70–80 per cent in Germany—were bonds issued by financial institutions (public as well as private).[3]

The difference in the size of the stock markets in the two countries derives not so much from a different propensity of German and Japanese firms to rely on equity finance as from a complex of historical reasons. Before the major upheavals of war mobilization and occupation, as recently as the 1930s, Japanese corporations were more clearly shareholder-controlled and stock-market-financed (rather than bank-controlled and bank-financed) than were German corporations. It was the war which gave the banks a similar crucial role in both countries. More recently, continuing family ownership and control has been a good deal more prevalent in Germany (as in Italy and France). Quite apart from the effects of the war and the deliberate dissolution of *zaibatsu* family holdings, ever since Mitsui and Mitsubishi started the process in the 1880s, Japanese firms have made the transition to public corporation more rapidly than elsewhere. That is to say, they have become bureaucracies, carefully recruiting carefully selected lifetime managers, while their founding families gracefully retire to rentier status—or, as in firms such as Toyota until recently, accept 'Emperor' status while Shogun managers actually run the firm. (Perhaps this is because of the long Confucian tradition of meritocracy: it is interesting that in Italy the word *meritocrazia* is primarily used apropos family management giving way to professional management.) Stock exchange quotation, as a symbol of achieving 'proper' corporate status, hence acquired in Japan a certain cachet. (Now, in both countries, that cachet attaches instead to achieving a listing in New York.)

Size apart, there are two senses in which both the German and the Japanese economies are far from being as stock-market-centred as the British and American economies. Overwhelmingly the most important one is that the equity market has hitherto served as a market only in income-yielding assets, not also as a market in corporate control. 'Rumours that Z was preparing to mount a bid for XY sent the latter's shares 8 per cent higher yesterday' is not the sort of thing one used to see in the press of either country.

There are two elements in that difference: corporate behaviour and saver behaviour. As for the first, mergers and acquisitions of any kind, however brought about, face greater 'enterprise culture' problems of integration than in Britain or the United States. German firms share some of the characteristics of communities which, as we saw, are so strong in Japanese firms. German workers do not identify with their company as much as Japanese workers. On the other hand, a worker who heard that the works council had been told that Siemens was selling his factory to Mannesmann would not be as indifferent to the change as a British worker who turned up on a Monday to find that his factory had been sold to British Aerospace by GEC. And for corporate strategists, the problems of integrating two corps of, if not lifetime-employed, at least long-tenured managers would loom as even more serious problems. Doubtless these considerations played some part in the decision by Daimler-Benz—whose CEO is known to be no lover of the trammelling constraints of co-determination— to incorporate the merged Chrysler/Daimler corporation in Germany rather than in the United States. The conformity of American managers and workers to alien regimes can doubtless be bought more easily.

So mergers of any kind can be problematic, and those that do take place depend not, as in a hostile takeover bid, on manager-financiers offering rewards to the mass of anonymous stockholders, but on managers getting the agreement, in face-to-face contact, of representatives of large blocks of holdings. And in both Japan and Germany these major shareholders usually have more concern with their business relationship with the company than with the profits they might derive from its shares. The Japanese cross-shareholding system and the important role in it of banks and life insurance companies have already been described at length. In Germany the banks are not only major shareholders in industrial firms themselves and frequently rep-

resented on firms' supervisory boards in that capacity, but also provide a safe-keeping service to, and vote the proxies for, large numbers
of private shareholders. Moreover, having long been the universal
banks that British, American, and Japanese banks are seeking to
become, their ties with the firms they serve have been multistranded,
covering insurance, securities underwriting, and trading and business consulting as well as the usual commercial credit and longer-term
finance. Their willingness to provide the last, of course, is frequently
recorded as a major strength of German manufacturing.

As in Japan, however, the role of the banks in corporate control is
far from being the whole of the story. There is also a dense network
of cross-shareholdings among industrial corporations. 'Corporations
themselves hold more corporate shares and more Board seats than
individuals, banks, investment companies, or any other type of investor.'[4] Indeed, some go so far as to speak of two distinct subsystems
in German industry: the companies with long-standing historical ties
to the banks, which category includes some of the major corporations
such as Siemens and Daimler-Benz, and those where non-bank cross-
holdings are more important. And there is some controversy as to
which is the more innovative and profitable arrangement.[5]

Either way, German firms for the most part have committed
shareholders. Takeovers by hostile use of market power remain a rare
phenomenon.

The second sense in which Germany, like Japan, has not been a
stock-market-centred economy is reflected in the minimal space that
the most commonly read middle-class newspapers devote to 'family
finance' (advice to investors) compared with, say, their British counterparts. Equity makes up a similarly small proportion of household
assets in the two countries—about 6 per cent in 1996, compared with
20 per cent in the United States. (Another calculation three years
later, at the height of the Goldilocks economy, put the value of the
average household's holdings of equity at 145 per cent of annual
disposable income in the United States, compared with less than 20
per cent in Germany and only slightly more in Japan.) Savers in both
countries are prone to put their savings into deposits or fixed-interest
bonds and forget about them. In Germany, given the insistence on the
'good banking practice' of matching maturities of long-term loans to
those of long-term fixed-interest deposits, this is a factor which has
greatly facilitated long-term lending to (and long-term thinking in)

industry. Trust in the Bundesbank's record for controlling inflation also contributed a great deal to the whole syndrome.

Furthermore, pension provision in both societies has minimized the role of the stock market. The public pension fund in Germany has been little more than a liquidity reserve for a basically pay-as-you-go system, but in any case has been formally forbidden from holding that reserve in equity. (The Japanese fund has become more substantial, but is used primarily through the Fiscal Investment and Loan Programme for development projects, only exceptionally, of late years, for *sub rosa* bolstering of stock market prices in so-called Price-Keeping Operations.) Corporate pensions in both countries are predominantly of the defined-benefit type, and pension funds play a much less prominent role in the stock market, since company pension funds are largely held within the firm (in Germany, protected against the firm's bankruptcy by a compulsory insurance system) and are one major source of long-term finance.

Signs of change

What are the trends in Germany running parallel to those we have observed in Japan? Here is a list of some of them in summary form:[6]

Many more firms are getting a stock market quotation, particularly since the Small AG law of 1994, which encourages smaller companies to make public issues of stock. The total market valuation of German quoted companies rose to some 55 per cent of GNP in July 1999, to be compared with 82 per cent in Japan, according to the *Nikkei Weekly*.[7]

Large firms, with high levels of self-financing and access to international securities markets, are becoming less dependent on bank finance, though the small and medium-sized firms (the *Mittelstand*) have strong-as-ever ties to their local house banks, particularly to the extensive network of public banks (the 17 *Land* banks and the 600-plus municipal banks—all mandated to pursue public-prosperity goals as well as profits) and to the nearly 3,000 cooperative banks.

Here there is emerging a sharp division between the public savings and the cooperative bank networks on the one hand, and the commercial banks on the other. The public system has changed least, particularly in relation to the financing of firms. In Eastern Germany, for instance, the *Land* banks have been almost alone in offering new equity participation to firms. But the major commercial banks, especially the big three—Deutsche, Dresdner, and Commerzbank—have been showing strong globalization effects. Their strategic planning has been dominated in recent years by the desire to become global players in the same league as the major American banks. 'For reasons related to national history and politics, German finance capital was historically less cosmopolitan in outlook and enjoyed less international market access than British capital.'[8] It is catching up fast. The Deutsche Bank's much-troubled acquisition of Morgan Grenfell and Dresdner's of Kleinwort Benson—purchases designed to strengthen their role as investment bankers—was one symptom of these new ambitions. Deutsche Bank's Managing Director was quite clear about his strategic directions in his annual report to shareholders in May 1996. Hitherto, he said, the bank had simply

> acted from Germany as an intermediary between those lending money and those borrowing it. But today's markets demand more . . . The forces driving change are information technology and prosperity, which is growing not just in the West. The process is being accompanied by the globalization of the world economy. The banking industry is undergoing a revolution . . . Competition is tougher than ever. Deutsche Bank aims not only to master it, but to emerge from it stronger.

And he goes on to set out three major aims: to be the leading European bank and one of the top ten worldwide, to become the prime European investment bank and catch up with the global leaders, and to maintain the bank's triple-A rating.

This shift of central strategic concerns, together with the publicly promoted growth of financial markets (see below) and the increased inter-bank competition and short-term bottom-line-ism which that competition induces, has made the commercial banks (a) more concerned about the yield on the assets they hold, and thus less enthusiastic about the relationship-cementing value of their equity holdings, and (b) more cautious/calculative about landing themselves with the risk of having to perform the traditional role of a major bank shareholder—namely, to bail out, or in extreme cases get involved in the management of, failing firms. This has resulted in the major large banks selling off, or reducing, some of their equity holdings in large firms. They remain major shareholders for the larger firms, but whether or not they will continue to serve to insulate firms from stock market pressures remains problematic. Deutsche Bank decided at the end of 1998 to create a separate subsidiary to handle its shareholder operations, thus creating a sort of deliberate Chinese wall between its operations as creditor and its operations as owner, making it clear that the units playing the ownership role would be primarily concerned with extracting shareholder value. The Deutsche Bank chairman insisted that it did not mean selling off these holdings. The Bank would continue to be a buyer as well as a seller of equity. These holdings have 'made money for our shareholders in the past and we hope to continue to do so'. But, continues the *Financial Times* reporting the announcement, 'analysts suspect the move . . . is the first step by Deutsche towards gradually jettisoning its non-banking business. Its close relationship with a wide spectrum of German industry is seen as increasingly unacceptable to shareholders, especially in the United States where Deutsche is keen to grow.'[9] The Dresdner Bank and Munich Re followed suit.[10]

There is also a collective and officially backed desire—indeed, campaign: the *Finanzplatz Deutschland* campaign, Germany's answer to Britain's Big Bang—to turn Frankfurt into a financial centre rivalling London; an ambition measurably furthered by Frankfurt's becoming the location of the European Central Bank. Through two omnibus Financial Market Promotion Laws in 1990 and 1992, new markets in options and futures and an over-the-counter unlisted share market were created. A new regulatory body was established (the Federal Supervisory Office for Securities Trading) to substitute for traditional cooperative self-regulation, and it showed exemplary zeal in cracking down on insider trading and setting up a computer system to detect it. It has also instituted new rules for disclosure of major shareholdings, publishes its own reference guide to such shareholdings, and has updated the takeover code to safeguard the position of minority shareholders (though without the effect of making the mounting of a takeover bid easier).[11] It has steadily strengthened its supervision of the investment brokers and asset managers who trade in securities (4,500 of them by July 1998). While attracting foreign capital may have been one object of this activity, the dominant aim has been to give private individual investors the same protection and the same information as was previously available only to the professional investor.[12]

Given this drive to construct effective financial markets, there was much rejoicing when the Frankfurt futures market registered more trades in 1998 than London's LIFFE. Involvement in this more intensive market competition (*international* competition: it was an American firm which made off with the contract to underwrite the flotation of Deutsche Telekom) has chiefly affected the large banks, in the ways just described, but it has also had some knock-on effects on the all-important public savings banks networks. Hitherto, banking was about dealing with people and firms, and could thus be territorially circumscribed. The public savings banks, for their part, were required by law to respect each other's local bailiwicks, while their associations and the regional bank of their own *Land* provided common services. The cooperative bank network did the same. Competition was between the two systems, and between them both and the commercial banks. Now, for the locally rooted banks, too, banking increasingly involves dealing in money instruments in national, or indeed international, markets. This has several consequences.

First, the solidarity of the networks is put in question. The stronger of the local banks have found themselves wanting to deal 'over the heads' of their local regional banks, and in competition with other local banks. The long-term effects of this erosion of the solidarity of the two systems are hard to gauge, but it is clear that it represents a diminution of the density and importance of relational banking.

More importantly, the public status of the savings banks and the regional *Land* banks is put into question—not least by the German private commercial banks, to which some of the most aggressive *Land* banks have become direct competitors over a whole range of corporate commercial business. The private banks have appealed to the European Commission to declare that the cheaper access to capital which the public banks get from their privileged status constitutes an unfair subsidy. The *Land* banks are 'fragmented, distorted by state subsidies, and unprofitable' and obviously ought to be privatized, is *The Economist*'s comment on the dispute.[13] It is not so obvious to those who want to retain the means of furthering industrial policy and investment in projects—infrastructure projects, for example—which have social externalities but are unlikely to make commercial rates of return. One solution which meets the unfair competition argument but retains scope for public activism is to split banks into two—a guaranteed part which does the public business and an unguaranteed part which competes commercially. Plans to do just that are under discussion in Baden-Württemberg.

It is not only at the European level that level-playing-field arguments are being used to force changes. The Basle committee of the Bank of International Settlements is currently revising its 1988 accord. The arrangements have as their ostensible purpose the enforcement of a uniform level of prudence which will make bank failures—and the possibility of a contagious international spread of bank failures—unlikely. Assets have to be matched by the bank's own 'core' capital, up to a percentage which depends on the asset's riskiness. Both the definition of core capital and the classification of assets by their riskiness are clearly points of potential contention, but the contention comes not so much from the degree of prudence that is assured, as from the fact that the banks of a country whose rules allow a loose interpretation of the 'capital' and 'risk' definitions in effect gain a competitive advantage. They have to mobilize less capital for their operations. German negotiators are currently in contention with their American counterparts and are accused of seeking advantages for German banks in general. Again, the *Land* banks in particular are under American fire. Their government guarantees can perfectly well substitute for capital reserves as a 'prudence' requirement. But those guarantees also clearly provide a competitive advantage, since they give them access to cheaper capital.

Herein is a clear illustration of the way in which the global operation of enterprises—in this case banks—and the strong fairness, level-playing-field arguments for reciprocal treatment by states of each others' firms require the framing of rules for that purpose which have to be based on some international consensus as to what sort of animals those firms are and what their objectives are. The dominant consensus about banks—assumed by British and American negotiators to be Revealed Truth—is that they are (a certain amount of discretionary charity activity apart) organizations devoted solely to making profits, regulated by governments to ensure prudence and transparency and to protect depositors through compulsory insurance schemes, but not guaranteed and not expected to serve any public purpose. The banking community in Germany, led by the private banks, may already be wholly converted to that consensus view, but those who want—like, presumably, the majority of *Land* governments—to preserve the right to have a different kind of bank with a cross-subsidizing mixture of public and private purposes come under strong pressure to conform.

I have made clear in Chapter 1 why I think that trying to preserve such a mixture is a perfectly reasonable position, but whether it will prevail or not is a matter of doubt, given the extent to which those who harbour such nostalgia for the nation-state, national cultures, and national economic systems are on the defensive. The gung-ho globalizers have already won over enough of the Tokyo and Frankfurt banking communities to make the effective deployment of such arguments unlikely.

And one more thing which makes it unlikely is that, while these changes are happening in the structure of banks and the strategic thinking of bankers, changes are also going on at the household interface. 'German savers and investors may grow more *rechenhaft*', wrote Streeck in 1997.[14] 'The good grey burghers of Zurich and Frankfurt are beginning to wonder what it feels like to win the jackpot with one spin of the roulette wheel', wrote Michel Albert in 1991.[15] Whether from calculation or the gambling instinct, they have. Markets are playing a slowly increasing part in personal savings. Time and savings deposits fell from 44 per cent of household assets in 1988 to 34 per cent in 1996, while equity holdings went from 3 to 6 per cent and holdings of other securities from 15 to 24 per cent. Although a cutback in state pensions is so far a matter of public discussion rather than an officially announced plan, more individuals are supplementing their retirement prospects with pension funds even though the taxation benefits which encourage this in Britain and the United States, and which are so avidly discussed in Japan, are not available. There are now 34 investment funds in Germany, of which 9 are of foreign origin.[16]

Chapter 9

The Co-determined Firm

CLEARLY of central importance is the structure of the firm and the objectives of managers that it conditions. In summary form:

- In a 'normal' (Anglo-Saxon) capitalist firm, capital, through its manager-agents, hires labour.
- In a production cooperative, labour, through its elected managers, hires capital.
- In a Japanese firm, autonomous managers hire capital under the constraints of the capital markets as modified by business ties, and they hire labour under the constraints of multiple conventions brought about primarily by the similarity of employment conditions between themselves as managers and other employees and the consequent sense of the whole body of employees being a sort of community of which they are the responsible elders.

In Germany, by contrast, it is not so much convention as law—laws which reflect an acknowledged starting-point of class antagonism—which governs the owner/manager/worker relationship. Through the twin devices of co-determination in the firm and the legal enforcement of bargained wage contracts in the industry, the system balances the rights and power of employees against those of shareholders, and thus constrains managers to be as concerned with the welfare of employees as with their duties to their shareholders, if not more so.

That the co-determination system is alive and well was shown in the events at the top of BMW at the end of 1998. The shareholders' favourite candidate for the CEO's job was forced to stand down as a result of opposition from employee representatives on the supervisory board. This system has roots in 1890s laws of catholic corporatist inspiration designed to promote works councils, thereby mitigating class conflict by institutionalizing the positive-sum elements of the capitalist employment relation. (This contrasts with the contemporary British answer to class conflict, as embodied in the Webbs' report on trade unions, of institutionally recognizing the *zero-sum* elements of the relationship and offering institutional means of reaching compromise.) Works council legislation was extended during the First World War—in a form which did not challenge property or authority structures—and re-enacted again in Weimar in a form which significantly did.[1] In its modern version it derives from arrangements reached in the immediate postwar period, pressed for by the revived Social Democratic Party and cemented by the authority of the occupying army in the British zone. Union opposition to works councils as an attempt to coopt workers and blunt the edge of their class militancy was not as strong then as it had been in Weimar. (Forty-two people were killed outside the Reichstag when machine-gun fire ended a protest march by 'revolutionary workers and militant trade unionists' against the Works Council Act of 1920.[2]) Nevertheless, the pull between class and enterprise has been a feature of the whole history of the system—the pull between works council members prone to develop the 'enterprise consciousness' which has become the Japanese norm and the unions trying to keep alive the transenterprise sense of class solidarity and stamp on any manifestation of 'enterprise egotism' which loses sight of the zero-sum elements in the capital–labour relationship. But more about that below.

German firms have a supervisory board and a management board. Briefly, co-determination comes in three forms. In the coal and steel industry, which was the first to be regulated and has the strongest, parity, form of co-determination, employee representatives have half the seats on the supervisory board (with a chairman elected by board members), and those representatives have veto-power control over the appointment of the labour relations director on the management board. About 400,000 employees were covered by such arrangements at the end of 1996, three-quarters of them actually in coal and steel, the rest in other industrial branches of firms predominantly—or once predominantly—in the coal and steel industries.

The second system established under the 1976 legislation for other large firms (over 2,000 employees), gives shareholders the edge over employees; shareholders have the same number of delegates as employees, but the chairman is elected by the shareholder representatives, and he has, if necessary, an extra casting vote (though there are cumbersome procedures for exercising it if the issue is the all-important one of appointments to the management board). The unions have long argued for the extension of full parity to all firms, but it is highly doubtful that Schröder's Minister of Labour, who once as a trade unionist gave expression to those demands, will be able to do more, in office, than continue to show himself sympathetic. In many firms the powers of the supervisory board have *de facto* become attenuated, and in some firms a dominant shareholder group deals directly with the management board, overruling the employee representatives as a matter of course whenever necessary.[3] The difference between the two systems is, however, not great, although some clearly deem it to be so: Mannesmann fought a long court battle in 1999 to establish that its coal and steel interests were now sufficiently minor to allow it to move from the first to the second system.[4]

In firms with fewer than 2,000 but more than 500 employees, employee representatives are entitled to one-third of the seats on the board. For even smaller firms, there are no legal requirements, and few of those which have formal structures of supervisory and management boards elect employee representatives to the former.

Many of these smaller firms do, however, have works councils—the other, and more important part of the co-determination system. Firms with more than 500 workers are obliged to establish such councils—one in each establishment and a central council for the firm. Employees are elected, irrespective of union membership. However, a common practice in many firms—the resolution of what was once, frequently, a tense conflictual relationship between the works council and union shop-steward committees—is to have a 'union slate' for works council elections. Unions belonging to the DGB still win some 80 per cent of the seats. The law lays on the works council the general obligation to cooperate in 'a spirit of mutual trust' for the 'good of the employees and of the establishment', and to negotiate with a serious desire to reach agreement, eschewing 'acts of industrial warfare'. Members are enjoined to maintain the confidentiality of any trade or business secrets with which they are entrusted, and some are required to be released full time for council duties—not more than one person in plants with below 600 workers, but at least seven in establishments with over 5,000. The electors include all employees except a small group of top managers, and voting turnouts hover around 80 per cent.

The establishing law distinguishes between those matters which are the subject of co-determination by the works council and those matters on which it has only the right to be consulted or informed. The former include practically everything to do with pay, hours, leave, etc., except for anything which would run counter to the arrangements set in industry-wide bargaining between the unions and the employers. Councils also regulate personnel matters, not only setting guidelines for recruitment, training, etc., but also having the right to veto certain individual personnel decisions. They also have extensive powers in matters of health and safety and of training. There is frequently a training standing committee of the works council as well as a finance committee, which gets monthly reports on the financial health of the firm.

Co-determination on supervisory boards and works councils is one half of the German 'dual system' of industrial relations (better called 'employment system relations', though even in Germany the top-down, manipulative business school term 'human resource management' seems more likely to take over). The other half is the system of bargaining over wages and conditions between associations of employers and trade unions. Both employers' associations and trade unions encompass whole industrial sectors. The rationalization of the process introduced after the war—and the sheer size of the union of the engineering (metalworking) industry, IG Metall—gave it a position of wage leadership which convention has subsequently reinforced. The annual contracting takes place not only industry by industry, but also, formally, region by region. Again, however, the precedent set by a leading region—by Baden-Württenberg for the metalworking industry, for instance—tends to determine at least the crucial variable of the percentage wage rise for all the other regions, though substantial regional differences in wage structures, holiday arrangements, etc. can still survive, notably since the East German *Länder* joined the system.

Like the co-determination system, the wage-bargaining system has a strong legal base. *Tarifautonomie*, the right of bargaining parties to set their wage levels free from state interference, is even protected in the Constitution. But the contracts so struck and registered can be enforced in law. It is also open to the Minister of Labour of each *Land* to give legal authority to the terms of any contract and enforce its wage levels and conditions of employment on firms in the relevant industry which are not members of the employers' association (though the conditions for doing so are complex—application by both parties whose membership covers more than 50 per cent of the industry—and the provision is not in practice much used). Union members can sue employers belonging to associations which have put their signature to a contract for infringement of its terms. One point which has long been at issue, and which is of considerable importance for future developments, is whether the unions themselves should also have the right so to sue, when the affected employees are themselves unwilling to do so. Only recently, in 1999, did a Federal Labour Court decision appear by and large to grant that right.

There are two important differences between Germany and Japan, which crucially affect the responses in the two countries to moves to shift firms from an employee-favouring to a shareholder-favouring stance. The first is the degree of legalism or legal entrenchment. The German system is enshrined in law; the Japanese system primarily in convention. One small indicator is that new cases reaching Japanese labour tribunals number somewhat over 3,000 a year, in Germany 470,000.

The second difference lies in the implicit assumptions which inform the collective-bargaining process. The industry-wide bargainers in Germany define themselves primarily as representatives of wage-earners and profit-takers, respectively, engaged in a largely zero-sum trial of strength (the strong growth of profits contrasting with slower growth of wages was a major union argument in the tense 1999 IG Metall–Gesamtmetall negotiations,[5] for instance). Secondarily they see themselves as members of an industry who share a joint concern with that industry's overall competitiveness. Thirdly, they are German citizens who want a sound macroeconomy and, however much they may denounce the conservatism of the bankers, know from experience (including the fate of Oskar Lafontaine) that the European Central Bank will follow the Bundesbank tradition in severely punishing with deflation and increased unemployment any inflationary wage settlements.

The participants in enterprise wage negotiations in Japan see things differently. True, for some months before they get to the bargaining table for the annual spring negotiations they will have been engaged —or reading in the newspapers about people who have been directly engaged—in arguments about what would be a just and macro-economically affordable average wage increase across the whole economy, and both unions and managers will belong to federations which, on the union side, occasionally try to rally the troops with talk of 'winning victories in the struggle against capital'. But, although those arguments do set an 'expectations framework' for their bargaining, the union negotiators see themselves primarily as fellow-members of a particular enterprise, the one side representing the people who want money and benefits now and the other the people who have the responsibility for finding money for other things—investment, price reduction, and market expansion which they can justify as bringing better wages and benefits in the future. With dividends usually held to a standard percentage of par value, profits represent the cash available for investment or wage increases rather than the size of the capitalist's 'take'.

In short, class still counts for a lot in Germany. It is the enterprise which counts in Japan.

Attack and defence

The American investor-protection movement has its counterpart in Germany too. The two main organizations (one specifically for small investors) were founded in the 1960s. The more important one has close links with the Free Democratic Party and owes much of its strength to that party's recently much diminished fortunes. In the 1960s it was able to draw support also from the traditional left-wing criticism of *Finanzkapital*—deep-seated resentment of the *Macht der Banken*. Indeed, it prompted the Cartel Office to establish a Monopoly Commission which periodically reviewed possible abuses in bank control over industry. Both organizations are small bit-players on the political scene, but in recent years renewed impetus has been gained by the main organization, the German Foundation for the Protection of Security Ownership (DSW). This is a result (again a parallel with Japan) of a small number of business scandals—at Metallgesellschaft, Schneider, etc.—highlighting the weakness of supervisory boards' ability to curb devious, indeed criminal, behaviour on the part of runaway managers. In this, again, there has been no conflict of interest with the unions. They too have wanted to increase the powers of supervisory boards.[6]

But the other strand of the movement, the attempt to reverse the tendency of managers to be more concerned with their employees' welfare than that of their shareholders, is a different matter, and one that came to be a central issue only in the 1990s. There have always been German employers who envied the untrammelled 'right to manage' of their British and American counterparts and chafed at the restrictions which the co-determination system entailed. At the time of the 1976 legislation they succeeded in strengthening the powers of the management committee at the expense of the co-determined supervisory board. They became more vocal in the mid-1990s when one of their number, Hans-Olaf Henkel, former CEO of IBM Germany, became the president of the main employers' federation (the BDI) and a member of Daimler's supervisory board. Henkel frequently and provocatively made clear his view that both parts of the dual system—co-determination and the legislative support for industry-wide collective bargaining—badly need amendment to reduce trade union and worker power:

> For two decades, co-determination has shown it can bog down decisions, delay restructurings, block divestitures, suppress boardroom debate and even cause the creation of a cumbersome tier of shadow shareholder boards that hold preparatory meetings in private without union-elected members, Mr. Henkel said . . . Candidates for board positions become like politicians kissing babies to win votes of labour representatives . . .[7]

The time-wasting cost of democracy is a long-standing source of complaint, but the new thing about the 1990s expression of such sentiments was that it was frequently coupled—notably in statements by leading businessmen such as Schrempp of Daimler-Benz—with declarations of the need for managers to focus on the creation of shareholder value.

Towards the end of the Kohl regime, however, the stridency of such declarations diminished. One significant turning-point involved a piece of cost-reducing and worker-privilege-reducing legislation—responding particularly to the high level of sickness absenteeism in German industry—to reduce sick-pay compensation to 80 per cent from the 100 per cent specified by the existing law and reconfirmed in some current labour contracts. The metalworking employers' association, wanting to back up Kohl and put on a tough 'right to manage' front, urged its members to implement the change immediately on the grounds that the law superseded existing collective agreements. BMW refused: with full order books it did not want a fight with the union.

Daimler-Benz went ahead, faced intense internal conflict, and had to backtrack. The employers then approached the union to bring the 1996 bargaining round forward to get the issue settled, and a compromise was reached: the 100 per cent was restored, but the wage on which it was calculated was stripped of extras. The union also settled that year for what was seen as a modest wage increase.[8]

The prospect of an SPD government and the unlikelihood of the Kohl Government in its dying years being able to institute dramatic changes cooled off the debate. It was possible for middle-of-the-roaders, with the support of the Bertelsmann and the Hans-Böckler foundations, to gather a sufficiently representative group of business leaders, academics, and trade unionists to write what counted as an authoritative endorsement of the co-determination system during the election year.[9]

The report contains much discussion on the need for the system to adapt dynamically to change, the nature of which it spells out as follows:

- shorter product cycles and intensified pressure for quick decisions make it more difficult to 'offset extended consensus-forming times by short implementation times';
- the high-quality markets in which Germany specialized are increasingly subject to price competition, so it is more difficult to offset the difficulty of making process innovations because of the need for consensus by faster product innovation;
- co-determination is good at producing incremental innovations; less so the quantum-leap innovations the world now demands;
- the problem of unemployment: co-determination favours insiders; can it help with the problems of job-seekers too?
- decentralization of decision-making requires reassessment of the relationship between central and plant works councils;
- changes in employment patterns: greater heterogeneity of the workforce, more outsourcing, new pay systems and profit-sharing participation;
- reduced investor time-horizons and internationalization of capital markets 'force co-determined German companies to come to terms with investors who are increasingly demanding, short-term oriented, less loyal and willing to compromise, and who are used to indicating their preferences regarding corporate strategy and corporate earnings primarily via the capital market'.[10]

The report is short on concrete suggestions on what form this dynamic adjustment should take. No legal changes were necessary. The system of co-determination was flexible. What was necessary was 'embedding co-determination in a cooperative culture that corresponds to the specific characteristics of the firm and in which participants can rely on informal agreements based on mutual trust to a greater extent than previously'.[11]

But whatever the modifications co-determination might need or have forced on it, the Commission was clear that its main mission was to endorse it. And the 'trust' of that last sentence is at the heart of its reasons. 'As an insurance policy against breaches of trust in the workplace, German co-determination law has made a decisive contribution to creating and stabilizing a cooperative corporate culture.'[12] What this means in practice may be illustrated by a puzzling fact about German wage systems. Piecework payment is still quite widespread in German engineering. One reason is that piecework, unlike the basic-time rates, can be worked out at factory level between management and the works council, and so can be a legitimate means of paying more than the industry rates. But it seems not to be considered a problem, whereas in the British engineering industry it was a major problem and was almost universally abandoned in the late 1960s. Why should that be?

Piecework pay is a complex form of incentive, expensive to maintain. (Twenty people in a German factory of 1,500 employees were employed full-time on the accounting mechanics of operating it, and many more hours were spent on establishing the standard times for new operations.) Apart from that possibly contentious rate-setting, there is also the ever-present possibility of friction over several variables: the definition of the minimum *quality* necessary for work to count, the definition of defective material, the monitoring of downtime which is not the fault of the worker, and the time-rate to be applied for such downtime. In 1960s Britain, where each possibility of friction was likely to be exploited by a prevalent opportunism—the assumption on the part of many workers and their shop stewards that you got away with what you could because beating the bosses was the name of the game—the hassle (and the knock-on effects on other forms of cooperation) was seen as not being worth the incentive effects. German managers judge otherwise, and it is a reasonable assumption that this is because 'the cooperative corporate culture'—the shared concern with the firm's prosperity and its reputation for quality—is strong enough to create a set of consensual norms: cheating is defined in more or less the same way by both managers and workers. They have similar conceptions about what constitutes acceptable quality, and a similar pride in, and sense of conscience about, producing it.

The contrast with Britain is clear, but so also, in the other direction, is the contrast with Japan. German wages are linked to job functions, and although, over the years, unions have come to accede in annual contracts to a certain flexibility in strict rate-for-the-job pay systems (some of which have the effect *de facto* of rewarding seniority), that rate-for-the-job system contrasts sharply with Japanese rate-for-the-person career-pay systems and the pattern of incentives which they imply. In the early 1990s, when Japanese 'lean production' was all the vogue in the management press, there was strong resistance from German unions, both to 'team-work' which would blur the connection between individual effort and reward, and to any 'quality circle' suggestion of unpaid worker contributions to the firm's (i.e. to the employer's) prosperity.

Evolutionary change: managerial strategy

There seems, as a reading of the Bertelsmann–Hans Böckler report just quoted would suggest, little likelihood of much change in the legislative arrangements governing industrial relations and co-determination. What about actual changes in management behaviour? At the level of rhetoric there were some strident statements in the mid-1990s about the dominant importance of shareholder value by prominent chief executives of major companies, such as Schrempp of Daimler-Benz, who famously invited the senior managers he was addressing just after his inauguration to put their hands up if they knew at what price their shares were being traded that day. (Few did, which prompted a scolding and a declaration that things would be different from now on.) There has since been some back-tracking: as the CEO of Veba, a firm more deeply involved with foreign investors than most (they own 40 per cent of its shares), said in an interview with *Die Zeit*:[13] 'I don't use the expression "shareholder value" any longer. The connotation is too negative. For me the debate is about value-oriented company policy.' A merely verbal adjustment, perhaps, but it is noticeable that, as mentioned above, when Schrempp merged Daimler-Benz with Chrysler he chose to keep the combined company incorporated in Germany even with all the co-determination constraints on management that that implied.

In the long run more important are the changes in the pay and conditions of employment for managers which seem designed to sharpen the class-division line (around which co-determination is indeed built) between managers, who have to give priority to shareholder value, and the people they manage. One important factor is that enough German managers are in an international executive labour market to make a difference—not the case in Japan. This has some importance for management styles and the transfer of the ideologies and strategic assumptions of American business across the Atlantic. What it means to be a CEO, your power to shape a firm and its strategy, is indeed different in Germany from what it means in the United States. German management is still more collective, the CEO more like the 'speaker of the board' (the official title in the Deutsche Bank). But it is nevertheless closer to American practice than the leading-from-behind style of the typical Japanese company president. A Sommer can transit easily from running Sony Electronics in America to running Deutsche Telekom. The *New York Herald Tribune*[14] can evaluate the impact of a Werner Dieter on Mannesmann in exactly the same terms and by the same criteria as for that of Welch on General Electric.

The international-market effect pulls up executive salary levels, too, if not to American levels, at least not far behind the British—a factor which has some bearing on the degree to which there is a sense of the firm as community.

But more important are the modes of payment. Of the 30 companies in the Dax index, 18 had introduced stock options for managers by the end of 1998. And whereas in Japan there is a half-heartedness about stock-option schemes—more to impress American investors with the firm's 'modernity' than real incentives—in Germany they are more likely to be for real. There has also been a change in the bonus incentive system. Bonuses were once collective; if they were variable, they varied across the firm according to overall company performance. Now, they are more frequently linked to achieving profit targets in decentralized profit-centres.[15]

The creation of such centres was one major objective of the restructuring of large conglomerates which was so much a feature of the 1990s. One of the leaders in the process was Schrempp of Daimler-Benz, who took over in 1995 from a CEO predecessor committed to building up the company by diversification. Henceforth, he announced, policy was to close down any division which did not make a return on capital of 12 per cent.[16] Still, however, the extent to which restructuring in Germany involves the sale or closure of less profitable divisions is a good deal less than in the United States and Britain (the process has usually not been initiated by a takeover or a threat of takeover, for a start) but a good deal greater than in Japan. In Japan, of course, the process is slowed down by the fact that running down the workforce can, by common consent, be accomplished only by natural wastage. On the other hand, Japanese firms are inhibited only by their unions and employee sentiment: the business and political community and the whole of the press cheer on restructuring efforts.

By contrast, opposition to surgical restructuring is more vocal in Germany, and it is mobilized at the political level—one writer attributes the wave of restructuring plans at the end of the Kohl Government to fears that a new, left-wing government would increase job protection. But already, compared with Britain or the United States, dismissing redundant workers is not easy in Germany.

To start with, it is costly in terms of negotiating time in works councils and on supervisory boards, and sometimes, in consequence, in work morale and cooperativeness. An excellent study comparing restructuring at ICI and at Hoechst found this to be the main difference.[17] The co-determination law has specific provisions for 'changes in the company' which require agreement with the company central works council, and at Hoechst it is said to have taken nearly 18 months to work out the agreement. The company was at great pains, through all these negotiations, to safeguard its reputation as a socially responsible employer by maintaining its involvement in the apprentice training programme, but above all it had to make safeguarding the position of existing employees a consideration in all the reshuffles. For instance, a subsidiary set up to absorb the 1,000 researchers who were neither dispersed to operating divisions nor retired (out of the 14,000 originally employed at its central research centre) was seen primarily as a holding operation; many of them were expert in businesses from which Hoechst had exited. However, in restructuring, as in the 1992–3 recession, precedents and procedures have been established which make voluntary early retirement a major means of cutback; and although it is costly in redundancy compensation, the state bears a part of the costs, through provisions which allow part-payment of retirement pensions from the age of 57 onwards.

The restructuring drive seems clearly to be a part of the financialization process. It is a reflection of the new business ideology stemming from the United States, of which the first commandment is that enemy of any notion of creating a firm-as-community: 'Thou shalt not let unprofitable divisions be subsidized by profitable ones.' Away with conglomerates, stick to your core competence, beware diversification, be suspicious of 'synergies', hive off unprofitable divisions. Quite explicitly, in Germany as well as in Japan, the doctrine is seen as a reflection of the drive to short-term/medium-term profitability overwhelming all concern with corporate growth, with 'positioning' the company for a long-term future, or with gaining market share. According to the chief executive of the Frankfurt Stock Exchange, quoted in *The Economist*,[18] the growing dominance of this managerial strategy is reflected in the 'rebirth of the chief financial officer'. The drive behind Siemens' restructuring plans, for instance, is said to have come from its 'performance-minded new finance director'. It was clear that its quite extensive shedding of less profitable lines of business—all its semi-conductor and other electrical component operations, in all a seventh of the business, employing 60,000 people—was a response to a declining share price (a fall of 40 per cent relative to the Dax average between 1993 and 1998). 'Siemens appears to be indicating that shareholder value will be its topmost concern. [It] is breaking with the traditional reliance on banks as industry's main financier and stake-holder, in favour of an Anglo-Saxon market-orientated approach' was the *Financial Times*'s interpretation.[19]

It is the M&A bit of restructuring, the preoccupation with buying and selling chunks of productive capacity—and indeed the tendency to make this the core element of the enterprise strategy which top executives define as their role—which is a major factor in making a high share price a dominant managerial objective, at the expense, inevitably, of a concern for employee welfare. When company divisions are bought and sold, part-payment in the acquiring company's shares is common, and the higher the market valuation of one's shares, the cheaper acquisitions become. 'For years the typical German chief executive viewed the share price as a bit of entertainment. He might now see how it can work in his favour.'[20]

Hence, in Germany, where this kind of restructuring is becoming more prevalent than in Japan, seeking a high share price appears to be slightly more a matter of 'dry' pragmatic necessity than in Japan, where 'paying greater attention to the shareholder' is often more 'wetly' spoken of as a matter of moral or legal duty, and often has in mind the people who turn up at the annual general meeting rather than the tough managers of mutual funds.

M&A is not the whole of the story, however, as the Hoechst study shows. The restructuring process took place at a time of capital stringency. Internally generated funds were tight and interest rates in 1993–4 were high. Apart from wanting a high share price because a substantial part of the restructuring took the form of joint-ventures, in which it invested partly with its own shares, it was also hoped to raise cash from equity issues. And although 'stable shareholders' own over half of the issued shares (Kuwait Petroleum a quarter, employees and ex-employees over 30 per cent), according to the *Financial Times* managers had had to consider the possibility of a takeover bid and build defences against it.[21] At any rate, when the corporate headquarters were drastically slimmed down, by 40 per cent, in a decentralization drive, the only department which expanded was investor relations.

It still remains the case that, as a *Financial Times* leader said, commenting on the Siemens reconstruction:

> the German interpretation of shareholder value is scarcely red in tooth and claw. Hurdle rates of return on investment remain low by US standards even at companies that claim to pursue shareholder value. And despite the recent emergence of the odd hostile takeover, there is not yet an active market in corporate control.

Note the 'all the world is coming our way' assumption implicit in that 'yet'.

Evolutionary change: industrial relations

All these changes tending to enhance shareholder-friendly behaviour on the part of top managers are matched by changes which make them more employee-unfriendly—or at least organized-labour-unfriendly. This is not just because co-determination slows down decision-making;

there is still a widespread willingness to accept that as a fact of life and to appreciate the counter-advantages of cooperative implementation of decisions. Labour-unfriendliness stems more from the wide diffusion of the notion that Germany has arrived at a level of pay, holidays, and fringe benefits which it could once afford, when its quality products earned good market premiums, but is now beyond its means, given that its highly export-dependent and still, in industrial relations matters, dominant manufacturing sector faces a much more competitive outside world in which others have learned to match, or nearly match, its product qualities. In 1980 labour costs per unit of output were approximately equal in the Netherlands and Germany. By 1997 German costs were 27 per cent higher. The threat is that manufacturers are increasingly voting with their feet, putting their new plants in Poland and the Czech republic. Between 1990 and 1997 there was a modest rise in inward investment into Germany: from $111bn to $138bn. Meanwhile the stock of German investment abroad went from $152bn to $326bn.[22] Is Germany finished as a manufacturing nation? The so-called *Standort Deutschland* debate— Can Germany remain a viable industrial location?—has become a media cliché.

The intensity of this feeling was never more apparent than in the 1999 engineering industry wage negotiations. With some of IG Metall's more militant sections demanding a 10 per cent wage increase to compensate for years of what they considered unjustified restraint, and a million workers taking part in the first rounds of 'warning strikes', the threat of a more general strike was averted at the last minute by a final compromise settlement in Baden-Württemberg (3.2 per cent plus a one-off lump sum). It left much bitterness, with the employers' association complaining of blackmail and refusing to follow normal practice and recommend the settlement as a pilot agreement for the other regions. (Strike threats forced the other regions to follow suit anyway.[23])

The dispute took place in the context of a continuing concern about unemployment. The Schröder Government got the unions' cooperation in its December 1998 Alliance for Jobs only by accepting their refusal to have an explicit connection between wage moderation and job creation recognized. (The fact that high wages may be driving increased capital intensity at home as well as driving jobs abroad, both at the expense of jobs, is suggested by the productivity figures: 1.6 per cent annual growth since 1992, compared with 1.2 per cent before unification, with a 4 per cent shrinkage of jobs—compared with France's 1 per cent productivity growth and a 5 per cent increase in employment.[24])

All this has given a new edge of urgency to the tension between the union bargaining part and the works council part of the dual system of industrial relations. It may no longer show itself at the plant level in conflict between a militant union shop-steward committee and what the unions considered a too-cooperative works council—grass-roots militancy is nothing like what it was in the 1950s and 1960s. But what is called into question is the boundary-line between the industry-by-industry collective bargaining over standard wages and conditions on the one hand, and the bargaining between works council and management over the local application of collective agreements at the plant level on the other. The possibility that 'the distributional conflict' would be further shifted to the factory level was clearly the central preoccupation of the Commission on Co-determination quoted above. Many fear, and predict, a complete disintegration of industry-level bargaining. The market forces which have worked to erode centralized bargaining in every other industrial economy—from the United States to Sweden—are at work in Germany too.

The right to call a legal strike or lock-out in the furtherance of a dispute was, indeed, confined to the unions and employers' associations as the sole organs of collective bargaining, but the notion that collective bargaining was something the works councils had nothing to do with always was a fiction. Until the 1990s, however, the main deviations from a 'one-size-fits-all' wage system had been in extra premiums in wages and bonuses—over and above levels set in the collective agreement. These were paid, after negotiations in their works councils, to workers in the bigger, more successful firms—not something the unions would have ever had any reason to oppose. Since unification and the recession of the early 1990s, however, the predominant deviation has been what Streeck calls 'wildcat cooperation'—*lower* wages and *worse* conditions than those set out in the collective agreement, in less successful, less profitable enterprises. Some of these local arrangements are sanctioned by 'opening clauses' in the collective agreement itself, allowing concessions under certain conditions which the union retained the right to monitor. This was notably the case in East Germany. Some are the 'illicit' product of concession bargaining within works councils—agreement by the workforce to sacrifice bonuses or holiday pay or to work extra hours, usually in return for a promise of job security. One survey found such undercutting of collective agreements in firms which were supposed to adhere to them in 16 per cent of West German, and 30 per cent of East German firms.[25] Breaking collective agreements with such arrangements is in theory something condemned by both unions and employers' associations. Firms which do so often offer to resign from the employers' association but usually receive sympathetic reassurance rather than acceptance of the offer. The unions' opposition is more vigorous, but unless they can persuade a union member in the firm in question to break ranks and sue the employer—which they frequently cannot do—they are powerless. Their long-standing demand for the right of the union to sue independently has become more strident lately, and this important bolstering of the system was in fact included in the coalition agreement with the Greens and may well be enacted.[26] A recent Federal Labour Court decision may have that effect even without legislation. Whether such a change would be effective in shoring up the system, or alternatively add to the incentives to employers to abandon it, remains to be seen.

The Commission on Co-determination took a 'since you can't stop it, limit damage by controlling it' line. The collective agreement itself should allow works councils to 'incorporate provisions on working time and pay that are normally regulated by collective agreement into a joint package of measures to maintain competitiveness and employment at the production location' where this is a precondition for 'medium-term investment commitments by the employer' and will 'safeguard existing and create new jobs'. But to prevent a 'race to the bottom' by competing employers, such agreements should require the ratification of the regional union and employers' association.[27]

The spectre which haunts the unions is that employers will desert their employers' associations en masse; there will be nobody left to bargain with; collective agreements will become meaningless, and the only way they can prevent a free-for-all (and the only way regional union staff can preserve a *raison d'être* and their jobs) is to exercise such a strong claim on the loyalty of their members as to gain, plant by plant, control over the bargaining process in the works council. Defections from the employers' associations have been growing, particularly in Eastern Germany, where many firms which joined when they were in Treuhandanstalt hands left as soon as they were privatized. The IAB research institute calculated that the coverage of collective agreements fell between 1995 and 1997 from 53 to 49 per cent of firms, employing respectively 72 and 65 per cent of private sector workers in West Germany, and to 26 per cent of firms, 44 per cent of employees in the East. The process of attrition has been aided in some regions by employers' associations which have set up a special class of membership allowing firms which wish to defect from the bargaining process to continue to enjoy the legal, insurance, and advice services which the association offers.

So we have the slightly curious spectacle of unions trying desperately to maintain the solidarity of their counterpart employers' associations, their leaders warning anxiously against any triumphalism when the unions come out of negotiations with what they could count as a victory.[28]

The crucial determinant of the future shape of German firms is the choice managers make about leaving or staying in their associations. And that depends on several factors:

1. Skilled labour is getting scarcer, especially in manufacturing, in Germany as elsewhere, as the learning-capacity (intelligence) demands of technology grow and an increasing proportion of those of above-average learning ability go into higher education and professional jobs. Already there are alarmist stories of skills shortages. Will high-technology firms face a competitive bidding-up of wages if industry-wide agreements collapse?

2. Clearly there are firms, especially *Mittelstand* firms, where relations of trust between managers (often owner-managers) and the workforce are such that the concession bargains really do represent good bargains for both sides and are accepted by the workforce as necessary.[29] There are others where employers could well imagine that, if there were no overarching collective agreement, union militants in the workforce, backed by the regional union organization, would take over the bargaining process and the firm would be worse off. Would lingering class consciousness, which the unions would seek to ignite, and which the 1999 bargaining round showed to be far from extinguished, win out over enterprise consciousness *à la Japonaise*? Might the mood among their employees be such that they would not be able to refuse an offer by the union of a separate agreement no

better, or worse, than the industry one? Volkswagen, which has long had such an arrangement, pays over the odds; on the other hand its separately negotiated agreement has provided for a considerable measure of flexibility in formally negotiated wage/hours/job security trade-offs. Striking out on one's own does not necessarily mean being able, unhindered, to strike a deal with one's own workforce.

3. The prospects of reaching a Japanese-type internalized accommodation with workforce representatives depend greatly on the extent to which the long-tenure, job-security pattern is continued. The new pension arrangements which are being negotiated in a number of industries could reinforce such patterns. Schemes to supplement state pensions, not with market free-for-all, tax-privileged schemes such as Britain's Individual Savings Accounts and America's 401(k) plans, but with voluntary enhanced company-organized pensions, have been promoted by the Minister of Labour and worked out in collective bargaining, already, for instance, for the insurance industry. Similar arrangements are under negotiation in construction.[30] Even if pension rights remain portable in principle, they could still serve to enhance 'stakeholder consciousness'.

4. Defection from an employers' association would get a firm nowhere if the *Land* Minister of Labour decided to give legal force to the terms of the collective agreement, though the limited use of these legal powers makes this a minor consideration.

5. The supervisory board part of the co-determination structure can also play an important role. Although wage bargaining does not get discussed on supervisory boards (the conflict of interests would be too obvious), where the employee representatives include a union organizer—as can be the case especially in large firms—they, with a different constellation of interests from the employees on the works councils, might exert pressure to keep the firm in the employers' association.

6. The professional staffs of employers' associations, like those of unions, obviously have strong personal interests vested in the system. But the elected business representatives also matter, and the balance, within industries, between small firms and large firms can affect policy. Small firms have been taking over the leadership in many regional associations recently, and it is probably the small firms which, on balance, see themselves as having least to lose—or, if they do have a committed loyal workforce, most to gain—from decentralization.

7. Considerable importance, therefore, attaches to the extent to which the *Mittelstand* small and medium firms, hitherto predominantly in family ownership, retain their characteristics and retain their weight in the industrial structure as a whole. As in other countries in Europe which saw a baby-enterprise boom in the postwar years, German firms have, for the last decade or more, been facing family succession problems. But there are two factors which seem to indicate that they might come through those problems more intact than was the case in other countries. One is stronger 'dynastic pride' (should one call it?). A recent survey showed that, of all European countries, German enterprises were most likely to pass to other family members, or to existing mangers, and least likely to be sold out to larger firms. Secondly, the options for family firms are extended in Germany by the popularity of a loose form of conglomerate structure—the 'management holding' *Konzern*. This gives considerable autonomy to its constituent firms, which, even as part of an AG joint-stock company, can retain their semi-private GmbH character and their identity as separate 'legal persons'.[31]

8. These various interest-rationality calculations apart, one should not overlook the consequences of long-term social change. One factor, which may be changing, is the braking effect on defections of what is still, in Germany, a strong sense of social obligation—obligation not to free-ride, but to play one's part in the organizations which produce public goods. (A small illustration: there is a German Chamber of Commerce for German firms with establishments in Britain. The bottom-line-relevant benefits are not great compared with the membership fee. Nevertheless, most firms headed by a German manager join. Most headed by a British manager do not.) With increasing financialization inducing stronger concern for the bottom line, and with the internationalization of German managers and German business, this sense of obligation may erode. But how quickly?

9. The ethic of responsibility, the sense that free-riding is something to be ashamed of, is a factor affecting union membership too, and hence the likelihood that employers going it alone would face stroppy union-led works councils. Worker identification with the union depends not just on calculation of advantage, but also in part on sentiments of altruistic solidarity and shared indignation at oppression by the capitalist class. Those sentiments have been attenuated in a Germany whose workers can hive off to Tuscany for three weeks a

year, as much as in any other country. The collective-bargaining system is living off (to adapt Fred Hirsch's graphic phrase) 'the declining moral legacy of class conflict'. One can chart some of the epiphenomenal landmarks: in 1920, 42 people militantly protesting against the Works Council Act were shot outside the Reichstag as only one episode in a bloody class war finally resolved by Nazi repression in 1933. In the 1950s there were many violent strikes. In the 1960s and 1970s there was perennial conflict in many factories between the works council and the shop stewards' *Vertrauensleutekorper*, with, not infrequently, election contests between 'coopted' and militant unionists. By the 1990s the shop stewards' committees were almost everywhere subordinated to the works council, and a 1991 North Bavarian study reported that only 20 per cent of works council members saw themselves as members of the union/working class first and members of their local workplace second.

10. Another part of the equation is the quality of union leadership. In the 1950s and 1960s in countries such as Germany, Italy, and Sweden where unions became a part of the established order—in Germany, the ordo-liberal order—at a time when socialist ideals were still alive among the young, unions offered attractive careers to some of the brightest, best educated, and most vigorous members of their generation. Germany would be exceptional among industrial countries if its unions were still able to attract such people, or indeed if they had been able to do so for some time. Someone close to these things remarks of the union representatives in the Alliance for Jobs that they are 'uniquely unoriginal. They look as if they are playing a "labourist" end-game'. Even if there were no decline in the 'pool of ability plus idealism' available to anti-establishment movements, in a world where radicalism has been greened the competition from environmentalist and other good-cause organizations is far greater. And, as was noted about Japan, any decline in the quality of union leadership will affect the loyalty of members and the respect accorded by opponents.

Why should the strains set up by a one-size-fits-all centralized collective agreement be greater now than they have ever been? Once again the comparison with Japan is illuminating. In Japan, where recruiting for lifetime jobs takes place largely in high-school staffrooms and professors' offices, teachers tend to channel their brightest pupils to the most prestigious high-wage firms. This well-known social fact—known only too well to the school-leaver who hoped to get into a first-class firm but ended in a third-rate one—helps to legitimate the well-known wage gradient: workers in Toyota get 30–40 per cent more pay than people in one of Toyota's second-tier subcontractors doing similar jobs in the same automobile industry. In Germany, partly *because* the collective agreement enforces the same wage on assemblers and subcontractors, there is no general assumption that there are differences in worker quality between them—which in turn reinforces the legitimacy of enforcing a one-size-fits-all wage policy. But it is reasonable to suppose that there is a tendency for an increasing dispersion among enterprises in any particular industry in the value-added per worker out of which wages have to be paid.

A primary reason, of course—since value-added depends on product prices—is the increase in opportunities for outsourcing, particularly abroad in the high-skill, low-wage parts of Eastern Europe, so close at hand. The wage differential between large firms and small in Japan is, of course, one of the reasons why outsourcing is so much more common in Japan—as numerous international studies of the automobile industry have shown. Western Germany had a relatively stable, if more restricted, system of outsourcing with rough equality of wage costs (though it was the large assembler firms, rather than their suppliers, which paid wage premiums above contract level). But in the 1990s, with opportunities for much cheaper procurement from Eastern Europe and tougher pressures on costs in the post-unification recession, *Mittelstand* suppliers of intermediates, parts, and assemblies have been under stronger pressure to reduce costs in order to compete—hence the greater importance of being able to trim the wage bill.

It is also reasonable to suppose (though it is hard to adduce any concrete evidence) that the cumulative increase in the sophistication of the technology used in production places an increasing premium on the skills and intellect necessary to manage it efficiently, and that this leads to increasing dispersion of productivity levels within the same industry through the differences in managerial and worker quality. One would suppose that the following mechanisms might be at work:

1. Entry into managerial ranks. In the initial boom period of industrialization many founders of *Mittelstand* firms came into them through family connections, or through working themselves up from

skilled-worker ranks. Now the majority (including often the sons of those men) are recruited from the graduate market, in which the larger and the more prestigious the firm, the brighter and the better the people they can recruit. The spectrum of managerial quality consequently widens, and is increasingly correlated with enterprise prestige/size.

2. A similar process at work among blue-collar and white-collar employees. In a German environment, where the virtues of training and the obligation to train and to be trained are so universally ac-knowledged, differences in skill level are likely to reflect primarily dif-ferences in trainability ('native ability', as shaped by early family and school experience as well as by genes). The distribution of trainability among firms in the 1950s and 1960s, particularly among blue-collar workers, did not correlate much with firm size—working-class children were likely to take an apprenticeship in a local factory as a matter of course. This 'campanellismo effect' has steadily diminished. The car has widened the 'life-sphere', and the labour recruitment market, even of small-town working-class families. More children—and especially children of higher levels of academic ability—enter labour markets after higher education—and markets which are geographically more extensive. At the same time, the premium placed on trainability (be-cause of tougher technological requirements) makes enterprises more selective in their admissions to apprenticeships. Hence the correlation between workforce trainability ('quality') and the size/prestige of firms increases. It has long been clear that top German firms quite rigorously select entrants to their apprenticeship programmes. They have always had a large field of the best applicants, but whereas many of those applicants might formerly have been primarily concerned to enter the labour market and look for a job elsewhere with an 'I did my apprenticeship with Siemens' label attached, there is reason to suppose that the other forces at work (see below) are making it more attractive for them to stay with Siemens.

The stresses and strains in the system are apparent. It is unlikely that it will return to the old equilibrium of unquestioned authority for whatever *Tarifautonomie* bargaining produces. A recent joint declara-tion by the important chemical industry union and representatives of the 22 sectoral employers' associations (mining, shoemaking, rubber, etc.) with which it bargains has two clauses. One affirms the value of the system and rejects 'all efforts to limit or destroy' it; but what is more surprising is that the union should put its name to the second one, calling for *more* 'opening clauses' to allow 'for differentiation and flexibility at company level'.[32]

The system could eventually reach the alternative equilibrium—a stable system of enterprise bargaining with a greater or lesser degree of outside union support for employee-representative bargainers, leading to considerable intra-industry and intra-occupational wage differentiation. Many managers might well opt for that solution if the system could become a Japanese type of equilibrium—that is to say, if bringing the nasty zero-sum bits of the employment relation back into the firm could be accomplished without spoiling the level of trust and cooperation they can at present achieve in part because most of the conflictual work is hived off to the collective-bargaining system—if, in other words, they could count on a consensus as to what is a fair level both of wages *and* of profits.

But would they be able to do that in a Germany where managers are increasingly defining their role as the maximization of shareholder value?

There are clues in a recent survey which showed that a majority of works councillors did not want an end to central industry bargaining since they saw the industry contract as providing authoritative reference points—statements of their rights—which they in their works councils could use in bargaining with their employer. (Twelve per cent actually did want more decentralization—rather more in big firms than in small—but 36 per cent did not, and 41 per cent felt ambiguous about it.[33]) One conclusion to be drawn from this is that works councillors do not trust the managers not to take advantage of them if they lose that negotiating weapon, and that therefore employers would find it difficult to achieve the level of trust and cooperation of what was just described as the Japanese-type equilibrium.

But if managers were happy instead to achieve an Anglo-Saxon type of equilibrium based more overtly on coercion, with strong management and relatively weak union bargaining power, then, the survey shows, employers would gain in bargaining strength if they were to go it alone. The defenders of the industry-wide bargaining system seek to shore it up because they see it as an essential element of the *soziale* part of the *soziale Marktwirtschaft*, which it undoubtedly has been. As they have to put more and more fingers in the dike, however, one may doubt whether in the long run they will be successful.

What is at stake?

The industry-wide bargaining system is central to unions' concerns, much more so than the other half of the dual system—workplace co-determination. On any objective reckoning, the chances of preserving the *soziale* character of Germany's market economy would seem to be greater from a progressive evolution of the co-determination system—towards what I have called the Japanese-type equilibrium—than from a last-ditch, and increasingly embittered, defence of *Tarifautonomie*. The crucial point, surely, is whether or not corporations come to place shareholder interests so far above those of their employees as to effect a major shift in current income distribution. The *Financial Times*, commenting on the Deutsche Bank's diffidence about continuing its close relations with industrial corporations, concluded a leading article: '. . . it is worth remembering the Achilles' heel of the German system. Its capital is used much less productively than in the English-speaking economies'.[34]

'Much less productively': the phrase was clearly used as a synonym for 'produces lower returns to investors'. A better measure of 'using capital productively' would be the value-added (sales less the cost of raw materials and bought-in services) per unit of capital employed. There is no evidence that German firms are laggard in that regard. So how have they differed from British firms? As is suggested by a study of the 1991–4 accounts of the 82 firms which figured among the European top 100 in each of those four years,[35] the difference is that in Germany (as also in France, Switzerland, and the Netherlands) rather less of the value-added gets left as profits attributed to shareholders, or as interest payments to lenders and bond-holders, because proportionately more of it is paid out in wages and salaries to employees.

Therein lies one, and probably socially the most important, difference between a shareholder-favouring and an employee-favouring firm.

Chapter 10

The Organized Community

Business has shown a high capacity to coordinate and cooperate through a dense network of industry associations, local chambers of commerce and industry, and extensive interlocking directorates and shareholdings between banks and non-financial companies. This coordination capacity has helped business pursue its collective interests in the political arena, to participate in the provision of collective goods important for restructuring such as skill formation, and to help avoid the kind of destructive price competition that has plagued adjustment in other countries.[1]

T HIS description of Germany might equally well have been given of Japan, though there are several differences in the pattern of associational constraints:

1. Again, as with co-determination, much of the associational network has legal backing. It is 'state-enabled' in Streeck's terms.[2] The fact that membership in Chambers of Commerce is required by law in Germany but not in Japan is only one outstanding example.

2. These chambers not only provide common services to their members, represent business interests on taxation and other matters, etc., but are also expected to play their part in the provision of public goods in the interest of the society as a whole rather than just of their members. In negotiations between, say, MITI and the Japan Iron and Steel Federation, the same kind of appeal to the *national* interest as well as to the interests of Federation members may well be made and heeded. But this is on an ad hoc basis. There is nothing comparable to the institutional involvement of both types of *Kammern* (the artisanal and the industrial), along with the unions and the local educational authorities, in maintaining the apprenticeship training system for which Germany is justly famed.

3. While both Japan and Germany had a strong system of artisanal and mercantile guilds in their preindustrial economies, there are

fewer traces of direct continuity of that tradition in today's Japan. The discontinuities involved in the fact that Japan was Westernizing as well as industrializing in the late nineteenth century meant that when the law began to get involved in framing associational patterns—the Industrial Cooperatives Law of 1896, for instance—it took its models from the West rather than from its own traditions. German nineteenth-century guilds grew more organically into modern associations, and often received legal protection in doing so. Such is the origin of many of the trades and professions (over 130 of them) now inscribed in the Artisanal (*handwerks*) Chamber—including architects, for instance, and a good number of the *Mittelstand* firms which the courts deem to belong to the artisanal rather than the industrial category because they are operated 'in an artisanal fashion' (a criterion whose definition has evolved over time).[3] The licensing of these activities (enforced by the prosecution of the unlicensed), and the involvement of the licensed in the licensing process through their control over training, in effect gives monopoly rights. It is a version of 'old corporatism': the granting to a civil corporation of a share in governance, conferring material privileges on it in return for its promise to act in the public interest— to ensure standards of competence, suppress cheating, and charge a fair price. In this case, there was an additional 'public purpose' which prompted Bismarck to reinforce and legalize—and often create— these protective privileges at the end of the nineteenth century. He hoped to call a halt to the potentially dangerous proletarianization of the skilled-craftsmen artisans. The threat to social stability as factory production, using unskilled workers, came to invade many markets formerly dominated by the family-based, self-employed skilled artisan was clearly perceived.

What Japan and Germany have in common is the deep involvement of the state in establishing and maintaining levels of skill competence —in contrast to countries like Britain where state involvement (apart from in fields carrying clear public safety issues such as airline pilot licences) really began, with the competitiveness scare, only a decade ago. The differences are, first, that in Japan the use of legal backing for licensed skill monopolies is sparing, and largely confined to issues of public safety (airline pilots, structural engineers) or agreed national economic objectives (energy conservation managers in factories), though the social importance attached to state examination certific-ates of skill competence (the bicycle repairer exhibiting his bicycle repair certificate) is great. Secondly, Japan has protective subsidy policies for small and medium enterprises of a similar Bismarcko–Jeffersonian inspiration to those of Germany, but they are entirely unconnected to the practice or the ideology of the skill-training system. In Germany, by contrast, for licensing as a *handwerk* enterprise, the owner—or his production manager—has to have a certificate of competence equivalent to the *Meister* level. He has to show—a word with Lutheran overtones—that he has a *Beruf*, a calling.[4]

4. Modern *Berufe* such as engineering—the word means 'profession' as well as 'trade'—have also created their own professional associations—spontaneous, non-state-sponsored creations with no original guild roots. These too have a much greater strength in Germany than in Japan, where organizational affiliation overwhelms professional affiliation. Unless he or she is a researcher who belongs to something like the Semiconductor Material *gakkai* (a research association usually with an academic base), a Mitsubishi electronics engineer is unlikely to meet his or her counterpart in Sharp. In contrast, a Siemens engineer may well frequently meet a Mannesmann engineer at meetings organized by the VDI, the German engineering association. In this, Germany more closely resembles Britain, but the differences are, first, that the VDI has greater prestige and is more institutionally involved in standards and business regulation than the British Institutions, and secondly, by the same token, that it is imbued with a stronger sense of having a social mission and a mission to further German interests. Germans have the chairmanship of over half of the technical committees determining European standards. The VDI has its origins in agitation by 'concerned engineers' over the Great Steam Boiler Question—the safety standards that needed to be legislated to protect workers from exploding boilers.[5]

5. German industry was once famed for its cartels—sanctioned alliances, designed to prevent competition reaching mutually destructive levels, but monitored by public authority to curb the extent to which they could act as conspiracies against the public. Finally, after a decade of the so-called cartel-wars, postwar ordo-liberalism, much aided by American pressure, rejected this tradition and in 1957 created, in the politically independent Cartel Office, a mechanism for keeping cartel-like understandings within bounds. Like Japan's Fair Trade Commission, it has powers, denied to more 'liberal' economies' anti-trust organs, to search unannounced for incriminating evidence.

And, again like Japan's Fair Trade Commission, it did not rule out collaboration between competitors which might be deemed to promote public purposes, though there was nothing quite as formal in Germany as Japan's recession cartels, agreeing cuts in production across whole industries, or its investment coordination cartels in the big-plant industries such as chemicals and steel.

Nor did intra-competitor coordination have quite the same external-trade efficacy as it had in Japan, where the steel industry, say, by appeal to its customers and coordinated blacklisting of 'disloyal' customers, could fairly effectively keep out cheap imported steel. The Japanese are much more prone to see themselves as being racially and culturally different from the rest of mankind. Having sea and not land frontiers also makes a difference. Hence, of the two ingredients such action requires (namely, a sense of being fellow-steelmen and a sense of being fellow-Germans or fellow-Japanese), Germans, for the reasons already discussed—much deeper involvement in international labour markets, different perspectives on the war, etc.—have a somewhat more attenuated sense of the latter.

Falling apart?

All of these factors have affected the extent to which the deregulation drive, and the reassertion of the virtues of competition, have impacted on both the prevalence of stable, mutual-obligation-loaded trading relations and the traditional 'publicly coordinated' character of the German political/social economy. How far has there been a real change in economic behaviour?

To begin with the former, outsourcing in Central and Eastern Europe, offering 20 per cent savings, not the 3–4 per cent savings from switching from one German supplier to another, has obviously affected the stability of trading relationships in intermediate goods, and the freight of mutual trust and consideration which they bore. The much publicized arrival of Lopez (renowned for his ruthless purchasing policy) at Volkswagen, and his equally well publicized departure, highlighted these changes, but it is hard to estimate their extent. Another factor is the diminishing role of family owner-manager control in the *Mittelstand* as generation change sees many firms absorbed into large concerns with more impersonalized managerial traditions, more prone to arm's-length trading relations.

Internal impulses to greater competition are much magnified by pressures from the European Union, where the principles of deregulated trade borrow the moral force of the greater European integration project. In late 1999 retail price maintenance in the book trade was under direct attack from Brussels, as telecommunications and electricity generation had been earlier—with, reportedly, 30–40 per cent reductions in both electricity and long-distance call prices over twelve months. The same report also points out that as the euro takes hold and the transparency of price differences between Spain, say, and Germany becomes greater, pressures for greater deregulation and competition are bound to increase.[6] On the consumer side, the efforts to make shopping a pleasurable leisure occupation rather than a painful necessity are only just beginning. The attack on the social regulation of shop opening hours has hitherto seemed half-hearted, though the Chamber of Commerce and the Christian Democrats are now in favour of a relaxation of the rules, and the number of court cases against shops which use some pretext or other to defy the rules is increasing. As for the entry regulations, there are many complaints that one cannot engage in novel occupation X unless one is a certified *Meister* in some antiquated and irrelevant trade Y whose bailiwick one might be deemed to be invading; but there is little erosion of the controlling regulations.

Germany perhaps differs from Japan in that the attacks on different aspects of 'the German model', although they often come from the same quarters—the Kiel University Economics Department has long been famous for its 'true believer' neoclassical economists, for instance—are not part of a concerted reform movement concerned with deregulation, shareholder value, privatization, a reduced role for the state, etc.—the whole neoliberal package across the board. Where, however, corporate bottom-line-ism does directly impact on one of the more institutionalized forms of social cooperation is in the key area of social partner concertation, namely vocational training, which is worth looking at in more detail.

Few things have been as extensively touted in Britain as the merits of Germany's 'dual system'—on the one hand apprenticeship training supplemented, on the other, by part-time schooling. The latter in itself is dual-purpose: partly the theory to go with the factory practice, partly general education. The system served Germany well in past decades. One condition for its success was the system of secondary education, which siphoned off about a fifth of the age group (by the twin criteria of middle-classness and academic ability) into *Gymnasium*, which gave their pupils a high-quality academic education and left them, at the age of 19, qualified for further education or for one of the more intellectually demanding apprenticeships. This siphoning-off of largely, but not entirely the brightest segment still left many very able children, most especially from working-class families where university attendance was a barely considered possibility, to enter apprenticeships in their mid-teens in the more skill-demanding, learning-ability-demanding metal-working and white-collar trades. They came from the two other streams: the 'practical' schools (*Realschulen*) and the *Hauptschulen* (formerly *Volksschulen*) high schools. The former absorbed most of the more able children. About 20 per cent of school-leavers in the early 1980s, mostly the least able children from the *Hauptschulen*, were not able to, or chose not to, enter an apprenticeship, even in the less intellectually demanding trades such as hairdressing and baking which were under the jurisdiction of the artisan (*handwerks*) rather than the industrial chamber.

The key ingredients of the system were: (*a*) national coordination of training standards and of standard testing, in spite of a good deal of local control over syllabuses and testing procedures, thus giving national validity to apprenticeship qualifications; (*b*) the acceptance by the firms which took apprentices that they had a duty to establish youngsters in a *Beruf* as the national standards defined it, that is, to give them the necessary general training and not simply training in the specific skills their own production processes required.

The shift in skill requirements with changes in technology has given rise to much-discussed problems in both areas, but there is the additional problem—the problem which has hit apprenticeship systems nearly everywhere—that this shift in technology is accompanied by a shift in the distribution of perceived life-chances, and also of values, on the part of 16-year-olds. Affluent Germany too is moving from the era of mass secondary education to the era of mass higher education—the transition that Japan went through in the 1960s. The 50-year-old *Meister* on whose skills and pride-in-skill the reputation for quality of German manufacturing depends entered an apprenticeship in the mid-1960s with a sense of embarking on an assured career in the country's key industry, proud of his success in competing for a good apprentice-ship in a firm with a good reputation. Two things are different today.[7] Sixteen-year-olds from the same segment of the learning-ability range as that *Meister* are now likely to be bent on higher education either at a university or at one of the growing number of technical high schools and not to be seeking apprenticeships, though—a countervailing tendency—there is an increase in the number of apprentices entering high-level service sector or advanced manufacturing apprenticeships after a *Gymnasium Abitur*.

Secondly, for those who are still entering apprenticeships, manu-facturing has lost its glamour. An apprenticeship in Siemens must surely be one of the most competed for in manufacturing. A conversa-tion with one of those who succeeded in the competition: 'How did you come to choose Siemens?' 'My marks in German literature weren't good enough to get me an apprenticeship in a bank.'

Although there are vacant places, there are still some in every age group who do not seek, or who are not accepted for, an apprentice-ship, though that proportion seems clearly to be declining. (Figures for age cohorts are not easily available, but of the total male workforce the proportion 'without qualification', which was 25 per cent in 1982, was down to 13 per cent—former western *Länder* only—in 1997.) The decline in the quality of apprentices' learning ability and motivation which this and the growth of the higher-education alternative imply —for the manufacturing industry in particular—is more discussed over beers than in the training literature, but it is an important com-plication of the other problems such as the adaptation of the appren-ticeship curriculum. The latter, of course, lags behind technical change and, naturally, in Germany as elsewhere, adaptation is hampered by arguments over whether, in this age of computer-controlled machines, metal-working apprentices still need to learn the whole range of tradi-tional turner's skills in order to get a real 'feel' for metal. Nevertheless, sensible adaptation, it appears, happens without too much delay.

In the key area of engineering (metal-working) skills, the curricu-lum changes have been generally in the direction of lesser specificity and at the same time more emphasis on cerebral rather than manual skills, more intended to provide the foundation for future polyvalence than final competence in a particular skill.

Given both these limitations—the decline in the learning ability of the average apprentice and the more preliminary nature of what apprentices are taught—it is not surprising that firms have begun to question the value of the apprenticeship system. Increasingly their real skill requirements are being met by the market outside the apprenticeship programme itself. They recruit those who have received higher levels of basic theoretical training from the public higher technical schools and private-enterprise vocational schools, while ad hoc in-house specialist training and upgrading training are provided by outside consultants.

Even though the apprenticeship system may be playing a less dominant role in the total picture of German training, it is still of great importance, not only for the skills it develops, but also symbolically—as a social induction, social-inclusion mechanism, giving a large section of the not-so-very-gifted members of German society a sense of holding a 'stake' in society. It is partly recognition of this fact which keeps firms cooperating with the system, not only in taking more apprentices than they would choose to take if they did not also have a sense of civic obligation, but also in sticking to the obligation not to skimp on general training in order to concentrate on firm-specific skills. How proof will this sense of civic obligation continue to be against relentless bottom-line-ist pressure from top management? Training officers in larger firms usually have two calculations showing the net balance between the cost of training apprentices on the one hand, and the estimated work contribution of lower-wage apprentices on the other. One calculation, showing a positive gain, is for the Board, telling them that they should not be too worried about losing money on this exercise in civic cooperation. The other, showing a negative balance, is for the industry Chamber's training officials, showing that the firm is really doing its bit at some cost to itself and should not be pressed to take more apprentices. (Common wisdom has it that while, indeed, in some of the *handwerk* trades—hairdressing, baking, etc.— the employer does indeed gain handsomely from the apprenticeship system, this is far from being the case in the more sophisticated industrial sector.)

Nevertheless, the fear of defections is clear. There had been such problems in earlier decades (as early as the 1970s there was talk of introducing a training levy which would penalize non-cooperators), but the sense that a real crisis of cooperation is at hand has recently been much stronger. Once again, the entrenchment of the co-determination system may be an important factor in sustaining the apprenticeship system, since a reduction in apprentice numbers would have to be discussed with works councils (though it is not hard to imagine that older workers, deploring the fecklessness of modern youth, would be susceptible to the arguments that the poor quality and lack of seriousness of purpose in the apprentices they get would justify the firm withdrawing). But a second brake on defection is the tripartite structure of the local *Kammern* themselves. One-third of the members of their governing bodies must be employee representatives, and they doubtless put pressure on firms to keep the system functioning via employee representatives on the works council.

Once again we come back to the importance of legally entrenched institutions. Compared with Japan, Germany, with its ordo-liberal background, its greater degree of individualism, and its much more internationally mobile businessmen, seems 'closer' to contemporary Anglo-Saxon moods and values. But the institutions which make Germany different are, compared with Japan, much more formally entrenched in law. That is no guarantee that they will not be subverted by individual defection to the point at which the institutions themselves are formally changed. But legal entrenchment does slow down the process.

— PART IV

Conclusion

Chapter 11

Nice Guys Finish Last?

THIS book so far has been about the processes of change and their causes, with an underlying evaluative bias which the reader could hardly have failed to detect. The bias has been the result of a pre-occupation with the 'good society' question and has sprung from the belief that, and the desire to show that, the processes of marketization and financialization are a bad thing.

That is not by any means to say that I find—to concentrate on Japan, which I know more about—everything in that country whole-somely admirable. Habits of cooperation and social devices intended to avoid conflict and confrontation may do more than just keep the peace and spare people's feelings; they may help to achieve com-promises between conflicting interests which all parties, even those with less bargaining power, can consider fair and reasonable. But, as our jokes about 'political correctness' acknowledge, they can also produce a lot of hypocrisy, dishonesty, and obfuscation. Japan could do with a bit more plain speaking. It would also be a better place if the corrupt use of political power for private purposes were reduced to, say, British levels (though I am not convinced that more democracy, British-style, with politicians having more and bureaucrats less power, would help very much to bring that about). It would indeed be an advantage if professional auditors had a more arm's-length relationship with the firms whose accounts they audit. Deregulation does sometimes justly attack the privileges of fat cats who might quite reasonably be expected to exert themselves more on behalf of consumers and expose themselves to competition from newcomers. The Japanese strategy of tolerating and containing bullies like the *sōkaiya* and the real estate thugs is not obviously better than going after them as enemies of society. The sense of belonging to a national community which sustains cooperation within industries, and makes possible inclusive, and redistributive, educational and social welfare systems, almost by definition entails xenophobia, and that xenophobia, while quite harmlessly defensive on what is conventionally defined as the political left, can become nastily aggressive on the right.

So there are many things which could with advantage be changed. But not those changes central to the intentions of those whom I have called 'reformers' in Japan and Germany, which have a tendency to increase inequality, increase the ruthlessness of competition, destroy the patterns of cooperation on which social cohesion rests, and thus promise to degrade the quality of life. At least, they degrade the quality of life for anyone who, in addition to valuing individual freedom of choice, also values the right to live in societies with few public and no private policemen, societies in which social relations span a spectrum from intimacy to friendliness rather than to hostility and fear, and societies which possess the degree of equality and sense of citizenship which are necessary to make the institutions of democracy less like manipulated fictions and more like functioning reality.

But, going beyond sermon or jeremiad, this chapter confronts two final questions: the realistic prospect question and the efficiency question.

First the forecast. How is it likely to pan out? Probably—from my point of view—badly. Michel Albert's paradox—Rhenish capitalism seems so much superior to the Anglo-Saxon version, but it is the Germans who are trying to be like Americans not vice versa—remains true today. And outcomes are not just in the hands of elite decision-makers. The people are voting with their feet and their pocket books, in a way that makes the processes of financialization and marketization seem at present unstoppable. The latest issue of one of the major Japanese business magazines which arrived as I started this chapter carries the legend, splashed across its cover, 'Personal savings: the great migration' (i.e. from bank deposits to mutual funds).[1]

The reader may recall that in Chapter 2, I argued for the 'system-ness' of the Japanese socioeconomic structure. The four features I singled out—the structure of the corporation, relational trading, inter-competitor cooperation, and a strong role for government—were said to be held together by (a) institutional interlock and (b) motivational consonance. But neither inhibits change, though they may slow it down. Institutional interlock means that change induced in one sphere is likely to spread to others: a change in the role of government industrial policy has implications for the industry associations and inter-competitor sodalities; mutual feedback means that a shift in these can set off further changes in government. Similarly with motivational consonance. 'Dryness preference' can spread. Managers who are constrained—by, say, ineluctable, exogenous financial factors—to start treating their employees less considerately get 'hardened hearts' and find it easier to treat their subcontractors in the same way.

But if there seems, at the turn of the century, little doubt about what direction these mutual feedback effects are taking, one can also see the possibility that, just as the 1930s depression prompted the postwar attempts at the social regulation of capitalism, so, if the coming bursting of the Wall Street bubble is more cataclysmic than a 'correction' and real depression in the dominant economy gives enough backing to 'global capitalism in crisis' talk, things could change. There could, once again, with Japan and a German-led Europe in the vanguard, be various attempts to reassert the nation-state's power in the name of society, to 'embed' the economic activity within its borders in norms and social structures that amount to something more than mere monitoring of free and fair markets. Short of such an event, the financialization/marketization process will probably continue and bring, in the end, the flexible labour markets, the arm's-length trading patterns, and the bottom-line-ism in management which characterize the globally dominant society, the United States. In both Japan and Germany the transition will doubtless be long and painful, given the force of custom and habit, modal personality dispositions, and regulations entrenched by powerful interest coalitions (the institutional gridlock to which Olson[2] attributed the economic decline of nations). But, if the hiccups in the system are not greater than, say, those produced by the 1987 Black Monday stock market fall, in the long run vice will prevail over virtue.

And, it can be argued, it will not be just a matter of admiring imitation of the powerful. I have only to re-read what I wrote in Chapter 3 about the processes of individuation and the erosion of egalitarian sentiment in Japan to be reminded of the arguments of those who have written of the 'depleting moral legacy' and the 'cultural contradictions' of capitalism. Fred Hirsch argued two decades ago that capitalism was founded on trust, yet has an inevitable tendency to erode trust; Daniel Bell that it was founded on what I have labelled 'productivism', but can only work by promoting consumerism.[3] This book, then, is like one of those fairy stories about the search for an elixir of life—an expression of nostalgia for what was, after all, a passing evolutionary phase in the history of two societies which just happened to start their industrialization with more fully evolved communitarian institutions than the others, and to preserve some of that legacy to more advanced stages of economic growth. No more, in short, than another example of cultural lag.

Of the two societies, Japan is the one which has the greater chance of resisting incorporation into American-led global capitalism and preserving its own distinctness. First and foremost, because (except for a tiny minority of children living overseas who have spent extended periods at foreign schools) Japanese have a much stronger sense of their country's cultural, and racial, distinctness (only cultural in Beijing, where their faces merge with the crowd's; in London or Berlin cultural distinctness gets a racial tinge). That *this* is Japanese and *that* American can become an argument for preserving the 'this' far more potent than similar arguments in Germany. Anyone arguing in a committee in Germany that such and such should be defended because it is part of a valued and specifically *German* heritage is liable to be devastated by an opponent who jeers, 'Yes, we know. As Kaiser Wilhelm said, "Am deutschen Wesen soll die Welt genesen!" ' (German ways will heal the world). As those who have analysed the way the two societies have dealt with war guilt have frequently pointed out, Germans have much more willingly disowned their national history than the Japanese, and in doing so eroded one major source of their sense of Germanness.

In a recent Japanese best-selling novel based on Japan Airlines,[4] the chairman of a textile company is finally and very reluctantly persuaded by the Prime Minister to take over the ailing enterprise. He had been called up as a student but kept in Japan as a military trainer while his class-mates went off and got killed in China. After refusing twice to take the job he is again put under heavy pressure. He can think of all sorts of sensible reasons for refusing, but, 'As the only one in his class who had not gone to the war, had survived, he had a debt to pay. How could he refuse? "All right. My second call-up I suppose you could call it." ' And he goes on to clean up the airline by the power of his saintly honesty and dedication to the public good. Hardly a typical modern Japanese, but it is clear that readers of younger generations are expected to read this with sympathy and understanding. There is not the slightest trace of irony.

Such a marrying of survivor's guilt and patriotism might just be found in a few officer-class families in Germany, but the rejection of the last war as a morally acceptable experience has been far more complete. And it is not only the war which is disowned. It is also the searing experience under the Nazis of the conformity-demanding aspects of community in a much more coercive and bloody form than the Japanese experienced in the 1930s. (Japan, after all, had only a handful of political prisoners, no concentration camps.) Germany may have had the legal-rational bureaucratic traditions which enabled it to 'constitutionalize' social obligations, but if they are not rooted, at the informal level, in some kind of 'spirit' of community, they can more easily be deconstitutionalized.

A second (intricately interlinked) factor which makes Japan more likely to resist global capitalism is that its 'corporatism', to use the term loosely, has been more 'holistic'. That is to say, it has depended more on all compromising parties sharing some sense that they have to 'think for the nation', and less on a simple horse-traded class compromise between opposing interests in a zero-sum game. I once examined closely the arguments used in the 1973 Spring Offensive wage-bargaining round—at a time when unions still had a powerful strike weapon available and were accustomed to use it.[5] Before, that is, the post-oil-shock stiffening of employer resistance prompted the unions to restrain and then to lose their bargaining clout. It was remarkable to what extent union arguments too were framed in terms of what would happen to the macroeconomy and why the wages they were asking for were not just a matter of justice, but the best thing for growth of the national economy as a whole. In Germany, by contrast, the attempt at true concertation of the kind that worked and still works in the Netherlands and Austria failed. Inflation control depended on the way that the *Tarif-autonomous* unions and employers accepted the discipline of unilateral action, and the threat of unilateral action, by the Bundesbank. Schröder's present problems with his Alliance for Jobs spring in large measure from the unions' unwillingness to move beyond their self-defined mission to maximize the interests of their members, rather than to 'think for the nation'. A case in point is their refusal to discuss plans to use the energy tax to encourage low-wage employment by reducing payroll taxes selectively—much more drastically for low-paid workers. They want across-the-board cuts. Anything else, they say, will compromise Germany's position as a high-wage economy.

This is simply to repeat the point made earlier that German co-determination does not spring from an original communitarian character of enterprises. It is a class compromise, quite deliberately arrived at in order to avoid a repetition of the class conflict of the 1920s and early 1930s, and enshrined in powerful legislation which sets limits to that conflict on the assumption that, in what realistically had to be considered a zero-sum game, it would not go away.

One does not, then, have to go back to medieval feudal traditions to explain the difference between the two countries in the propensity for 'holistic' corporatist thinking, even if such deeper roots are not to be ruled out. It is enough to hark back to the 1920s. Japan, too, had its militant unions. They had to face, not only employers, but also the police and the violence of hired thugs. People were killed. But the violence was on nothing like the scale that Germany saw—or even America, for that matter. Nor was the shaping of the postwar institutions as influenced as it was on the union side in Germany by returned exiles with vivid memories of that violence. The tiny number of returned exiles from China and Russia were vastly outnumbered in the postwar Japanese unions by people who had earlier made their compromises in the Patriotic Labour Front within which the prewar unions had been incorporated.

That history still counts. It means that there is greater scope in Japan for propagating the notion that there is a national and not just a class interest in preserving established institutions and protecting them against the pressures of global markets, global firms, America-dominated global institutions.

A third reason why Japan might put up stiffer resistance is because of its neighbours. There are great similarities between Japan and Korea, on the one hand in employment institutions, business practices, and views of the state's role in the economy, on the other in the debates currently under way over the extent to which 'Americanization' should be allowed to go. China's state-owned enterprises, for all their diminishing contribution to GNP, are still norm-setters, and their employee-favouring orientation is not in doubt. Neither is China's nationalistic propensity to resist American 'corruption' of its Confucian socialist soul (its 'market socialism with Chinese characteristics'). Both Korea and China are still some way from Japan's industrial maturity, still growing at a fast rate. Another decade or two and the weight of East Asia in the whole world economy could seriously eclipse that of the United States and of Europe. And that could have profound consequences. At present the Japanese are in no mood to think of preserving their institutions because of some valued quality of Asianness. For the vast majority of Japanese, Asianness is backwardness, contrasting with American modernity. That may not always be so.

Efficient? Competitive?

And so to the second, and the main, question for this chapter. Suppose that something more catastrophic did happen to the global system and there were to emerge a general consensus in either Japan or Germany that, in the interest of maintaining the quality of social and political life, marketization and financialization should be resisted. It would require calling a halt to some of the processes of globalization, and there would have to be a reworking of the commitments to the IMF, the BIS and the Basle Committee, and the WTO. Germany could not do that without agreement with its European partners—agreement which might come from France and Italy, but hardly from Britain. However, just suppose for the moment that the political will to do those things could be mobilized, even over the dead bodies of a few bankers and the bulk of the economics profession.

If that did happen, one condition for sustaining such a course would surely be that these 'good societies' should also be not so much less efficient—competitive—than the other more marketized, more financialized societies. If the result were that Japan and Europe continued over a long period to have average growth rates of 1 per cent while the Anglo-Saxon economies had a trend growth rate of 2–3 per cent, it is unlikely—given the intensification of nationalism and the enhanced preoccupation with competitiveness which are paradoxically (unlike free trade) one of the irreversible consequences of globalization—that this consensus could long survive.

Hence, 'good society' questions apart, it is important also to ask the question which is the central question of (usually the only question considered in) much of the 'hard-nosed' literature which this book has drawn on. Would the 'Japanese model' and the 'Modell Deutsch-land', if they were preserved, be able in the future to make Japan and Germany as competitive with the Anglo-Saxon economies as they manifestly were in the 1980s?

The complexities of this question are often obscured by the simpli-fied stylizations that it has bred over the last decade—for instance, a distinction between a 'high road' to competitiveness involving high skills, high product quality, and high wages, and a 'low road' of low skills, low wages, and price competition. Or the attribution of success to a more rapid forward-looking shift from mindless 'Fordist' mass production to 'flexible specialization' or 'diversified quality produc-tion', characterizations often liberally tinged with romantic nostalgia for the *Gemeinde* of the cooperative industrial district and the produc-tivist ethic embodied in the small entrepreneurial firm. It is true that it is primarily in one-off or job-lot production systems of machine tools and precision engineering that the competitive advantage of both Japanese and German manufacturing has seemed most marked. But they have also done well in the mass-production industries of auto-mobiles and consumer electronics.

It is worth remembering just how much growth in Japan and Ger-man has depended on productivity growth rather than on growth in labour inputs. The figures in Table 1 are for the period 1972 to 1992.

Table 1. Sources of economic growth, 1972–1992

Country	Real GDP ($ at purchasing power parity (PPP))	Employed persons	Working time per person (1992 hours)	Productivity per hour (1992 output per hour, $PPP)
Germany	1.625	1.100	0.851 (1,618)	1.735 (20.1)
Japan	2.192	1.256	0.882 (1,965)	1.980 (14.9)
USA	1.552	1.387	0.957 (1,825)	1.169 (20.9)

Sources: I owe these calculations to Gregory Jackson. They are based on OECD, *Employment Outlook*, various years and data provided by the Institut für Arbeits-maktforschung, Bundesanstalt für Arbeit, and US Bureau of Labor Statistics. US employment data have been corrected for multiple-job-holders based on BLS estimates.

Capital: patient or flighty?

One view of the sources of competitive strength emphasizes the role of corporate finance. Competitive strength depends increasingly on the power to innovate. Innovation is risky and takes a long time; it requires the sort of organizational learning which only stable organizations can provide. Organizations which are capable of such innovation need patient capital, not flighty capital; commitment not liquidity. A hard core of stable shareholders and an absence of hostile takeovers conduce to innovation; pressure from shareholders solely interested in short-to-mid-term results, backed (via the effect on share price and market valuation) by the threat of takeovers if they do not get them, is an innovation-inhibitor.[6]

An alternative view is that one needs to distinguish between different kinds of innovation. The above argument applies to intra-paradigm incremental innovation. In that, indeed, the patient-capital, long-term commitment model excels. But it does not apply equally to innovation which implies a paradigm shift. Take this analysis of the Lufthansa turnaround in the early 1990s:

> Consensus decision-making and secure employment prospects for managers appear to provide an advantage for adjusting to an industry environment of continuous change that can be dealt with effectively by accumulating technical skills . . . and by equitably splitting the economic gains of programmable productivity increases . . . However, in an environment requiring a radical change in the company's set of skills, in the power structure, and in the company's capacity to make rapid decisions involving risk and uncertainty about the mode and success of implementation, a system of consensus top-level decision-making and of lifetime employment for managers may prove disadvantageous.[7]

Have aeroplanes really changed that much?

What has brought radical change, the need for a paradigm shift, is, according to a common view—a view more or less accepted in the Bertelsmann–Hans-Böckler report discussed in a previous chapter—the emergence, in the shape of electronic computing, of a new generic technology comparable to steam power in the early nineteenth century and electricity in the twentieth in heralding a new 'long-swing' cycle. At such moments—look at the flood of resources into Internet stocks—it is, indeed, so the argument goes, the fluidity of resources which counts. A market-oriented form of capitalism 'is better able to respond to the changes in relative prices of all resources that occur more significantly and frequently when new technologies are being adopted rapidly, and when global independence is accelerating and competition is intensifying world-wide'.[8] However, goes one twist to the story, while the Anglo-Saxon model may show superior results in the turbulent short term, as the pace of innovation changes in the maturity phase the German/Japanese model will come into its own again.

As one who has always been sceptical of Kondratieff-type cycle theories, always found the distinction between fundamental and incremental innovation protean, and always been impressed by the consistent incremental gradualism of such steady, evolutionary upward trends as the percentage of GDP devoted to research and development, or the shortening of product lifecycles, I find such predictions less than convincing.

But let us grant to the above arguments at least the truth of the proposition that the 'competitiveness' which determines long-run relative growth rates has a great deal to do with the capacity of corporations to innovate—to get, and to acquire a reputation for getting, a stream of new products rapidly on to the market at favourable quality/price ratios.

The cyclical factors

Such capacity is not unaffected by cyclical—or what hitherto we have thought of as cyclical—swings in the macroeconomic climate. It may well be that the brains required to do the inventing, or to see the possibility of using the inventions of others, or to imitate and improve on others' use of inventions, are available, properly equipped, and efficiently managed. It may be, too, that the organization to translate the ideas they generate rapidly into products works smoothly, and that the resources to finance that translation are easily available. But the will to commit those resources can well be affected by (*a*) the best rational expectations of future market developments and (*b*) the general 'mood', the diffuse optimism–pessimism, confidence–anxiety balance which those expectations breed. There is no better illustration of this than the contrast over the last eight whole years between a gloomy Japan, with falling asset prices and a savings–investment imbalance which has led it to send large quantities of capital into reserves or abroad, and a gung-ho United States, with buoyant asset prices, which has compensated for a negative savings–investment balance and a rapidly deteriorating balance of payments by sucking in a large proportion of the world's liquidity (thus maintaining an invigorating level of consumer demand).

The unpredictable nature of these swings is such that there is only one thing to say: that the United States/Japan comparison once looked very different, and there seems to be no fundamental change in the working of market economies to convince one that it cannot be different again. Just one relevant observation about a difference between Germany and Japan: Japan can still run a budgetary deficit of 9 per cent of GDP by way of Keynesian demand stimulus (even though still, at the time of writing, with no certain prospect of success). With the (for the moment binding) Maastricht stability pact in place, Germany's armoury of macroeconomic policy weapons would be much more limited and in any case would have to be coordinated with its fellow-Europeans.

Business strategy: monopoly power

Beyond these business-cycle effects, what are the long-term factors which will affect outcomes? Clearly, the capacity to innovate quickly and produce efficiently. But before we consider that, a brief word on one strategic advantage enjoyed by countries with 'community-like' firms over those with firms devoted to the pursuit of shareholder value—an advantage particularly in those industries, such as telecommunications, where oligopolistic market power can be of decisive importance. Where it is shareholders which count, all one has to do to bring off an acquisition is to offer them a good price (plus, perhaps, side-payments for senior managers in the form of golden handshakes, chairmanships, etc.) and the deal is done. Where, however, other stakeholders have a legal (Germany) or socially recognized (Japan) right to interfere, even the most attractive tender offer may not bring off a hostile takeover. Thus Mannesmann had no difficulty in buying the British Orange, but British Vodaphone's attempt to buy German Mannesmann is fraught with difficulty and, at the time of writing, of uncertain success. The gain to the winner in this contest—in terms of the ability to set technical standards and prices, to bargain down suppliers' prices, etc.—will be very great.

This asymmetry, of course, is denounced by the British press and by Tony Blair as grossly unfair. However, it is not altogether clear to me why possession of this 'natural immunity' to takeovers should be seen as more unfair than so many other advantages countries have thanks to nature and history—such as all that British natural gas in the North Sea or America's power to absorb armies of clever Chinese graduate engineers.

Skills, cultures, and organizations

But let us return to the question of those features of German and Japanese (manufacturing) industry which were supposed, in the heady days of the 1980s, to give them competitive advantage. It was not just a matter of having patient capital, no fears of takeover, and managers able to devote their time to running their business rather than M&A wheeling-and-dealing. The ability to make use of the opportunities that patient capital affords rested on other features which they supposedly had in common. Such as:

- a high level of skill in the average worker, which is in content a mixture of cognitive and manual competence, and of conscientiousness, backed by effective training (albeit of very different patterns in the two societies), but rooted also in moral qualities—seriousness of purpose, self-discipline, notions of a duty of self-development—for which families and primary schools are probably more important than training on the shopfloor;
- similar orientations in engineers and their ability to embody the routines developed by such workers for producing high-quality products (plus a lot more evolved out of their own inventive problem-solving heads) in hardware which makes skill less necessary, is proof against momentary lapses of attention, and also allows much more customer-tailored product diversity within mass-production systems;

- the customer orientation plus 'perfectionism as end-value' (i.e. as something which is not just an instrument to obtain profit, and can sometimes reduce it—think of the curious word 'overengineering') which make top managers *want* to utilize to the full the above characteristics of workers and engineers;
- the long tenure of managers and their consequent identification of their own interests with the long-term future of the firm, a factor which enables them to make full use of the availability of patient capital—long-term planning, a low time-discount, low hurdle rates for investment;
- the ability to mobilize conscientiousness and cooperation among employees—workers, engineers, and the planners of company strategy—conditioned by the fact that the firms are run as much for the benefit of their employees as for that of their shareholders.

These qualities do not disappear overnight. But they do have two cumulative long-run consequences. Inasmuch as they confer a competitive advantage and faster growth rates (as they did for Germany and Japan in the 1970s and 1980s)—and inasmuch as a part of their recipe is to be more egalitarian in income distribution—wage costs, and consequently prices, rise faster than those of competitor countries. Secondly, the quality-guaranteeing improvements in production techniques, which may start off as tacit knowledge and skills on the shopfloor, frequently get embodied in hardware and in teachable organizational routines. As such they diffuse to competitors. I have already quoted one German manager's estimate: 'quality used to give us a 20 per cent premium on the price: now it's about 5 per cent'.

But Japan and Germany are stuck with wage levels predicated on that 20 per cent premium, and in the medium-to-long term—unless the dollar remains for ever the only 'safe haven' currency and the yen and the euro remain weak—that threatens their competitive power. A lowering of the national standard of living, or at least a slowing-down of wage increases until competitors catch up, is one recipe. Another is the hollowing-out transfer of a lot of production to low-wage countries, leaving predominantly the high-value-added, design, and new-product functions at home. That too can be an effective way of maintaining market share and GNP.

As far as lowering, or more likely holding back, the standard of living to get closer to competitors does become necessary, Japan is at an advantage. Its company-level wage-bargaining system is more flexible, and it can still engineer its own inflation inside its own currency zone. Germany by contrast has powerful central unions which prove strongly resistant to requests for sacrifice in the national interest, though, through Alliance for Jobs contracts, the unemployment problem can to some degree provide an effective argument to evoke concessions. As far as inflation/devaluation is concerned, Germany now can only enjoy the same inflation rate as Italy and Spain, though the weakness of the euro at the time of writing (which has provided exchange rate advantages and greatly eased German cost pressures) has been the result of mechanisms which have nothing much to do with inflation.

But discussion of the wage rate cannot nowadays be divorced (at least in Germany, and now, increasingly, in Japan) from discussion of unemployment, and not just as a bargaining tool in wage settlements. Maintaining competitiveness through hollowing-out—keeping up GNP but not necessarily GDP—would only exacerbate unemployment problems, which are in any case already produced by the fact that German manufacturing industry's success in raising productivity (by over 1.5 per cent annually in the first half of the 1990s) was far greater than any possible increase in output—thus swelling unemployment. A similar increase in productive efficiency is probably available in Japan, but it is masked there by the fall in capacity utilization and output and the much stronger lifetime-employment guarantee, which has meant that instead of higher headline unemployment rates (though they are still rising at what is considered an alarming rate) there is more waged idleness, ritual retraining, and other forms of concealed unemployment in lifetime-employing firms. It is doubtful whether the recovery of the economy will be followed by a fall in unemployment. The ratchet effect has probably already started to work.

But that brings us back to 'good society' problems self-generated within the original German/Japanese models themselves. When they lose their capacity to give jobs to those who want them, their claim to enhance the overall quality of life may become suspect. But it is not clear that the Anglo-Saxon economies, if one looks behind their currently better headline unemployment rates, are any better. And in any case, the relevance to the present question—what change or non-change does to competitiveness and the growth rate—is not entirely clear. The 'job-less growth' arguments, that in modern economies large segments of the unskilled labour force are technologically redundant—with the implication that finding them jobs would add little to GDP or the capacity for growth—may be exaggerated, but it is clear that the employment question and the growth question can be separated.

And, for the growth question, the capacity for innovation is clearly of the greatest importance.

Where ideas and capital meet

There are two parts to the argument that neoliberal economies are better at innovation because of their flexibility and mobility of resources: the speed with which they off the old, and the speed with which they find and produce the marketable new. Of the first there can be no question. Where the Anglo-Saxon economies clearly excel is in the destruction part of Schumpeterian creative destruction. Upsizing profits is quickly achieved (if only in the short term) by downsizing staff.

What is not so clear is whether this is the reason why they excel (if they do indeed excel) at the creation bit. In spite of all those tales of the sacked engineers from IBM and Boeing providing the nucleus for much of Silicon Valley's success, it is not at all clear that the rapid release of resources through destruction without compunction is a factor which conduces to effective innovation, much less *the* essential precondition. Compunction or ruthlessness has a clear effect on distribution issues; but not so obviously on the production side. The opportunity cost of the resources 'wasted' in the kindlier and gentler way the Japanese ran down the coal mines in the 1960s, or the numerous industries hit by the oil shock in the 1970s, seems not to have been much of a growth inhibitor. And again, as one of the least conformist of Japanese economic commentators remarked in 1999,[9] chiding the 'blood-on-the-floor' advocates of restructuring for dynamic innovativeness: if Japan were operating at full employment, and with a scarcity of capital, they might have a point. But it is clearly not such supply-side constraints that today inhibit the growth of new ventures or the launch of new products by old ventures. It is something else.

One part of the 'something else'—the confidence that markets will be there for new products—we have already dealt with. The other part is the organizational part; what is often called the 'national innovation system'.[10] Those Japanese who make the standard argument about the Japanese economy being admirably structured for catch-up but no good for the new stage of innovation-at-the-frontier frequently make clear that their ideal is Silicon Valley, the place where individual technological brilliance and daring creativity combine with business entrepreneurship and venture-capital financing—the winning combination for which Japan has no answer, and which all the attempts over the last decade to promote venture business have failed to emulate.

There does, indeed (still concentrating on the Japan/United States comparison) seem to be a big difference in the dominant innovation paradigms. The sources of creativity remain elusive, but clearly the originality needed to make either breakthroughs or incremental improvements has to be combined with the high-grade learning ability needed to get rapidly to the frontiers of existing knowledge—in short with high IQ. In the United States, a high proportion of people with such talent go into university doctoral programmes which are also fed by large numbers of bright students from overseas, many of whom become American citizens. Some of these 20- to 30-year-olds develop ideas during their doctoral and postdoctoral spells in well-funded academia which they subsequently take out to found entrepreneurial firms on Route 128 or Silicon Valley or one of the other industrial parks close to universities. Others go into corporate laboratories—to which they are usually recruited specifically for the expertise they have acquired—and may well, later on, 'spin out' to become founders of entrepreneurial firms. This often gives rise to charges that in spinning out they have taken commercial secrets with them, thus providing lawyers with much lucrative business. (One hard-disk manufacturing firm which captured a goodly market share from IBM was founded by someone who had worked on a new hard-disk generation inside IBM. He compounded the offence by getting his funding from a venture capitalist who drew substantial investment from the IBM pension fund.) Others—particularly in the health, pharmaceuticals, and biotechnology fields—spin out from national laboratories with ideas largely developed within them, giving rise to complaints that though 90 per cent of the development work was done with public money, 100 per cent of the profits are private.[11] In the electronics field, in which the United States has leapt ahead in the last decade, the role of public money, via defence contracting, is even greater. Thanks to a new Minister of Economic Planning and his 1999 Economic White Paper, the economic philosophers of Japan have found a new buzz-word to replace the 'tension' about which I wrote in Chapter 4. It is risk (*risuku*: untranslatable into traditional Japanese contexts without overtones of—nasty—speculation!). What the Japanese do not take into account when they speak so admiringly of the American ability to take risks is the extent to which it is not only the easy acceptance of bankruptcy as a device for starting again, but also assured income from defence contracts which often substantially reduces what the risk-taker is laying on the line.

The essential ingredients of this recipe, then, are a strong role for universities at the frontier of innovation; a strong role for individual profit incentives provided by strong individual property rights in inventions; great mobility of engineers and scientists in response to those incentives; and a good deal of covert public spending. And what makes all this work is the financier, the venture capitalist who specializes in taking (and spreading) high risks for the prospects of occasionally very high, and usually on average high, returns.

The Japanese recipe is very different. To start with, doctoral courses in science and engineering departments of universities typically re-cruit only a limited number of aspirants to an academic career—at the top universities often the very brightest students, but few of them. Most of the people of comparable IQ levels to the leading participants in the American innovation system stay in graduate school only for a taught Master's degree, which nowadays is seen as a part of basic training, a necessary supplement to what is usually no more than two years of specialist disciplinary study in the undergraduate degree. Thereafter, typically, they go immediately into the research lab of a major corporation. They may subsequently be sent abroad for a spell at an American graduate school, or they may do a part-time Ph.D. at a Japanese university—nowadays a major form of collaboration be-tween universities and corporations—but the majority, even of the very brightest, remain committed to the firm they have joined and expect to make their career within it, not necessarily exclusively in research. Much of their work is done in teams, collaborating with colleagues with whom they build up cooperative relationships over a period of years. In most firms they will be named as inventors in any of the patents (the firm's property) to which they have contributed, and they may for particularly meritorious work get material rewards. (The inventor of a particular artificial fibre process on which the prosperity of a major firm is founded is said to get a $50,000-a-year bonus on top of his salary.) But, as with R&D everywhere, much of their work ends up, after considerable expense, with no commercially viable product. Equally high-risk is the launching of new products through the corporation's own procedures for entrepreneurial initiatives, integrating research, design, production planning, and marketing. Finance for the whole risky process is found from the corporation's own deep pockets.

Two quite different recipes, then: the graduate-school whiz-kid/entrepreneurial individualism/venture capital/eventual IPO recipe and the corporate research/corporate finance/corporate commercialization recipe. The German pattern, like the Japanese, is overwhelmingly of the latter kind, but perhaps with rather closer links between academic institutions and firms, and with rather more small-firm start-ups in some fields. But the difference is not great compared with the difference between both countries and the United States.

To be sure, a careful count would almost certainly show that in the United States, too, it is in fact the latter, corporate recipe which produces the overwhelming bulk of innovation activity. (Innovation producing increments in added value, that is, if not the extraordinary share capital values generated by Silicon Valley and Internet hype. Though the American computer industry may have a productivity growth rate of an amazing 40 per cent per annum, in 1999 it still represented only 1.2 per cent of American GNP.[12]) However, for all that the Japanese tend to exaggerate its importance, it seems obviously true that the venture recipe does play a substantial part in the American pattern and a very small part in Japan—probably with considerable variation among industrial sectors, however. Innovation in pharmaceuticals is more likely to follow the same predominantly corporate pattern in both countries than innovation in electronics.

So the first observation (a much more sophisticated version of the argument that the Japanese/German pattern is all right for catch-up but not suited to the fluid flexible New Economy of the Third Industrial Revolution) is that if there are areas in which the entrepreneurial start-up recipe has manifest advantages over the corporate recipe, and others where the opposite is true, then overall economic growth rates are likely to depend on the future structure of production worldwide and the viability of individual country specializations. On this the literature is large and growing—and inconclusive. Two recent papers which compare, not Japan, but Germany with the United States concur in seeing the strength of the Japanese/German pattern as lying in those fields where the learning and inventing are cumulative rather than one-off discrete.[13] (German biotechnology is strong on 'platform technologies' rather than specific therapies; custom software for business is a field in which Japanese and German firms seem to do well, while marketed package software is more suited to the risk-taking entrepreneur.) Beyond that, the analysis in both papers suffers from what seems like ad hoc rationalization of observed patterns of technological and trade specialization. The factors listed above which serve as strengths of the Japanese/German pattern—worker involvement, stable relations with suppliers, patient capital, the commitments of insider managers—play out in such a wide variety of ways in different industries that deterministic predictions seem hazardous.

A second question, doubtless, is whether the glittering attraction of the American model will make the Japanese corporate recipe unviable in the long run, even in those areas where it clearly offers advantages. *The Economist* notes that Japan has no shortage of talented software engineers but 'most work for large electronics firms, not independent start-ups'. Clearly an aberration, thinks *The Economist*, and concludes: 'missing from all the talk about embracing the Internet [in Japan] has been any mention of stock options, spin-offs and IPOs. How long before the clever young programmers at Fujitsu, Toshiba and NEC decide to go it alone?'[14]

Industrial policy?

Germany is clearly closer to the Japanese than to the American pattern in its balance of the two recipes: apropos software just mentioned, a recent article points out that two of its big firms (Siemens–Nixdorf and a subsidiary of Daimler-Benz) have been gaining market share in IT services/custom software in recent years after a poor beginning, though, as just noted, Germany (like Japan) does less well in packaged software. It is harder to compare these countries with respect to another important dimension in national systems of innovation, the much disputed question of the role of industrial policy. The simplest measures—the volume of public funding in the total research effort, for example—are difficult to compute. It is hard enough to compare the costs, let alone the effectiveness, of (a) the small injection of funds but larger injection of hands-on bureaucratic effort of the centrally funded Japanese pre-commercial research consortia (some of which appear to be successful, some not), (b) the numerous disparate initiatives of the *Land* governments and their *Landesbanken* in Germany, and (c) the (probably in total much larger) sums spent by the American federal government, partly in such overt 'competitiveness-boosting' schemes as Sematech and partly under the guise of the defence budget for 'dual-use' technology, or in the form of generous public procurements which cross-subsidize civilian R&D.

Intellectual resources

It is no use having good organizational recipes for transforming brainpower into commercially successful product innovation if you do not have the brainpower in the first place. Here again the difference in the recipes outlined above is not irrelevant, since the high-powered university graduate schools which play such an important role in the United States are one factor—together with the English language, the openness of American society, and America's role as cultural hegemon and the Mecca of the world's scientists—which explains the migration of a great deal of scientific talent to the United States. Look through any list of leading American scientists and engineers and you will find a considerable number from Asia, Europe, and Latin America who did their first degrees in their native country. Both Japan and Germany, as less attractive places to migrate to (especially Japan, with its lifetime-employing corporations), seek alternative means of tapping foreign sources of talent by setting up corporate R&D establishments in Europe and the United States. Japan in particular will probably do so increasingly in China, and may well, until Chinese salaries get a good deal higher, attract a good number of R&D researchers from China as well. And it is worth remembering that, on the assumption of similar gene pools, when China with its vast population reaches the same level of educational provision and merit-based selection as Japan, for every Japanese who scores, say, three standard deviations above the mean on IQ tests, there will be ten Chinese; for every such American, there will be six Chinese.

Conclusion?

This is perhaps a good place to stop—with that reminder of the possibility that, just as Japan went in two decades from registering 4 per cent of the patents filed in the United States to a more than 25 per cent share, there is a good chance that in 20 years' time it will be China which is the world leader in scientific research, and in product and process innovation. And China by then could well have such a weight in the total world economy that the form its capitalism takes will have a considerable influence on the rest of the world, not least on its Asian neighbours.

By that time there will be a good deal more evidence to judge whether or not the 'decent quality of life' virtues which I discern in Japanese—and in German—society are likely to be endangered by a lack of competitiveness in international markets and an inability to achieve growth rates comparable to those of other societies. Germany will clearly lose much of its separate identity as it is absorbed in, or absorbs, Europe. Japan will still for a long while to come be a much more autonomous entity. All that can be said in summation of the comparisons made in this chapter is that there is no reason to suppose—and, indeed, simple measures like the recent US patent registration record give one no reason to suppose—that the underlying strengths of the Japanese economy which were responsible for its earlier success have disappeared. Neither the 'end of catch-up' theory, nor the 'wrong kind of creativity' theory, nor the 'growth fatigue' theory seems convincing. Japan clearly needs not to take too long to recover national self-confidence, to stabilize its asset prices and its expectations of future asset prices, and to get its savings rate down in line with its investment needs. Should it do so, even if (or rather, *especially if*) it calls a halt to some of the incipient processes of financialization and resists the siren voices of those who promise that tough structural reforms will lead to quick salvation, there is no reason to suppose that those strengths should not be apparent once again, and once again deliver respectable growth rates.

Notes

Chapter 1. Introduction

1. *Flexible Rigidities*, London: Athlone and Stanford: Stanford University Press, 1987.
2. *Taking Japan Seriously*, London: Athlone and Stanford: Stanford University Press, 1988.
3. Armonk and London: M. E. Sharpe, 1999.
4. Roy Jenkins, *Gladstone*, London: Macmillan, 1995, p. 305.
5. Richard Young, *Restructuring Europe: An Investor's View*, Goldman Sachs International, May 1997.
6. J. K. Galbraith, *The New Industrial State*, London: Hamish Hamilton, 1967.
7. Andrew Shonfield, *Modern Capitalism: The Changing Balance of Public and Private Power*, Oxford: Oxford University Press, 1965.
8. James Burnham, *The Managerial Revolution* (1941), Penguin Books, 1945.
9. A. Berle and G. Means, *The Modern Corporation and Private Property*, New York: Macmillan, 1932.
10. Robin Marris, *The Economic Theory of 'Managerial' Capitalism*, New York: Free Press, 1964.
11. *The Economist*, 7 August 1999, p. 19.
12. Paris edn., 27 July 1999.
13. D. Yergin and J. Stanislaw, *Commanding Heights: The Battle between Government and the New Marketplace That Is Remaking the Modern World*, New York: Simon and Schuster, 1998.
14. 'Rethinking free trade', in R. Morgan *et al.* (eds.), *New Diplomacy in the Post-Cold War World*, London: Macmillan, 1993; and 'Convergence for whose benefit', in Suzanne Berger and Ronald Dore (eds.), *National Diversity and Global Capitalism*, Ithaca, NY: Cornell University Press, 1996.

Chapter 2. A Society of Long-Term Commitments

1. A survey organized by an academic committee of the think-tank of the Rengo trade union, reported in F. Suzuki, 'How top managers see the Japanese corporation', paper for the Corporate Governance Conference, European University Institute, June 1999.

2. For details of share-cornering operations, see Paul Sheard, 'The economics of interlocking shareholding in Japan', *Ricerche Economiche*, 45 (1991): 428–9.

3. For a sample of the left-hand column theory, see John Kay, *Foundations of Corporate Success: How Business Strategies Add Value*, Oxford: Oxford University Press, 1993, and the work of theorists such as Oliver Hart on which it draws. For Aoki's work, see M. Aoki, *The Cooperative Game Theory of the Firm*, Oxford: Clarendon Press, 1984.

4. There is now a considerable economics literature on Japanese firms' promotion systems which seeks to model the way in which they are 'rational'. Being entirely individualistic, as all such models have to be to be calculable, let alone respectable, they have no place for—and in fact are often explicitly motivated by the desire to deny the importance of—what are called here 'altruistic collective incentives'. A survey of such models, and of their inadequacies, may be found in H. Itoh, 'Japanese HRM and incentive theory', in M. Aoki and R. Dore (eds.), *The Japanese Firm: Sources of Competitive Strength*, Oxford: Clarendon Press, 1994. See also H. Odagiri, *Growth through Competition, Competition through Growth: Strategic Management and the Economy in Japan*, Oxford: Clarendon Press, 1990.

5. Chalmers Johnson, *MITI and the Japanese Miracle*, Stanford, CA: Stanford University Press, 1982.

6. Karl Polanyi, *The Great Transformation*, New York: Rhinehart, 1944.

7. On the tedious methodological question of why I prefer to talk of 'behavioural dispositions' rather than of 'culture', see Ronald Dore, 'The distinctiveness of Japan', in Colin Crouch and Wolfgang Streeck (eds.), *Political Economy of Modern Capitalism*, London: Sage, 1997.

8. W. G. Runciman, *A Treatise on Social Theory*, 3 vols., Cambridge: Cambridge University Press, 1983–97.

Chapter 3. Sources of Change

1. R. Taggart Murphy, 'Tinkering or reform? The deregulation of Japan's financial system', Hotel Okura, *The Tokyo Report*, June 1997.

2. James Shinn, 'Corporate governance reform and trade friction', mimeo, Council on Foreign Relations, March 1999.

3. *Japan Echo*, Autumn 1999; from *Chūō Kōron*, January 1999.

4. Nakajima Shūzō, *Kabushiki no mochiai to kigyōhō* (Cross-shareholding and company law), Tokyo: Shōji Hōmu Kenkyūkai, 1990, pp. 265–73. The book is a printing, with afterthought comments, of a 1977 Masters thesis.

5. The foil for his arguments is Itami Hiroyuki, *Jimpon-shugi kigyō* (The Human-capital-ist enterprise), Tokyo: Tokyo Chikuma Shobo, 1987. See also Itami's paper in Kenichi Imai and Ryutaro Komiya (eds.), *The Business Enterprise in Japan*, Cambridge, MA: MIT, 1994, and the introduction to that book by Whittaker and Dore.

6. R. Dore, *British Factory: Japanese Factory*, London: Allen & Unwin and Berkeley: University of California Press, 1973, pp. 282–3.

7. Heidi Gottfried and Jacquline O'Reilly, 'The weakness of a strong breadwinner model: Part-time work and female labour force participation in Germany and Japan', draft paper for W. Streeck and K. Yamamura (eds.), *Germany and Japan in the 21st Century*, forthcoming.

8. See R. Dore, *City Life in Japan*, London: Routledge, 1958 and Hastings: Paul Norbury, 1999, ch. 11.

9. Keizai Kikakucho (Economic Planning Agency), *Kokumin seikatsu hakusho* (White Paper on the people's livelihood), 1995, p. 116.

10. Masayuki Tadokoro, 'The end of Japanese egalitarianism', *Bulletin* of the Committee on Intellectual Communication (American Academy of Arts and Sciences), no. 3, 1999.

11. Suzuki Yoshio of Gōdō Seitetsu, writing in the *Nihon Keizai Shimbun*, 17 July 1997.

12. Andrew Gordon, *The Wages of Affluence: Labor and Management in Postwar Japan*, Cambridge, MA: Harvard University Press, 1998, pp. 25ff.

Chapter 4. Corporate Governance

1. See e.g. Keizai Dōyūkai (Japan Association of Corporate Executives), *Kigyō Hakusho 12-kai: Nihon kigyō no keiei-kōzō kaikaku* (Enterprise White Paper no. 12: Reform of the management structures of Japanese firms), May 1996, and *Kigyō Hakusho 13-kai: Shihon-kōritsu-jūshi keiei* (Enterprise White Paper no. 13: Management which prioritizes the efficient use of capital), April 1998; Nihon Kōporēto Gabanansu Fuorum (Corporate Governance Forum of Japan), *Kōporēto Gabanansu gensoku: Atarashii Nihon-gata kigyō-tōchi o kangaeru* (in an oddly out-of-focus translation, an English version is available as *Corporate governance principles: A Japanese view*), 26 May 1998; Shakai Keizai Seisansei Hombu, Seisansei Kenkyūjo (Social and Economic Productivity Council, Productivity Research Centre), *Nihongata Kōporēto gabanansu kōchiku ni mukete no toppu manējimento kinō no kadai* (The function of top managers in working towards a Japanese pattern of corporate governance), June 1998; 21-seiki no kōporēto shisutemu ni kansuru kenkyūkai (Study Group on the

Corporate System Needed for the Twenty-first Century: a MITI-convened group, though the report bears no trace of the fact), *Hōkokusho* (Report), March 1998; Nikkeiren Kokusai Tokubetsu Iinkai (Japan Employers' Federation, Special International Committee), *Nihon-kigyō no kōporēto gabanansu kaikaku no hōkō: Shihon-shijō kara mo rōdōshijō kara mo sentaku sareru kigyō o mezashite* (Directions for reforming the governance of Japanese corporations: Towards corporations favoured by both capital and labour markets), August 1998; Jiyū-minshutō (Liberal Democratic Party), 'Kōporēto Gabanansu ni kansuru Shōhōtō kaisei shian kosshi' (Outline draft for revisions of the corporate governance provisions in the Commercial Code and other legislation), *Seimu Chōsakai, Saishin Jōhō*, 8 September 1997, and comments on that draft: Keidanren (Federation of Japanese Business Organizations), 'Kōporēto gabanansu no arikata ni kansuru kinkyū teigen' (An emergency proposal for the reform of corporate governance), 16 September 1997, reprinted in *Jurisuto*, 15 October 1997; and Keizai Dōyūkai, 'Jiyū-minshutō no shōhō ni kansuru shōiinkai ". . . Shian-kosshi" ni tsuite' (A comment on the Jimintō's outline draft), also issued on 16 September 1997.

2. Keizai Dōyūkai, 'Jiyū-minshutō no shōhō ni kansuru shōiinkai ". . . Shian-kosshi" ni tsuite', p. 6.

3. Nikkeiren, *Nihon-kigyō no kōporēto gabanansu kaikaku no hōkō*.

4. OECD, *Corporate Governance: Improving Competitiveness and Access to Capital in Global Markets*, Paris: OECD, April 1998. This working group report was subsequently eclipsed by a report endorsed by the Council of Ministers, much less tolerant of deviation from the Anglo-Saxon mainstream: *Principles of Corporate Governance*, Paris: OECD, 1999.

5. Ministry of Finance, *Hōjin kigyō tōkei nempō* (Year-book of enterprise statistics), various years.

6. John Kay and Aubrey Silberston, 'Corporate Governance', *National Institute Review*, August 1995: 86.

7. *Tōkyō Shimbun*, 27 January 1998 indictment of Koike Ryūichi.

8. See M. Aoki and H. Patrick (eds.), *The Japanese Main Bank System*, Oxford: Clarendon Press, 1994. The whole book is permeated by the 'corruptions of insiderness' assumption, but it is suggested that the 'functionally necessary' external control is subject—in the pattern of economic development almost everywhere—to evolutionary development: there is a natural progression from main bank control to control through the discipline of the market.

9. Tachibanaki Toshiaki and Nagakubo Ryōtaro, 'Kabushiki mochiai to kigyō-kōdō', *Financial Review* (Okurasho: Zaisei Kinyū Kenkyūjo), November 1997: 158–73.

10. Wakasugi Hiroaki, 'Makoto no gurobaru-kigyō o mezashite: kabunishi-rieki to jūgyōin-rieki no chōwaron' (Towards the truly global firm: Harmonizing shareholder interest and employee interest), a contributed essay in Keizai Dōyūkai, *Kigyō Hakusho 13-kai*, p. 12.

11. NLI Research Institute, 'Kabunushi kōsei to kōporēto gabanansu' (Shareholding structure and corporate governance), July 1999 (www.nli-research.co.jp).

12. Keizai Dōyūkai, *Kigyō Hakusho 12-kai*.

13. Osaki Akiko, 'Dare no tame, nan no tame no kaikei kansa ka' (Auditing for what, for whose benefit?), *Tōyō Keizai*, 31 January 1998.

14. Ibid.

15. Ueno Masahiko, 'Nippon Koppaasu jiken to sono hanketsu' (The Nippon Koppas case and its judgments), *JICPA Jaanaru*, 487 (February 1996).

16. NLI Research Institute, 'Tōshika-shokō ni henkaku suru kigyō kaikei seido' (Towards an investor-oriented accounting system), August 1999 (www.nli-research.co.jp).

17. Sōmuchō Tōkei kyoku, *Rōdōryoku Nempō*, 1997.

18. Figures from Tōyō Keizai, *Kaisha Shikihō*, spring 1998.

19. *Financial Times*, 9 November and 21 December 1998. I owe this observation to an unpublished paper by Martin Fransman.

20. Keizai Dōyūkai, *Kigyō Hakusho 13-kai*, pp. 22–4.

21. Nissei Kiso Kenkyūjo, 'Kabushiki mochiai jōkyō chōsa 97-nen' (Survey on interlocking shareholdings 1997), August 1998.

22. Keidanren, 'Mochiai-kabushiki no kōkanseido ni kansuru teigen o tori-matome' (Summary of proposals regarding the mutual exchange of cross-holdings), statement (*Kurippu 84*) of 5 August 1998. The proposal, according to the *Financial Times* (7 October 1998), was drawn up 'after consultation with US investment banks'.

23. Robert H. Frank and Philip J. Cook, *The Winner-Take-All Society: Why the Few at the Top Get So Much More than the Rest of Us*, New York: Penguin Books, 1996.

24. Three drafts have been published, dated respectively 8 September 1997, 16 April 1998, and 1 June 1998. The first two bore the title *Kōporēto gabanansu ni kansuru shōhōtō kaiseian kosshi* (Outline of draft legislation for the amendment of provisions of the civil code etc. relating to corporate governance). For the third—a late burst of linguistic purism, perhaps—the Japanese word *tōchi kōzō* was substituted for 'corporate governance'.

25. Kobayashi Hideyuki and Kondō Mitsuo, *Kabunushi daihyō soshō taikei* (Every aspect of the shareholder representative suit question), Tokyo: Kōbundō, 1996, p. 232.

26. Keizai Kikakuchō (Economic Planning Agency), *Keizai Hakusho* (Economic White Paper), 1998, p. 380.

27. MITI, Sangyō seisaku-kyoku, sangyō-shikinka, Kigyō-hōsei ni kansuru kenkyūkai (Study Group on Company Law, Finance Section, Industrial Policy Bureau), 'Kabunushi-daihyō-soshō-seido oyobi torishimari-yaku no sekinin-seido no genjō to mondaiten' (Study group on the shareholder representative suit system and the responsibilities of company directors), reprinted in Kobayshi Hideyuki and Kondō Mitsuo, *Kabunushi daihyō soshō taikei*, p. 422.

28. *Nihon Keizai Shimbun*, 24 October 1997.

29. Fukao Mitsuhiro, 'Nihon no kinyū shistemu fuan to kōporēto gabanansu kōzō no jakuten' (Financial instability and the weak structure of corporate governance in Japan), Conference Paper 98-2-6 for the Symposium 'The Role of Markets and Government', 17–18 March 1998.

30. Nomura Shōken, Kinyū Kenkyūjo, *Keiei Chōsabu, Zaimu-senryaku Chōsaka* (Corporate finance research report), no. 18, May 1998, p. 1.

31. Ryūichi Yamakawa, 'Overhaul after 50 years: The amendment of the Labour Standards Law', *Japan Labour Bulletin*, 37(11) (November 1998).

32. See e.g. Michiyo Nakamoto, 'Revolution coming: Ready or not', *Financial Times*, 24 October 1997.

33. Rōdōshō, *Rōdō keizai Dōkō Chōsa* (Vital statistics of the labour economy), October 1998.

34. Rōdōshō, Daijin Kambō, Seisaku Chōsabu, *Nihonteki koyō-seido no genjō to tembō* (Present state and prospects for the Japanese-style employment system), 1995.

35. Dore, *British Factory: Japanese Factory*, p. 318.

36. Hiroyuki Fujimura, 'New unionism: Beyond enterprise unionism', in Mari Sako and Hiroki Sato (eds.), *Japanese Labour and Management in Transition: Diversity, Flexibility and Participation*, London: Routledge, 1998.

37. Keisuke Nakamura, 'Worker participation: Collective bargaining and joint consultation', in Sako and Sato (eds.), *Japanese Labour and Management in Transition*.

38. Hiroki Sato, 'Labour–management relations in small and medium-sized enterprises: Collective voice mechanisms for workers in non-unionised companies', in Sako and Sato (eds.), *Japanese Labour and Management in Transition*.

39. Nissei Kiso Kenkyūjō, 'Kabushiki mochiai jōkyō chōsa 97-nen'; and *Kaishō ga kasoku suru kabushiki mochiai* (Accelerating unwinding of cross-holdings), October 1999.

40. Fukao Mitsuhiro, 'Nihon no kinyū shistemu fuan to kōporēto gaban-ansu kōzō no jakuten', p. 7.
41. 18 December 1998.
42. *Nihon Keizai Shimbun*, 2 December 1998.
43. See *Tōyō Keizai*, 28 November 1998: 90–1.
44. Nomura Shōken, Kinyū Kenkyūjo, Keiei Chōsabu, Zaimu-senryaku Chōsaka. The survey covers finance managers of a sample of 100 firms, of which 66 had been included in the similar survey three years earlier.
45. 10 March 1999.
46. *Nikkei Shimbun*, 9 April 1998.
47. Tōyō Keizai, *Kaisha shikihō*, spring 1998.
48. 22 April 1999.
49. Figures calculated from Ministry of Finance, *Hōjin kigyō tōkei nempō* (Yearbook of corporate enterprise statistics), various years.
50. The firms were Toray; Jujo (later Nihon), Seishi; Mitsubishi Kasei; Bridgestone; Shin-nittetsu; Komatsu; Hitachi; NEC; Nihon Denso. Many thanks to Kamimura Yasuhiro for doing the count.
51. Chris Carr and Cyril Tomkins, 'Context, culture and the role of the finance function in strategic management decisions: A comparative analysis of Britain, Germany, the U.S.A. and Japan', paper for Management Accounting Conference, Siena, November 1996, appendix table 3.
52. The group is called the Keiei minshu-shugi network (Workplace Democracy Network), and the draft is contained in its journal *Keiei minshu-shugi*, 9 (October 1998).
53. Nihon Kyōsantō Keizai seisaku iinkai, *Nihon keizai e no teigen* (Proposals for the management of the Japanese economy), Tokyo: Shin Nihon Shuppansha, 1996.
54. *Financial Times*, 18 December 1998.

Chapter 5. Trading Relations

1. D. H. Whittaker, *Small Firms in the Japanese Economy*, Cambridge: Cambridge University Press, 1997, p. 199.
2. David Finegold and Karin Wagner, 'When lean production meets the "German model"', *Industry and Innovation*, 4(2) (December 1997): 207–32.
3. Chūshō Kigyōchō, *Chūshō kigyō hakusho 1998* (SME White Paper), p. 87.
4. 'Survey Japan', 9 July 1994, p. 10.
5. *Financial Times*, 13 October 1998.

6. Chūshō Kigyōchō, *Chūshō kigyō hakusho 1998*, p. 91.
7. Mari Sako, 'Supplier development at Honda, Nissan and Toyota: A historical case study of organizational capability enhancement', mimeo, Said Business School, October 1998.
8. *Nihon Keizai Shimbun*, 22 March 1998.
9. This was written, of course, before the November 1999 announcement by Nissan's new Chief Operating Officer, the 'Proconsul from Renault', of his plans to downsize everything—factories, head-count, cross-shareholdings, distributors, *and* commitments to suppliers.
10. Chūshō Kigyōchō, *Chūshō kigyō hakusho 1998*, p. 92.
11. T. Nishiguchi and A. Beaudet, 'Self-organization in chaos: The Toyota Group and the Aisin fire', Hitotsubashi University, Institute of Innovation Research, Working Paper 97-02, 1997, p. 2.
12. Mari Sako and Susan Helper, 'Determinants of trust in supplier relations: Evidence from the automotive industry in Japan and the United States', *Journal of Economic Behaviour and Organization*, 34 (1998): 387–417.
13. Kōsei Torihiki Iinkai Jimukyoku (Fair Trade Commission, Secretariat), *Nihon no roku daikigyōshūdan, Sono soshiki to kōdō* (Japan's six large enterprise groups: organization and behaviour), Tokyo: Tōyō Keizai, 1992, pp. 151, 153.
14. *Financial Times*, 29 December 1998.

Chapter 6. The Industry as Community

1. Quoted in Kobayashi Michi and Sakamoto Mamoru, 'Dango'tte nan daro', *Sekai*, December 1993, pp. 37–46.
2. Nishiguchi and Beaudet, 'Self-organization in chaos'.
3. A term made popular by Oliver Williamson; see almost any of his writing, e.g. *The Economic Institutions of Capitalism*, New York: Free Press, 1985.
4. Sato Taiji, *Ore wa Tsūsanshō ni barasareta* (MITI tore me limb from limb), Tokyo: Tairyūsha, 1986.
5. As Michel Albert pointed out in his discussion of (British) 'marine' and Swiss 'mountain' insurance traditions in *Capitalism against Capitalism*, London: Whurr, 1993 (transl. of *Capitalisme contre capitalisme*, Paris: Seuil, 1991).
6. Conducted by the author together with Professor Takeshi Inagami of Tokyo University. Questionnaires were sent to 311 industry associations listed in various directories; 99 replied.

Chapter 7. The Role of Government in the Economy

1. Steven K. Vogel, 'When interests are not preferences: The cautionary tale of Japanese consumers', *Comparative Politics*, 31/2 (1999): 187–209.
2. Adrian A. R. J. M. van Rixtel and Walter H. J. Hassink, 'Monitoring the monitors: *Amakudari* and ex-post monitoring of private banks', London: Centre for Economic Policy Research (CEPR), Working Paper 1785, 1997.
3. Gyōsei-kaikaku Iinkai, Kisei-kanwa shōiinkai, *Sōi de tsukuru arata na Nihon*, 5 December 1996.
4. Yambe Yukio, *Itsuwari no kiki: Honmono no kiki* (False crises and real crises), Tokyo: Tōyō Keizai, 1997.
5. Sōmuchō (General Affairs Agency), *Kisei kanwa hakusho (97-nen-ban)* (Deregulation White Paper 1997), August 1997.
6. Ulrike Schaede, *Cooperative Capitalism: Self-Regulation, Trade Associations, and the Antimonopoly Law in Japan*, Oxford: Oxford University Press, 2000. See also her 'The benefits from *Shinboku*: leveraging information exchange in Japanese industry associations', in Horst Albach, Ulrike Gortzen, and Rita Zobel (eds.), *Information Processing as a Competitive Advantage of Japanese Firms*, Berlin: Sigma, 1999.
7. For an account of how this works on the ground see my *Shinohata: Portrait of a Japanese Village*, Berkeley: University of California Press, 1993.
8. *Nihon Keizai Shimbun*, 6 September 1999.

Chapter 8. *Finanzplatz Deutschland*

1. Dentsū Sōken, *Dainikai Kachikan kokusai hikaku chōsa* (Second international study of value systems), Tokyo, 1999.
2. Steven Casper and Sigurt Vitols, 'The German model in the 1990s: Problems and prospects', *Industry and Innovation*, 4(1) (June 1997). A good deal of the account of recent German developments derives from the symposium which this paper introduces.
3. Figures taken from Bank of Japan, *Kokusai hikaku tōkei* (Comparative economic and financial statistics), 1997.
4. John Griffin, 'Institutional change as a collective learning process? A U.S.–German comparison of corporate governance reform', paper for the 1995 American Political Science Association meeting, Center for European Studies, Harvard.
5. Ibid.
6. Much of what follows derives from another paper in the symposium

mentioned in note 2: Richard Deeg, 'Banks and industrial finance in the 1990s', *Industry and Innovation*, 4(1) (June 1997).

7. 25 October 1999.

8. Wolfgang Streeck, 'German capitalism: Does it exist? Can it survive?', *New Political Economy*, 2(2) (1997).

9. 17 December 1998.

10. Ulrich Jurgens, Katrin Naumann, and Joachim Rupp, 'The political economy of shareholder value: The German case', paper for Workshop on the Political Economy of Shareholder Value, London, April 1999. Schröder's capital gains tax reform of January 2000 seems designed to facilitate the unloading of bank shareholdings.

11. *Financial Times*, 17 July 1995 and 4 December 1995.

12. BAW (Bundesaussichtsamt fur den Wiertpapierhandel), press release, 30 July 1998.

13. *The Economist*, 22–28 May 1999.

14. Streeck, 'German capitalism', p. 255.

15. Michel Albert, *Capitalisme contre capitalisme*.

16. Jurgens *et al.*, 'The political economy of shareholder value'.

Chapter 9. The Co-determined Firm

1. Gregory Jackson, 'Origins of corporate governance in Germany and Japan', mimeo, Max Planck Institute, Cologne, 1999.

2. Walther Müller-Jentsch, 'Germany: From collective voice to co-management', in J. Rogers and W. Streeck (eds.), *Works Councils, Consultation, Representation and Cooperation in Industrial Relations*, Chicago, IL: University of Chicago Press, 1995.

3. Mark J. Roe, 'German "populism" and the large public corporation', in R. M. Buxman *et al.* (eds.), *European Economic and Business Law*, Berlin and New York: Walter de Gruyter, 1996, p. 252.

4. Eiro Online, 'Court sets stricter limits on coal, iron and steel co-determination', March 1999 (www.eiro.eurofound.ie).

5. Eiro Online, 'New collective agreements signed in metalworking', March 1999.

6. Griffin, 'Institutional change as a collective learning process?'.

7. *International Herald Tribune*, 30 June 1997; see also *Die Zeit*, 9 May 1997.

8. Kathleen Thelen and Ikuo Kume, 'The future of nationally embedded capitalism: Industrial relations in Germany and Japan', paper for Max Planck Institute Conference, Cologne, June 1999.

9. Bertelsmann Stiftung and Hans-Böckler-Stiftung (eds.), 'Mitbestim-

mung und neue Unternehmenskulturen—Bilanz und Perspektiven',
Bericht der Kommission Mitbestimmung, Gutersloh, 1998. An English
summary entitled 'The German model of co-determination and cooperative corporate governance: An evaluation of current practice and
future prospects' is available from the Max Planck Institute Cologne
(www.mpi-fg-koeln.mpg.de/bericht/endbericht).

10. Ibid., paras. 28, 36.

11. Ibid., para. 35.

12. Ibid., para. 10.

13. 6 September 1996; quoted in Jurgens *et al.*, 'The political economy of
shareholder value'.

14. 1 June 1999.

15. Jurgens *et al.*, 'The political economy of shareholder value'.

16. *The Economist*, 16 March 1996.

17. Ansgar Richter, 'Corporate restructuring in Britain and Germany',
Ph.D. thesis, London School of Economics, 1998.

18. 21 November 1998.

19. 8 November 1998.

20. *The Economist*.

21. 9 June 1993; cited in Richter, 'Corporate restructuring'.

22. Martin Wolf, 'Emu: German handicap', *Financial Times*, 31 March 1999.

23. Eiro Online, 'New collective agreements signed in metalworking'.

24. Wolf, 'Emu: German handicap'.

25. Eiro Online, 'Unions seek right to bring cases against employers contra-
vening agreements', January 1999, and 'Growing numbers of "employment pacts" at establishment level', February 1999.

26. Eiro Online, 'Growing numbers of "employment pacts" '.

27. Bertelsmann and Hans-Böckler report, English summary, para. 11.

28. Thelen and Kume, 'The future of nationally embedded capitalism', p. 37,
quote the head of IG Metall after the hard-fought Bavarian conflict of
1995: 'No *Schadenfreude*. Collective-bargaining autonomy requires strong
bargaining partners.'

29. e.g. Viessmann, a manufacturer of gas heating units (see Michael
Fichter, 'The German system of labour relations: Still a model or a passing phenomenon', paper for a WZB workshop, June 1997), or Heller, a
family firm near Stuttgart (see Ronald Dore, 'Unions between class and
enterprise', *Industrielle Beziehungen*, 3(2:2) (1996)).

30. Eiro Online, 'Insurance sector agreement', April 1999.

31. J. R. Griffin 'Ownership, governance and the impeded politics of corporate creation in Germany', paper for the State and Capitalism Seminar,
Harvard Center for European Studies, May 1996.

32. Eiro Online, 'IG BCE and employers adopt joint declaration on partnership and branch-level bargaining', February 1999.
33. Eiro Online, 'Majority of works councillors unconvinced about decentralisation of bargaining', February 1999.
34. 20 May 1997.
35. Henk de Jong, 'European capitalism between freedom and social justice', *Review of Industrial Organization*, 10: 410–20, and 'The governance structure and performance of large European corporations', *Journal of Management and Governance*, 1(1) (fall 1997): 5–27. The wage/salary share of value-added in Britain went from 70 per cent in the recession year of 1992 to 60 per cent in 1994; in Germany it was over 85 per cent in every year. (The third recipient of value-added, besides labour and capital, is, of course, the state and local authorities in the form of taxes. The authorities had a higher share in Britain because profits are so much higher, even though tax rates are lower than in Germany.)

Chapter 10. The Organized Community

1. Casper and Vitols, 'The German model in the 1990s', p. 2.
2. Streeck, 'German capitalism'.
3. Wolfgang Streeck, 'The logics of associative action and the territorial organization of interests: The case of the German *handwerk*', in Wolfgang Streeck, *Social Institutions and Economic Performance*, London: Sage, 1992, pp. 105–36.
4. Streeck, *Social Institutions and Economic Performance*.
5. J. Nicholas Ziegler, 'Institutions, elites and technological change in France and Germany', *World Politics*, 47(3) (April 1995): 351.
6. John Schmid, 'Germans feel tough new climate of competition', *New York Herald Tribune*, 5 November 1999.
7. The prime source for what follows is Colin Crouch, David Finegold, and Mari Sako, *Are Skills the Answer: The Political Economy of Skill Creation in Advanced Industrial Countries*, Oxford: Oxford University Press, 1999, pp. 140 ff.

Chapter 11. Nice Guys Finish Last?

1. *Shūkan Tōyō Keizai*, 29 May 1999.
2. Mancur Olson, *The Rise and Decline of Nations*, New Haven, CT: Yale University Press, 1982.

3. Fred Hirsch, *Social Limits to Growth*, London: Routledge, 1997; Daniel Bell, *The Coming of Post-Industrial Society*, New York: Basic Books, 1973.

4. Yamazaki Toyoko, *Shizumanu Taiyō*, Tokyo: Shinchōsha, 1999.

5. R. Dore, M. Sako, and T. Inagami, *Japan's Annual Economic Assessment*, London: Campaign for Work, October 1991.

6. Mary O'Sullivan, 'The political economy of corporate governance in Germany', mimeo, Fontainebleau: INSEAD, March 1998.

7. Mark Lehrer, 'German industrial strategy in turbulence: Corporate governance and managerial hierarchies in Lufthansa', *Industry and Innovation*, 4(1) (June 1997): 138.

8. Kozo Yamamura, 'Germany and Japan in a new phase of capitalism: Confronting the past and the future', forthcoming in W. Streeck and K. Yamamura (eds.), *Germany and Japan in the 21st Century*.

9. Richard Koo, 'Kōzō-kaikakuronsha no musekinin na hatsugen' (The irresponsible urgings of the proponents of reform), *Tōyō Keizai*, 5 June 1999.

10. Chris Freeman's term (*Technology Policy and Economic Performance*, London: Pinter, 1987) subsequently taken up by Richard Nelson and others (e.g. Nelson, *National Innovation Systems: A Comparative Analysis*, Oxford: Clarendon Press, 1993).

11. Edward Luttwak, *Turbo Capitalism*, London: Weidenfeld & Nicholson, 1998, p. 160.

12. *The Economist*, 24 July 1999, p. 20.

13. Steven Caspar, Mark Lehrer, and David Soskice, 'Can high-technology industries prosper in Germany?', and Andrew Tylecote and Emmanuelle Conesa, 'Corporate governance, innovation systems and industrial per-formance', both in *Industry and Innovation*, 6(1) (June 1999).

14. 7 August 1999, p. 57.

Index